Republic of Noise

Republic of Noise

The Loss of Solitude in Schools and Culture

Diana Senechal

ROWMAN & LITTLEFIELD EDUCATION
A *division of*
ROWMAN & LITTLEFIELD PUBLISHERS, INC.
Lanham • New York • Toronto • Plymouth, UK

Published by Rowman & Littlefield Education
A division of Rowman & Littlefield Publishers, Inc.
A wholly owned subsidiary of The Rowman & Littlefield Publishing Group, Inc.
4501 Forbes Boulevard, Suite 200, Lanham, Maryland 20706
http://www.rowmaneducation.com

Estover Road, Plymouth PL6 7PY, United Kingdom

British Library Cataloguing in Publication Information Available

Library of Congress Cataloging-in-Publication Data
Senechal, Diana.
 Republic of noise : the loss of solitude in schools and culture / Diana Senechal.
  p. cm.
 Summary: "In this book, Diana Senechal confronts a culture that has come to
depend on instant updates and communication at the expense of solitude. Schools
today emphasize rapid group work and fragmented activity, not the thoughtful study of
complex subjects. The Internet offers contact with others throughout the day and night;
we lose the ability to be apart, even in our minds. Yet solitude plays an essential role in
literature, education, democracy, relationships, and matters of conscience. Throughout
its analyses and argument, the book calls not for drastic changes but for a subtle shift: an
attitude that honors solitude without descending into dogma"— Provided by publisher.
 Includes bibliographical references and index.
 ISBN 978-1-61048-411-4 (hardback) — ISBN 978-1-61048-413-8 (electronic)
 1. Reflective learning. 2. Classroom environment. 3. Education—Effect of
technological innovations on. 4. Solitude. I. Title.
 LB1027.23.S46 2011
 370.15'23—dc23   2011035358

∞™ The paper used in this publication meets the minimum requirements of American
National Standard for Information Sciences—Permanence of Paper for Printed Library
Materials, ANSI/NISO Z39.48-1992.

Printed in the United States of America

From far away I heard you speak today,
the way we hear bells in a slant of sun,
knowing they ring at five: the calendar
itself makes words, the very rays make chords.

A teacher must have rushed there after school,
arrived breathless, flopped in a seat, arranged
her coat and hair, leaned into heed, and found
a rampart in the very listening.

Something to sit up for, something to hold
one's head up for, a time to put aside
one's foibles for, even a distant time,
this came my way today, a reckoning.
I grasped that there was loneliness in gold
and gold in air, and debt in everything.

This book is dedicated with gratitude to Diane Ravitch.

~

Contents

Acknowledgments

M y gratitude goes to all my former students and colleagues at the two New York City schools where I taught. I am likewise indebted to my students from previous years and summers: in Bishkek, Kyrgyzstan; at Trinity College in Hartford; at Yale University (when I was a graduate student there); and on the Crow Indian Reservation in Montana.

I would like to thank my wonderful teachers from high school, college, and graduate school, and the people who were and are my teachers without knowing it.

I would like to thank Lisa Hansel, editor of *American Educator*, for her encouragement and wise comments, and for publishing an early version of chapter 6. Thanks also to the blogs and journals that have published my work and allowed me to try out ideas, especially *Education Week*, *American Educational History Journal*, *Educational Leadership*, *The Core Knowledge Blog*, *Joanne Jacobs*, *The Answer Sheet*, *Double X*, and *GothamSchools*.

I am indebted to everyone who read chapters or parts of chapters and offered comments: Lara Allen, Claudia Allums, Mary Ann Bandiola, Victor Bers, Lenore Boling, Jed Buchwald, Peter Carpou, Louise Cowan, William Deresiewicz, Carvel Gold, Lauren Gold, Arthur Goldstein, E. D. Hirsch Jr., Carol Jago, Susan Jacoby, Rita Lipson, Hannah Marcus, Donal O'Shea, and Ginny Scholey. Their insights and careful reading have honored the book and helped me; each person deserves more acknowledgment than I can give here. All errors of fact and interpretation are, of course, my own.

x   ～   Acknowledgments

I am indebted to Caroline Stark, who not only read and commented on my second chapter but offered her own translations of some of the quoted passages from Petrarch's *De vita solitaria*. These translations made the chapter sharper and are treasures in themselves.

Various people have helped me make contacts, locate sources, and obtain information. Special thanks to Shermaine Andrew, Deborah Gentile, Bina Mancini, Aaron Oberstein, Harvey Sherer, Patricia Tseng, Paul Woodruff, and the staff at the Yale University and Dartmouth College libraries.

This book owes much of its existence to Diane Ravitch, the first person to hear about the idea. In August 2008, when I told her that I was considering it, she encouraged me heartily and suggested the title *Republic of Noise*. From then on, I knew that I would write the book. She read chapters and offered comments along the way, and her books were great companions and resources.

It has been a joy to work with Kristina Mann, my editor at Rowman & Littlefield Education. She appreciated the book from its early versions onward and was helpful at every stage. Thanks also to Lynn Weber, the production editor, and Gail Fay, the copyeditor, for their expert handling of the book, and to Barbara Hendra, my publicist, for her sage advice and support.

Deep gratitude goes to my mother and Stan, and my father and Ann, for their encouragement and understanding, for giving me so many opportunities, and for doing such interesting things with their lives.

Finally, I am grateful to my sister, Jenna, who urged me to tell her stories night after night when we were little, and who wouldn't let me stop in the middle of a story I had begun.

~

Credits

Grateful acknowledgment is made for permission to reprint the following:

Excerpt from "Dar neištirpusį ledyną" by Tomas Venclova, in *Pašnekesys žiemą: Eilėraščiai ir vertimai*. Published by Vaga. Copyright © 1991 by Tomas Venclova. Reprinted by permission of Tomas Venclova.

Unpublished translations of selections from Petrarch's *De vita solitaria* by Caroline Stark. Reprinted by permission of Caroline Stark.

Excerpt from "The Book of Ephraim" from *The Changing Light at Sandover* by James Merrill. Copyright © 1980, 1982 by James Merrill. Used by permission of Alfred A. Knopf, a division of Random House, Inc.

Excerpts from *Antigone* by Sophocles, translated by Paul Woodruff. Copyright © 2001 by Hackett Publishing Company, Inc. Reprinted by permission of Hackett Publishing Company, Inc.

Excerpts from *Antigone* by Sophocles, translated by Wm. Blake Tyrrell and Larry J. Bennett, in *Diotima* (http://www.stoa.org/diotima/anthology/ant/). Copyright © 1996 by Wm. Blake Tyrrell and Larry J. Bennett. Reprinted by permission of Wm. Blake Tyrrell.

Excerpt from *Antigone* by Sophocles, translated by Kelly Cherry, in *Sophocles 2: King Oedipus, Oedipus at Colonus, Antigone*, edited by David R. Slavitt and Palmer Bovie. Copyright © 1999 by the University of Pennsylvania Press. Reprinted by permission of the University of Pennsylvania Press.

Excerpt from *Antigone* by Sophocles, from *The Three Theban Plays* by Sophocles, translated by Robert Fagles. Copyright © 1982 by Robert Fagles. Used by permission of Viking Penguin, a division of Penguin Group (USA) Inc.

Excerpt from *The Antigone of Sophocles, an English Version* by Dudley Fitts and Robert Fitzgerald. Copyright © 1939 by Houghton Mifflin Publishing Company and renewed 1967 by Dudley Fitts and Robert Fitzgerald. Reprinted by permission of the publisher.

Excerpt from *Antigone* by Sophocles, translated by Nicholas Rudall. Copyright © 1998 by Ivan R. Dee, Publisher. Reprinted with permission of Ivan R. Dee, Publisher.

Excerpt from *Antigone* by Sophocles, translated, with notes and an introduction, by Ruth Fainlight and Robert J. Littman. From *The Theban Plays: Oedipus the King, Oedipus at Colonus, Antigone.* Copyright © 2009 by Ruth Fainlight and Robert J. Littman. Reprinted with permission of The Johns Hopkins University Press.

Excerpt from "Love and Learning" (unpublished essay) by David Coleman. Reprinted by permission of David Coleman.

Excerpts from *The Principia: Mathematical Principles of Natural Philosophy,* by Isaac Newton. Copyright © 1999 by the Regents of the University of California. Published by the University of California Press. Reprinted by permission of the University of California Press.

Excerpt from letter from Mother Teresa to Father Neuner, written before January 8, 1965, published in *Mother Teresa: Come Be My Light; The Private Writings of the Saint of Calcutta,* edited by Brian Kolodiejchuk (New York: Doubleday, 2007). Copyright © 2007 by the Mother Teresa Center. Reprinted by permission of the Mother Teresa Center.

Excerpts from *Notes from Underground* by Fyodor Dostoevsky, translated by Michael Katz. Copyright © 2001, 1989 by W. W. Norton & Company. Reprinted by permission of W. W. Norton & Company.

Excerpt from *Charlotte's Web* by E. B. White. Copyright © 1952 by E. B. White. Text copyright © renewed 1980 by E. B. White. Used by permission of HarperCollins Publishers.

Excerpt from "Letter to John Selby," excerpt from "Letter to A" from *The Habit of Being: Letters of Flannery O'Connor,* edited by Sally Fitzgerald. Copyright © 1979 by Regina O'Connor. Reprinted by permission of Farrar, Straus and Giroux, LLC.

Excerpt from a notebook of Robert Frost, ca. 1937–1942, Dartmouth College, Rauner Special Collections Library, Robert Frost Collection,

1

~

Introduction:
The Chatter of the Present

In June 1976, at age twelve, I traveled alone to Ithaca to visit a scientist, his wife, and their two-year-old daughter. During the previous school year, when they lived in my town, I babysat the daughter; I was with her, day by day, as she seized new words and learned the alphabet with glee. At the end of the year, when we said goodbye, they invited me out to Ithaca. Weeks in advance, I sent daily postcards to the little girl, counting down the days until the trip; from the first day of the visit, I wished *its* days would not count down. It seemed no life could be more delightful, no house more mind-warming than theirs, with the cozy living room and the deck overlooking the gorge. We talked about science and inventions, ate Marmite (a very salty spread, popular in Britain), listened and laughed to Tom Lehrer songs, and went water-skiing (I barely stood up on the skis, once). The daughter made sense of the world in new ways every day. She had always called me "Danana" (*Dah*-na-na), but one day, out of the blue, on the motorboat, she carefully pronounced my name, keeping the stress on the first syllable (*Di*-a-na). Upon returning home and sitting down for supper, she proudly lifted a banana and said, "*Bi*-a-na!" Of course: if Danana was really Diana, then a banana must be a biana.

While I was there, an article appeared in a national magazine, with a few paragraphs about the scientist; it said, more or less, that he spewed out fanciful and outrageous theories by the hundreds without regard for their truth. This seemed unfair and rude; his theories may not all have proved correct, but many did, and he did not form them casually or irresponsibly. He had

1

knowledge of a wide range of fields and drew connections that others did not immediately understand. The scientist and his wife discussed the article in low tones; I became agitated as I listened. I revered the scientist and wanted to defend him. How could he have been treated this way? I wondered. How could the writer have been so snide? A few minutes later, I heard the scientist whistling. He had put the matter behind him.

I was amazed by his calm and cheer; I must have made a comment. His wife explained to me that he could not afford to worry too much about what others thought; he had his work to do. "Many scientists are not fully recognized in their lifetime," she pointed out. Her tone was matter-of-fact, without pity or martyrdom. Of course he had won recognition in his lifetime; of course this mattered. Of course negative reviews could sting. But he and she kept all of this in perspective. A scientist's work pushes up against the unknown; it may be decades, even centuries, before its value is fully apparent. To take the long view—to work without excessive concern for the judgment of others—is to recognize the solitude in one's work and life.

Many years later, I read W. H. Auden's essay "Yeats as an Example" (1948). It expresses something similar to what I learned in Ithaca. Auden begins by explaining why poets are limited in their appreciation of other poets: they are less concerned with a poet's value than with what the poet can teach them about their own writing. A poet, he explains, "will often prefer an inferior poem from which he can learn something at the moment to a better poem from which he can learn nothing." Thus, the young poet begins with "an excessive admiration for one or more of the mature poets of his time." But then he becomes disillusioned with his heroes; his admiration "is all too apt to turn into an equally excessive hostility and contempt." This leads to his statement:

> I shall not attempt, therefore, in this paper, to answer such questions as, "How good a poet is Yeats? Which are his best poems and why?"—that is the job of better critics than I and of posterity—but rather to consider him as a predecessor whose importance no one will or can deny, to raise, that is to say, such questions as, "What were the problems which faced Yeats as a poet as compared with ours? How far do they overlap? How far are they different? In so far as they are different, what can we learn from the way in which Yeats dealt with his world, about how to deal with our own?"[1]

"That is the job of better critics than I and of posterity." Auden acknowledges that he is not in a position to judge William Butler Yeats, as he lacks adequate perspective. What he *can* do is examine how Yeats responded to the problems that faced him. This recognition makes room for the poetry of

Yeats and for a remarkable essay. Similar tones and ideas pervaded my childhood; adults reminded me that many authors, artists, and scientists lived in obscurity or mixed popularity and that the meaning of their work came clear only over time. If it wasn't common wisdom, it was in the air, in the books. It may even have been a cliché, but people sensed the truth in it. If they hadn't read Auden's words on Yeats, at least they had borrowed something of his humility. They knew—or at least believed up to a point—that the chatter of the present, about the present, cannot always grasp the present.

I heard, likewise, that being popular wasn't everything, that having many friends often meant having no good friends. It is more important to have a few true friends, people said, than to be surrounded by crowds; it is more honorable to make judgments on one's own than to adopt those of a group. Of course, people fell short of this most of the time; children my age were exceedingly concerned with popularity and conformity, and those who did not fit in (including myself, until high school) fell prey to bullies and jeering cliques. I was often bewildered by social codes that my peers regarded as all-important: wearing just the right jeans, standing and talking just so, being seen with the right people, watching the right TV shows. Nor was this only child's play; I often heard stories about adult hypocrisy, gossip, and pettiness—in academia, in small towns, and elsewhere. All the same, I carried the knowledge that some of the kindest and most gifted people lead lonely lives and find company in books, faith, music, or their own thoughts. I read *Jane Eyre*, and to this day remember the words of Helen, "If all the world hated you, and believed you wicked, while your own conscience approved you, and absolved you from guilt, you would not be without friends."[2]

Later I learned the other side of the matter: recognition by one's contemporaries, and acceptance by one's peers, does count for something. It can make the difference between a published book and a manuscript in a filing cabinet. It can allow a recording to wend its way to listeners around the world. It can bring comfort and cheer. It can break a trail for lasting friendships, not just fleeting acquaintanceships. Conversely, much unrecognized work is actually atrocious; much of what critics ignore or debunk deserves no better. Some social outcasts are hateful and cruel, not just victims of a prejudiced society. Yet, even with this understanding, I remained convinced that I should not depend too much on others' approval or applause, and that I must judge people and things with my own mind and conscience.

Today it is hard to do much of anything without learning—and, involuntarily, caring—what the wider world thinks of it. We subject ourselves to instantaneous appraisals, having forgotten about the limited value of popularity and the importance of the long view. Go online to the *New York Times*, comment on an article, and others will recommend your comment (or not). As you scroll through the comments, you can see how many votes each one received. Other websites have similar options. Some of this is justified: comments on the Internet vary so widely in quality that it helps to have some way of ranking them. Nonetheless, we lose the private relationship with the written word. Just about everything is subjected to a group forum, a rushed judgment—always present, always a little bit in the way. Those with mobile gadgets can check their "friends'" ratings of just about everything they buy, visit, or attend—a concert, a book, a restaurant, a neighborhood. Everyone can fit David Riesman's description of the "inside-dopester"—the person who is in on the latest chatter, the consensus of the group, the gossip, the hits, the scores—and yet is moved by nothing.[3] To be moved by something, one needs to think and feel on one's own.

THIS BOOK EXAMINES ways in which individuals, schools, and culture are pushing solitude aside. It looks at what solitude is; why we need it and avoid it; and what can happen when we drive it away.

At the outset I should take on the notion of "we." It is one of the trickiest words in the book. When I use "we" to describe a cultural tendency, I recognize that there are many outliers. Personal observations, psychological and sociological studies, and historical and literary works help define this "we"—but how can I claim to be part of this group when, by virtue of writing about it, I stand outside it? I answer that I am part of this "we" even as I view it from the outside. I am more affected by the current culture than I would like. The concept of "we" is complex, and I will return to it over the course of the book. I wish there were a more fitting pronoun, something between "we" and "I." There is "one," of course, but one can only use "one" so often before one starts sounding awkward. For now, "we" refers to a general societal tendency with many variations and exceptions. On the whole, in schools, work, and life, we are driving solitude to the edges, even as we become lonelier and more isolated in some ways.

Our public schools, which should encourage students to see beyond the claims of the moment, have instead caved in to the immediate demands of the larger culture and economy. Convinced that the outside world calls for collaboration, school leaders and policy makers expect teachers to incorporate group work in their lessons, the more of it the better. They do not pay enough attention to the ingredients of good collaboration: independent thought, careful pondering of a topic, knowledge of the subject, and attentive listening. State standards—such as those of New York and Washington—devote large sections to group work and social interaction while failing to name a single literary work that students should read. Instead of structuring their curriculum around literature itself, schools focus on processes and strategies.[4] As a consequence, students lose both the quiet thought and the things worth thinking about.

One telling example in elementary school is the "turn and talk" activity, where a teacher pauses in a story she is reading aloud, asks a question, and has the students talk to their partners about it. When they are done, they join hands and raise them in the air. Instead of losing themselves in the story, they must immediately contend with the reactions of their peers. Many districts require small-group activities, throughout the grades, because such activities presumably allow all students to talk in a given lesson. Those who set and enforce such policies do not consider the drawbacks of so much talk. Talk needs a counterbalance of thought; without thought, it turns into chatter.

Outside of school, young people and adults surround themselves with "friends" they have never met or have met but do not know personally: strangers who "friend" them on Facebook or connect with them on some other network. Not only have the meanings of "friend" and "like" become trivial, but people judge themselves, at least somewhat, by the number and status of friends and followers they can amass. Those who use online dating services may rely on "friends'" recommendations or votes. Those who keep a personal blog may take pride or shame in the number of hits or "visits" they receive every day, though they have no idea in what spirit those visits occurred—whether someone landed on their blog by chance, visited it out of boredom, or came to read it out of genuine interest. As a result, a person winds up with a lot of virtual "stuff"—data, personal connections, votes—but little sense of the value of these things.

Such clutter can take over one's life; as a result, some have fought back, opting out of online networks or protesting their policies. Some have called for a return to slowness: slow reading, slow action, slow living overall.[5] But it can be difficult to fight back; online networks have many enticements, and they create a nonstop social life, however illusory. There is always the hint that if you do not rush to respond to something, you may lose out. The idea of being at home alone in the evening, without logs and blogs and instant messages, seems overwhelming. There are many problems intertwined here, but most can be traced to our weakened capacity for being alone and our dwindling sense of any life beyond the immediate scramble.

We have become anxious about walking away from crowds, even for brief intervals. It is easier to stay in the mix. We deftly and swiftly navigate (fingers and feet) from one conversation to another, from one set of noises into another. As soon as the noise stops, we often lose our footing. Workers, students, actors, managers reach for their cell phones as soon as the rehearsal, class, or meeting is done; it is a way of saying, "I am with others now; I have a right to turn away." The cell phone relieves us of the obligation to face those around us, but also prevents us from being by ourselves. This is not to say that past generations were staunch in their solitude; it was probably always difficult to go off on one's own, perhaps more difficult in some ways than it is now. But they did not have so many societies to grab, so many messages blinking and jangling throughout the day. When two people said goodbye after meeting, they would walk their separate ways without being able to talk to anyone else immediately. They could reflect on their meeting with the person, prepare themselves for what they had to do next, or simply enjoy the walk. We have not given up quiet walks, but the sidewalks are noisy with cell phone conversations rushing by. It is hard to go anywhere—to a library, store, park, or restaurant—without seeing phones out and illuminated. What we miss are the minutes between conversations, not only ours, but other people's. Those minutes may have been peaceful or fraught with anxiety, but in any event they are scarce now.

It is difficult to measure or define the loss. Loss, after all, is continuous, and whatever we feel we have lost was probably lost long ago (or was never had). In 1931 the philosopher Irwin Edman wrote that the contemporary individual has "too little time for that steady contemplation which is an absorption in the world and in things; he has too many odds and ends of time for brooding, for the internal canvassing of his own doubts and insufficiencies."[6] If the loss of contemplation was felt eighty years ago, have we really lost it, or do we merely imagine we have lost it? Perhaps neither: we have not lost contemplation entirely, nor are we imagining things. Edman had no idea that one day our lives would be dominated by the distractions of TV and Internet; those "odds and ends of time" are no longer hours here and there, but minutes and seconds. Even brooding receives short shrift. Machines have relieved us of many tedious tasks; theoretically, we have more time to do what we want. Yet our lives have become noisier and more fragmented; we fail somehow to exercise our choices.

How to respond to the incessant polls, updates, ringtones, throbbing lights? Leaving society and taking up residence in the woods is one option, but for most of us it solves nothing. In libraries and bookstores we find loners' manifestos, hermits' diaries, and guides to survival in the wilderness, but they offer a specific lifestyle or retreat, not a way of living in the world. Most of us need others and wish to be involved in lives beyond our own. Even the so-called recluses throughout history had close relationships; they were rarely as isolated as hearsay has made them seem. Emily Dickinson had passionate friendships. Henry David Thoreau had guests in his hut and loved to go into town and strike up conversations. We should not have to choose between nagging buzz and lake-like stillness. There are flies buzzing on any lake, and lakes below every buzz.

It is not the isolation, but the consciousness that we need: the knowledge that an hour listening to a piano piece might give us more than a month of Internet-filled evenings. Besides consciousness, we need the strength to do what we find most rewarding. The strength takes time to build. Mark Bauerlein writes that today's "screen intelligence," while good for certain kinds of mental agility, "conditions minds against quiet, concerted study, against imagination unassisted by visuals, against linear, sequential analysis of texts, against an idle afternoon with a detective story and nothing else." Nicholas Carr puts it eerily: "What the Net seems to be doing is chipping away my capacity for concentration and contemplation." William Deresiewicz points to the desperation in our Internet habits: "a constant effort to stave off the possibility of solitude, a continuous attempt, as we sit alone at our computers, to maintain the imaginative presence of others."[7] The effects of this continuous company may be more damaging than we realize. We may become so accustomed to instant affirmation—from one source or another—that we stop daring to stake out with our thoughts. We may stave off pain and loneliness, but in doing so, we limit ourselves. Of course there is no need to suffer more than necessary, but a certain kind of pain reminds us who we are, what we think, and what we love.

The Internet answers and exacerbates our need for feedback; we rely on devices and services that seize, frame, and market the latest instant. If our minds become accustomed to jittery stimuli and quick answers, then we may come to resist the more meaningful activities. It is hard for us to give up the little attractions and distractions that fill the seconds of the day—and tempting to hold on to them. Instead of browsing the library stacks, we do a Google search. Instead of writing a long letter, we dash off a few lines in an email. We go against what we ourselves want; those who love the stories of Anton Chekhov may find themselves reading blogs, not Chekhov. Those who love long face-to-face conversations learn to content themselves with quick emails, Twitter updates, and cell phone check-ins, simply because habit and convenience take over, and because others are doing the same. The more quiet thought we give up, the less we remember of its contents, and the more we continue to give up. We are like the drunken man in *The Little Prince* who drinks to forget that he is ashamed of his drinking. In all this we become edgier and jumpier but lose our true leaps and edges. Deresiewicz writes that we "have made of geniality—the weak smile, the polite interest, the fake invitation—a cardinal virtue. Friendship may be slipping from our grasp, but our friendliness is universal."[8]

This loss of thoughtfulness creates a longing. Whatever the benefits of technology and teamwork, many lament the loss of time for study, contemplation, and daydreaming. A teacher needs time to work alone; not every moment outside the classroom should be spent collaborating or socializing with colleagues. An artist needs to be able to shut the door and focus on her work, without being subjected to hours of peer critique (in person or by email). A scientist needs to ponder a problem without worrying about the opinions of the team, department, or funding agency. A carpenter needs to be able to build a porch without constant interruptions on the cell. Many of us have wanted some ruminative time, some allowance for sifting things through, some relief from our self-willed crowdedness. Petrarch (Francesco Petrarca) wrote in 1346 that those caught up in the business of others "are ruled by the power of another man's nod and learn what they must do from another man's look. They can claim nothing as their own."[9] More than 650 years later, we have not lost the need to claim something of our own. We may be losing the means, as we fill our moments with quick communications from people close and distant.

Part of the problem is a cultural tendency toward excess, a desire to see salvation in each new thing. We don't know how to say "enough." In her most recent book, *Alone Together*, Massachusetts Institute of Technology (MIT) professor Sherry Turkle quotes a high school student's comment that "technology is bad because people are not as strong as its pull." If children knew how to take time away from their devices and away from their peers, then a bit of social activity and digital communication in the classroom wouldn't hurt. But the amount of time students spend with digital devices is staggering. In 2009, a national study by the Kaiser Family Foundation found that students from ages eight to eighteen devoted an average of seven hours and thirty-eight minutes daily to the use of media, much of which is spent on two or more devices at once. Students are online, chatting, telling their latest updates to groups of "friends," picking up flashes of gossip, watching video clips, posting quick comments to blogs and Facebook, sending text messages, calling friends on their cell phones, watching TV, and maybe doing a bit of homework. Then they enter the classroom and begin chatting all over again. There is little respite from wireless social activity, little time alone with a book or a piece of music. Yet instead of giving students a break from the buzz, many schools try to "catch up" with the kids, bringing in more technology, using cell phones in class, and encouraging the use of online networks. A video used in teacher training sessions offers a principal's grim advice, "If you can't beat 'em, join 'em."[10]

The constant chatter affects our behavior; the good habit of shutting up is on the wane. Our media, technology, and networks not only blur lines of privacy but can turn into tools of rudeness. I have been in lecture and performance halls where, despite repeated reminders, a cell phone would ring again and again. While the event was in progress, I would see the flash of devices as audience members checked their text messages or sent out Twitter updates. Many assume they have the right to communicate with others at all times. On trains, conversations over cell phones can be long and loud, as though intended for a mass audience. Some trains have quiet cars; we may be seeing more of those. It takes determination to stake out some quiet; it is a fight for internal land.

Technology can be a boon if it serves rather than dominates us. I marvel at the sixteenth-century books that I can download. I envy those studying foreign languages today, especially Russian; there are many ways to read and listen to the language online. The Internet also lets us track down long-lost friends and acquaintances who might otherwise be hard to locate. In some ways it can offer us quiet; instead of having the phone ringing constantly, we can put thought into an email at our own convenience. The Web can connect us with others who have similar interests; it provides community for those who live in isolation. Yet we give up much in return for these services. We become so accustomed to quick answers that we lose the habit of slow browsing and reading. We give information about ourselves, often unwittingly, and put up with animated advertisements and other intrusions. We are just starting to tackle the privacy issues and other complications of recent technology. We may come to grips with them, over time, if we stand back and consider what we are doing.

Standing alone is not easy or always enjoyable, but we would flail without some room for solitude. We cannot have meaningful relationships with others unless we know how to stand apart. We cannot learn unless we make room for learning in our minds. We cannot make sound decisions unless we are able to examine the options on our own, in quiet, along with any advice or information at hand. We cannot distinguish fads from sound ideas if we have never questioned social pressures and fashions. We cannot participate in a democracy without deep understanding of the issues at stake. We cannot accomplish anything of beauty unless we are willing to spend many hours working on it alone. We cannot endure disappointment, rejection, bereavement, or distress unless we have a place to go in ourselves. Without solitude, our very thoughts tend toward one-liners. Without solitude, we set ourselves up for halfhearted pursuits. The catch is that solitude, by its nature, cannot be a movement. Each person must find it alone.

WHAT IS SOLITUDE? The second chapter will offer a long definition. For now, let solitude be our aloneness even among others. It is with us no matter what we do. We have solitude even in marriages, even in intimate friendships, even in collaboration. When we have no grasp of solitude, no respect for it, it may elude us or overwhelm us, and our social life at its liveliest will be lacking. But if we come to understand it, it will offer many riches. If it is filled with interesting things—poetry, puzzles, music, art, thoughts, projects, books—we may relish it. If it seems empty or frightening, we may still face it and learn from it. Petrarch points to three aspects of solitude: solitude of place, solitude of time, and solitude of the mind.[11] While all three aspects are important, the third is the essence of solitude, as it does not depend on external conditions. The primary solitude discussed here will be the solitude of the mind.

Our most important experiences, joyous or difficult, throw us back onto ourselves. In her 1892 speech "Solitude of Self," Elizabeth Cady Stanton said, "We ask no sympathy from others in the anxiety and agony of a broken friendship or shattered love. When death sunders our nearest ties, alone we sit in the shadow of our affliction. Alike mid the greatest triumphs and darkest tragedies of life we walk alone." (This comes from an activist and mother of seven children.) Such solitude may come clearer over time; as we grow older, we become familiar with the steps going down, far past the level of our friends and families, and start to welcome these descents. Harold Bloom writes that "as intelligence and awareness increase in us, we can believe that what is best and oldest in us cannot be known by others."[12] To honor what is "best and oldest in us," we must not be afraid when others do not greet it, cheer it, or comfort it. We must know how to hold it ourselves.

Solitude may be painful—not only because of the realizations it brings, but because of the very experience, for example, of picking up an instrument and playing just to play, not because anybody will hear it. When we do something like that, we may hear a call to go a little deeper, to make the notes sound richer, to change the phrasing. We may become aware of our faults; we may come to listen more closely to ourselves. With a little time, distractions drop away. It may come as a shock that there were so many distractions. We may find it discouraging that so much work needs to be done, that the instrument needs so much practicing. And there may be a frightening beauty—frightening because it needs no one in the moment.

Solitude does not always involve activity; far from it. There may be nothing to do, or nothing that seems appealing in the moment. What then? How to handle the emptiness? Some believe that the emptiness is the very thing needed. For some, it is an opportunity for meditation; for others, it is an ultimate truth. Perhaps we need times of emptiness in order to confront ourselves. Leo Tolstoy's *Death of Ivan Ilyich* is a tale of such a confrontation. Ivan Ilyich realizes while dying that his whole life has been a show; as he sheds the facade of his life, he sees something clear and beautiful for the first time. But perhaps emptiness has an everyday role as well. Maybe those "empty" moments are needed pauses. They may have a meaning; they may not. They are sometimes no better or worse than the full moments; they are simply there.

Some fear solitude because it seems selfish. It is individualistic and competitive, some say; it is Western and white, others say. We are surrounded with collectivist slogans, such as "There's no 'I' in 'team.'" It seems wrong to pull ourselves apart, when we could be doing something for others. It seems snobbish to work alone, when we could be part of a joyous society, a palpitating, productive whole. It seems rude to turn down invitations, to ignore the phone, to spend days on one's own. Yet if we lose the ability to say no or to leave a group, there can be no assent or community. If we cannot handle being alone, then our social activity becomes an escape. We may not face what is troubling or delighting us; we may settle for pale amusements and diluted truths. We may find excuses for treating others poorly, neglecting responsibilities, or avoiding the things we love to do. We may tangle ourselves in the talk, the activity, the rush to be up to date.

Solitude is an opportunity for reckoning with ourselves. In solitude we may recognize our shortcomings. We may see where we have gone wrong during the day and think about how to set things right. We may practice our work, arts, and hobbies; enjoy books; and hone our thoughts—without interruption, if we dare. We may become more capable of loving, as we grow stronger in ourselves. We may grow more compassionate toward those who suffer loneliness, confusion, and fear. We will not end loneliness, confusion, or fear, not in ourselves or others. But we will have a way to collect ourselves. Anyone can feel despair, but no one has to give in to despair, social pressure, or anything else. Solitude, understood and practiced well, can keep a person from giving in.

THIS BOOK IS not autobiographical or confessional. Yet a few words about my background are in order.

I have never been able to ignore solitude. I have always recognized its presence, whether I embraced it, resisted it, struggled with it, aspired toward it, saw it in others, recognized it in literature, or simply lived in it. For most of my life, my interests have been largely solitary but not exclusively so. Beginning in childhood, I spent hours a day practicing cello, writing stories, and reading. I had no idea how to belong to a social group, but I had a few wonderful friends. I attended many different schools, public and private, and spent two years abroad with my family: one year in the Netherlands, at age ten, and one year in the Soviet Union, at age fourteen. The schools I attended over the years ranged from experimental to traditional, from dreary to delightful. I adapted to each of them, to varying degrees, while pursuing interests on my own.

In high school, in Boston, I finally found the studies I had wanted so badly. I took classes in Greek, Latin, French, English, Russian, history, music, math, and physics. During this time, I formed friendships with classmates who remain in my life today. A group of us became close; sometimes we would have parties, go roller-skating along the Charles River, or feast on enormous sandwiches at Mississippi's in Kenmore Square. While I relished those get-togethers, I generally preferred spending time with individual friends. Group conversations sometimes confused me, and I found one-on-one conversations more satisfying. One exception was whole-class discussion of a work of literature. There, the focus was defined, and there was time to think, look into the text, comment, and listen. The teacher could direct the discussion by posing challenging questions or drawing attention to a particular passage. I was fortunate to have English teachers who showed how this could happen.

From a young age, I was torn between longing for solitude and longing for company; I wanted both and had neither, or so it seemed to me. In high school I admired a girl who spent many an early morning reading in the school library. She took Latin, Greek, and French, as did I. She had quiet spunk and a sense of humor. She got parts in the school plays (I did not). She showed me indirectly that solitude can hold many seeming contradictions (which often turn out not to be contradictions at all). I remain grateful for her example. My teachers had subtle or not-so-subtle forms of solitude: their particular tone of voice as they read a passage, or the glint in their eyes when they brought up certain ideas. There were many others: peers and adults who wrote poetry, played musical instruments, stayed silent in chants, spoke up in defense of a person or idea, or poked fun at jargon and dogma. And then there was the solitude of walking down the school hallway and suddenly hearing a chorus singing a madrigal, the different parts wending their way around each other and resting on a strange chord. For a minute or two it didn't matter where I was, what I had planned to do, or who was rushing past me. The sounds were my location and company.

In college, at Yale, my solitude fell apart for a little while. An intense loneliness took over. I can explain it in many ways, but I will probably never know exactly why it happened. I wanted to be part of a community; I tried churches, political groups, and various social groups. I thought that if I just found the right group, my loneliness would end. I devoted myself to relationships that barely existed or that were not what I imagined. Nothing quite worked. Any group I joined would disappoint me in the end, and I the group; its purposes and mine were not the same. The loneliness persisted in some form for many years, but slowly I found that when I stood my own ground, working on things I loved to do and did well, the terrible sense of loneliness would go away, and people would come to me. It took a long time for this to happen, and I would not reduce it to a cliché. People often say, "Love comes to you when you're not looking," or "You have to love yourself for people to love you"; these maxims are only partly true. Some people despise themselves yet somehow endear themselves to others; some self-sufficient people end up alone, precisely because they are self-sufficient. Loneliness is part mystery; it can attack even those who know better, and it can go away. There is also a certain joy in it; when you sit in a pit covered with branches you start to notice their triangles and trapezoids. Those irregular shapes, and the trembling of a leaf or needle, tell you that these are branches, not iron grating, and that you can actually get out of there.

Throughout my life I have read, memorized, and written poetry; I steeped myself in music and literature. I wrote my dissertation on Nikolai Gogol, who was strange and solitary and brilliant. I translated the Lithuanian poetry of Tomas Venclova, a project that demanded many hours of listening to tapes of the original Lithuanian and playing with possible words and phrases in English. I memorized some of the poems in the Lithuanian, and I still repeat them to myself. To this day I love to memorize poems; it is like adding an upper story to your house, as you can go into those rooms whenever you want. Memorizing is intensely solitary and contemplative; unfortunately many schools have written it off as "rote" learning.

I have worked in education, editing, computer programming, counseling, and cataloging. Each field or job had a different combination of society and solitude. I often found myself too rushed, with too little time for thinking or for independent projects. Throughout the years, people would ask me, "Why don't you teach?" I didn't want to teach at a college; it was a predictable path. My parents were college professors, and I grew up surrounded by teachers and students. I didn't want to have to confine myself to what was deemed scholarly or academic, or what pertained immediately to my field. I didn't like the careerism that I encountered in graduate school: the focus on building one's résumé, making the right impressions and connections, doing everything just so, and finally getting tenure (or not). But the idea of teaching in a public school did appeal to me. I had taught before, with great enjoyment—on the Crow Reservation in Montana for a summer, in Kyrgyzstan for a summer, at Trinity College in Hartford for a year, and at Yale as a teaching assistant. I thought public school teaching would draw on all that I had done before and allow me to combine many interests. In this I have not been disappointed, though I was in for a jolt or two.

I began teaching English as a Second Language (ESL) in the public schools in 2005, as a New York City Teaching Fellow. I plunged into the work and thrived in it, but it was not as thoughtful a profession as I had expected. The obsession with group work baffled me. In many of my education classes we were told to put our students in groups and have them engage in paired and small-group talk. This always had to result in "evidence" of learning, but the "evidence" could be as trivial as a list or chart. The actual topic of the lesson mattered less than the process, it seemed. As one education professor put it, the content of the lesson was a "vehicle for the strategy." The bias in favor of social activity—and the heavy overlay of jargon—pervaded faculty meetings, professional development sessions, and much of education writing.

The New York City Department of Education had mandated a "workshop model," in which the teacher was supposed to be not a "sage on the stage," but a "guide on the side." Students were supposed to learn from each other. Lessons had to follow a specific format, no matter what the subject: the teacher would write the "objective" on the board and present a "minilesson," seven to ten minutes long. This was followed by "guided practice," where the teacher would help the students apply the lesson to a specific text or problem. Then the students would practice in groups (or sometimes alone). Finally, in the last five minutes, the groups would "share out" what they had accomplished and learned.

During teacher trainings, teachers themselves were put in small groups and asked to perform activities together. Just as I started to ponder a topic, I had to move into my group and start working and talking. The work seemed superficial and rushed. It seemed, moreover, that the groups reached predictable conclusions about whatever they read or did. The instructor would move from group to group, listening to each discussion for a few minutes. When, at the end of class, she pulled together the insights of the day, it seemed that many of the finer points had vanished. The best way to challenge common assumptions, I found, was to speak out in the whole-class discussion; there, a point once made would not go away. Whole-class discussions can be intimidating for that very reason: they have a public feel, and the speech is unmitigated. That is one reason not to avoid them: they keep speech bare. When words are overly socialized, they lose their sharpness, truth, and error. We need the errors as well as the shining points.

I wondered why group work was emphasized to such a degree, given its obvious drawbacks. Part of it was the nature of the subject, ESL; students learning English need ample opportunity to speak, and teacher trainings rightly emphasize this. Yet group work reigned supreme across the subjects. I wanted to understand how this situation had come about.

I began to pursue this question on my own. I read books on the history of education, such as *Left Back* by Diane Ravitch. I was fascinated by Ravitch's description of the education philosopher Michael John Demiashkevich, whose writing sparkles with love of literature. Demiashkevich, who wrote in the 1920s and '30s, sharply criticized those aspects of the so-called New Education, which emphasized experimentation and activity over book-learning. He noted that not all of the New Education was harmful or even new; good teachers had practiced many of its principles for centuries. Its main flaw was its one-sided adherence to a philosophy of constant change; it downplayed the enduring aspects of education, the things passed down from generation to generation. Demiashkevich was admired by a few in his time but led a lonely life that ended in suicide. I tracked down copies of his books, read and reread them, and made a trip to Nashville to read the Demiashkevich Papers at the Vanderbilt University Special Collections. I immersed myself in those papers; some made me grin, and others made me cry. In his work and correspondence I found something kindred. This experience led me to write an article on his *Introduction to the Philosophy of Education* (1935).[13]

I could see how a philosophy of constant change continued to dominate education reform; reformers spoke disparagingly over the status quo, as though a thing's very stability made it wrong. Still, questions remained unanswered. Why have the mantras about cooperative learning gone unchallenged? Why do so many educators insist that "research has shown" the superiority of group work over individual study? I looked into research on cooperative learning and found that the researchers' arguments were often circular. Assuming that social interaction in school is inherently beneficial, researchers argue that group work leads to improved social interaction—granted, interaction that focuses on a task.[14] This may be so, but is the premise sound? Should schools hold social interaction high among their priorities—and, if so, what kind? What is good education, what ends does it serve, and what principles sustain it? Many assumptions need to be taken apart and reconsidered. Demiashkevich stressed the importance of knowing the philosophy behind an educational policy. If we understand the history of our ideas, if we understand what education is, we are in a better position to form and evaluate policy than we would otherwise be.

Other questions puzzled me as well. I noticed that education policy makers attached great value to "results" without considering what the results actually meant or what students were learning. If test scores went up, that supposedly meant a district or school was doing well, even if the tests contained very little of substance. There is currently a great push to evaluate teachers on the basis of their students' test scores and to publish the names and ratings—as though such ratings could tell us anything about what goes on in a classroom. One teacher might be teaching Shakespeare, another no specific literature at all—but if their students have similar scores on the test and are demographically similar, it is assumed that the two teachers have similar levels of "effectiveness." How did we lose sight of what we are actually trying to teach? How did "results" attain such high stature?

A related question had to do with curriculum. When I began teaching at a middle school, there was no curriculum for ESL. No one told me what to teach, but there were many directives about how to teach. In ESL and English language arts, the general assumption—which I found puzzling—was that teachers should decide for themselves which books to "use." What this meant, in practice, was that no one was really supposed to teach literature as a subject. The lesson was supposed to focus on a strategy, and students were then expected to apply the strategy to the books they were reading in groups or alone. Classroom libraries had very little lasting literature; most of the books were second-rate "chapter books," the kind one reads once and then forgets. Usually there was just one copy of a given book; sometimes they came in small sets. The storage room had a few class sets, but again, very little literature. Why so little attention to literature? Why did the setup almost preclude the teaching of it?

Education is a reflection of the larger culture, or a window into it, or a stethoscope onto it; everything from the curriculum to the bulletin boards comments on the values of the outside world in some way. Lionel Trilling wrote in 1952 that "it is a truism that universal education is one of the essential characteristics of modern democracy and that the quality and content of the education provided is a clear indication of the quality and tendency of the democracy that provides it." Sadly, much of education discussion is reactive, as Trilling points out; people across the ideological spectrum "live in a cave of self-commiseration into which no ray of true criticism ever penetrates."[15] Those who push for more group work are convinced that they must battle the bad old days of teachers doing all the talking. Others have decided that everything should be judged by the results (in terms of test scores and graduation rates), lest the results go down the tubes. These assumptions have led to skewed education goals and flawed initiatives. The jargon builds on itself; those pushing for one solution or another tend to latch onto familiar phrases, which can be difficult to crack.

Yet some educators have called the prevailing assumptions into question again and again. Thinkers such as Ravitch, Demiashkevich, William Torrey Harris, William Henry Maxwell, Alfred North Whitehead, William Chandler Bagley, Isaac Leon Kandel, George S. Counts, Boyd H. Bode, Mortimer Smith, and E. D. Hirsch Jr. (to name a few) have pointed out the transience, silliness, and destructiveness of educational fads. Some bloggers today write thoughtfully about education topics, cutting through the usual oppositions and raising important questions. To restore meaning and quality to education, we need a strong philosophy, the courage to teach and study excellent works, and a good nose for snake oil. We are fortunate to have a few excellent role models, past and present. Each of them has stood alone.

WHY IS THIS book about solitude, and not about privacy, focus, or quiet? Each of these subjects will have a place in this book. Yet solitude is at the center; it brings together every aspect of life. Privacy is largely an ethical and legal matter, though it has other aspects. Focus belongs to the field of psychology, at least in part. Quiet exists outside of human life—in nature, in the night, in inanimate things. Solitude is more than privacy, focus, and quiet, more than law, psychology, or the physical world.

But there is another reason for choosing this topic. The very word "solitude" has resonance and memories: *soledad* in Spanish, *vienatvė* in Lithuanian (from *vienas*, "one"), *odinochestvo* or *uedinenie* in Russian, *eenzaamheid* in Dutch, *solitude* in French, and so forth. I think of William Wordsworth's "I wandered lonely as a Cloud," in which solitude ranges between that strange first line and the lines written by his wife, Mary: "They flash upon that inward eye / Which is the bliss of solitude." Or the bleak yet contemplative lines of Tomas Venclova, "Riba, kur baigiasi jaunystė, / Ertmė, kur keičiasi vienatvė" (The boundary where youth expires, / The space where solitude evolves).[16] If I am to write a book, let at least the main word be a worthy word. Of the others, "quiet" comes the closest, but solitude is still more beautiful and difficult.

This book is not a regretful backward glance at a forsaken past where solitude was honored. It is true that we have become more distracted over time, but solitude was never easy or popular. Writing about the state of the printed word, Steve Wasserman, a literary agent and former editor of the *Los Angeles*

Times Book Review, stresses the importance of steering "soberly between the Party of the Future, whose members are true believers in the utopia they insist will bring us a new dynamic and open medium that will liberate the creative possibilities of humanity, and the Party of the Past, whose members fear that the dystopian tsunami now rushing toward us signals the death knell of civilization, the trivialization of the word."[17] When looking at solitude, I hope to steer between these two parties, neither of which holds a satisfactory answer. If I look frequently at literature of the past, it is because this literature remains vital. The farther we go along in time, the more literature we can draw out of the shelves, electronic files, and minds, provided we remember to do so.

I hope to draw attention to something invisible and wounded, something at the center of our existence that has been pushed to the periphery. I think of the student at the back of the room who likes to observe and think. I think of the courage it takes to leave the computer and go somewhere with a book or take a quiet walk. To find one's own words and thoughts is always a challenge; it is even harder when one's job is filled with rush, busywork, and jargon. So I hope that, by bringing up the subject of solitude, I will help make room for it. Many are concerned about raising workers' "quality of life"; we could be equally concerned about quality of thought.

A few words about collaboration. We hear so much about the virtues of collaboration: how it is needed in school, on the job, in a democracy, and in all sorts of voluntary associations. I agree that it is vital and wonderful. There are few things that I love as much as good collaboration. But we are pursuing it in the wrong way.

Collaboration is fertile when there is something worth collaborating over, and when the people come together out of genuine affinity. I have most enjoyed collaborating over something I cared about deeply: a translation, a book I edited, a musical piece or performance. In such projects, I did most of the work on my own and would then bring it to others. It would have been impossible to do this work through "hands-on" collaboration, that is, by actually doing it together. Certainly we worked out many parts together, but much of it we did on our own. Such collaboration has done much to inspire this book.

So to those who call for more collaboration in the schools, more networking, more emphasis on communication skills, I suggest that solitude makes such collaboration better. We "network" best out of strong interests, without even trying to network. We communicate best when we have wrestled with words and meanings in quiet. If we do not know how to sort through and refine our own thoughts, our communication will mean little. Ralph Waldo Emerson wrote, "Conversation will not corrupt us, if we come to the assembly in our own garb and speech, and with the energy of health to select what is ours and reject what is not."[18]

For a long time I told only one person about this book. I didn't want to contend with opinions—favorable, dismissive, or skeptical—until I had something on paper. I didn't want to talk myself out—to put so much into the conversation that there would be little impetus left for writing. Most of all, I wanted to "come to the assembly" in my own "garb and speech." Slowly, over the months, I told others. Solitude was essential to the book itself, and it was not absolute.

Solitude is not the answer to all things, or even many things; it is a knotty and complex part of existence. But to ignore it is to ignore our nerves and sinew. Let us take a closer look at what it is.

2

~

Definitions of Solitude

One could thumb through all the dictionaries for a definition of solitude, one could drink up all the literature, and yet no definition would do unless it tightened a gulp or unsheathed a grin. It makes no sense to rely on others for definitions; what kind of solitude does that? Yet it would be just as foolhardy to ignore the literature of solitude or to claim ancient ideas as one's own. What seems a modern definition of solitude may have existed for centuries; what seems a personal and unique definition may belong to thousands. The challenge is to scavenge for truth from within and without, turning over hint after hint until one or more of them grabs the mind and holds on. I am looking for solitude that does not depend on deserts or caves, solitude that is with us at all times, whether we recognize it or not. But that is only a beginning. Solitude cannot be grasped at once; it changes as one looks into it. Sometimes it comes closer, sometimes it retreats; sometimes it appears in two places at once. All of its apparitions are part of it—a tree glittering with ice, a cat walking alone, a cackle erupting from a cubicle.

Writers on solitude avoid fencing it in; many prefer to keep it undefined. Thoreau associates solitude with vast space, nature, and removal from society: "I have, as it were, my own sun and moon and stars, and a little world all to myself." Yet his solitude also involves human company: "Every day or two I strolled to the village to hear some of the gossip which is incessantly going on there, circulating either from mouth to mouth, or from newspaper to newspaper, and which, taken in homeopathic doses, was really as refreshing in its way as the rustle of leaves and the peeping of frogs." He turns the question of solitude around, asking not where solitude is, but whether there is anything but solitude: "What sort of space is that which separates a man from his fellows and makes him solitary? I have found that no exertion of the legs can bring two minds much nearer to one another." He suggests, in other words, that humans are separated no matter what they do. Moreover, they can find solitude anywhere—and in it, perspective: "By a conscious effort of the mind we can stand aloof from actions and their consequences; and all things, good and bad, go by us like a torrent."[1]

Like Thoreau, Emerson regards solitude as part of human life but rejects its extremes. We need solitude for integrity of thought, he writes; the "necessity of solitude" is "organic." Yet the "banishment to the rocks and echoes" is just as much a violation of nature as the lack of solitude. He points out that "society and solitude are deceptive names" and that what matters is "readiness of sympathy" and a "sound mind" that can "derive its principles from insight." Nonetheless, he points out, certain personalities and occupations demand solitude; if Archimedes and Newton had taken to clubs and dancing, "we should have had no Theory of the Sphere and no Principia." To be alone, in some cases, is to preserve one's vitality of mind; "each must stand on his glass tripod if he would keep his electricity."[2]

In the twentieth century, writers and scholars have offered a mixture of definitions. The novelist and lecturer John Cowper Powys refers to "a central core, a unifying force, an integral identity," which, through its insistence, "implies a constant renewal of our natal solitude." This "I am I" within us is "absolutely alone," he declares. "It is alone from the first moment of its awareness of life to its last moment on the threshold of what may be its final extinction." Anthony Storr defines solitude as "the capacity to be alone" (in reference to Donald Winnicott's article by that title); such capacity facilitates "learning, thinking, innovation, and maintaining contact with one's inner world."[3] Both Powys and Storr recognize solitude as inherent in human life; while Powys emphasizes its continual presence, Storr emphasizes our variable relation to it.

Many have probed the paradoxes of solitude. In *Solitude: A Philosophical Encounter*, Philip Koch explores the nature of solitude through literature, philosophy, history, and personal reflection. He describes solitude as "the luminous silent space of freedom, of self and nature, of reflection and creative power," existing in "a surprising companionship" with human encounter. Thomas Merton offers a particularly compelling idea. He states that a man "becomes a solitary" at the moment when he is "suddenly aware of his own inalienable solitude and sees that he will never be anything but solitary." This is a permanent yet somehow unattainable condition: "Actual solitude has, as one of its integral elements, the dissatisfaction and uncertainty that come from being face to face with an unrealized possibility." We must accept that solitude is unrealized in order to have it, he explains; we lose "the actuality of the solitude we already have" if we try too hard to find it in external things.[4]

The *Oxford English Dictionary*'s (*OED*'s) definitions of "solitude" have not changed since the first edition, completed in 1928. The *OED* offers four definitions, quoted here (without the examples). Definition 1(b) in particular is intriguing; the *OED* has deemed it "obsolete and rare," yet it may be the most important definition of all.

1. The state of being or living alone; loneliness, seclusion, solitariness (of persons).
    b. The fact of being sole or unique. *Obs. rare.*
2. Loneliness (of places); remoteness from habitations; absence of life or stir.
3. A lonely, unfrequented, or uninhabited place.
4. A complete absence or lack. *rare.*[5]

To illustrate this "obsolete and rare" definition, the *OED* gives two examples. The first is from Henry More's fascinating "Platonick Song of the Soul" (1647), which refutes the notion of the "souls [sic] strange solitude"—that is, the unity of all souls in a single soul. The second example is from Sir Thomas Browne's 1646 treatise *Pseudodoxia Epidemica* (translated as *Vulgar Errors*), which disputes the "solitude" of the phoenix—that is, its uniqueness.[6] We no longer use the word "solitude" to mean "soleness" or "uniqueness," so, strictly speaking, the definition is indeed obsolete and rare. Yet soleness and uniqueness are central to a conception of solitude. To make one's way through the world, one must be to some degree sole; to have a mind apart from others, one must be in some way unique. Ironically, this "obsolete and rare" definition is rather solitary itself, having been set apart by the dictionary's authors.

It seems that solitude must be primarily of the mind; how could it be otherwise? If it relied on external circumstances, on physical removal from others, it would be little more than a vacation spot. Moreover, as Thoreau has hinted, physical removal may have little to do with the matter. If I were separated from others physically but unwilling to think for myself, would I have solitude? It seems I would not; I might live in the woods but mimic everything I encountered, from buzzards to bulldozers. If, on the other hand, I were to sit in a lecture hall with hundreds of others and ponder the lecturer's words, then I would indeed have solitude. Solitude has many aspects, but the solitude of the mind must be at the center.

Solitude is threatened when one lacks the strength or will to honor it from moment to moment: when, out of rush, laziness, or insecurity, one grabs the opinions and company of others, in order to have something to say, or in order not to be alone. The loss of solitude is, at least in part, the capitulation to the judgment of others, the lack of strength or will to stand up for something or to stand apart from the group. It begins with lack of room for thinking: a frenzied life of meeting upon meeting, message upon message, obligation upon obligation. Without time to stand back, or strength to separate oneself, one has little opportunity to form one's own thoughts, let alone defend them. Thoreau warns us that "society is commonly too cheap. We meet at very short intervals, not having had time to acquire any new value for each other."[7] Solitude may be at times opposed to loneliness, for when we hold to our principles, regardless of what others think, we have at least the company of our conscience. But when we fail to stand up for something, or even to know and consider our own thoughts, we become our own outcasts, lonely when surrounded.

In this chapter, I approach the question of solitude's definition in two ways: first, by considering Petrarch's treatise *De vita solitaria* (*On Solitary Life*), and second, by offering some ideas that have arisen from experience, reading, and thought. I chose this combination because one can learn more from one work, closely read, than from fifty skimmed ones, and because solitude involves departure of a kind: going off on one's own and figuring out what is at stake.

WRITTEN OVER 650 years ago, Petrarch's *De vita solitaria* is warm, searching, and joyous, with brooding undertones at times. It associates solitude not only with tranquility, but with literature and friendship. It comes from a quiet but flamboyant poet who led the way into Renaissance humanism; wrote treatises and letters; studied Latin literature throughout his life and built a classical library; treated his friends with great affection and regard; wrote sonnet upon sonnet (as well as other kinds of poems) about love, politics, religion, and friendship; immortalized a certain Laura in verse; and opened up possibilities for poetry in centuries to come. Robert M. Durling notes that the "deepest tributes to Petrarch's influence are in poets great enough to make his lessons their own."[8] Their poems, in other words, came out of a meeting of solitudes; *De vita solitaria* likewise calls for such a meeting. At once religious and secular, the treatise sheds light on some of solitude's layers, contradictions, and uncertainties. A single reading is not enough; it is on the second and third readings that some of the meanings come through.

Jacob Zeitlin's 1924 translation of *De vita solitaria*, the first and only English translation, is a gift to those interested in the subject. Yet there is need for a more faithful rendition of the sound, logic, and life of the work. Sometimes Zeitlin neglects nuances of the original that could easily have been conveyed. Take, for instance, this sentence: "If you ask those very persons why they are ever anxious to be in the company of others, they will answer, if they are in a mood to tell the truth, that it is only because they cannot endure being alone." (*Quod si hos ipsos interroges, cur tam cupide cum aliis semper sint, si verum loqui volent, nil aliud respondebunt, nisi quia secum esse non possunt.*) "Alone" is not quite right; Petrarch expressly contrasts *cum aliis* (with others) with *secum* (with oneself). A clearer translation would be (emphases added) "If you ask those very people why they are always so eager to be *with others*, they will give no other answer, if they wish to tell the truth, but that they are unable to be *with themselves.*"⁹

Elsewhere Zeitlin's decisions distort the meaning on a larger scale; for example, he translates *solitarius* as "the retired man " ("retired" in the sense of "withdrawn" or "secluded"); "solitary" would clearly be richer and more appropriate. Moreover, he uses the term repeatedly for clarification, whereas Petrarch does not. After the first occurrence of *solitarius*, Petrarch refers to the solitary man as "this man" or "this one of ours" (*iste* or *hic noster*), implying the solitary man's closeness to the author and reader, in contrast with the busy man, "that man" (*ille*).¹⁰ A new translation could do more to convey the intensity, subtlety, and elegance of this work. Caroline Stark, a scholar of classics and Renaissance studies, has kindly offered new literal translations of select quotations for this chapter; the source of each translation is indicated in the notes.

A short summary of Petrarch's life is insufficient but will have to suffice here; those wishing to learn more may consult biographies such as Ernest Hatch Wilkins's *Life of Petrarch* and Morris Bishop's *Petrarch and His World.*¹¹ Petrarch was born on July 20, 1304, in Arezzo, Italy. Political conflicts forced the family to relocate several times; when Petrarch was eight, he, his mother, and his brother settled in Carpentras, Provence, near Avignon. In childhood Petrarch discovered Cicero and Virgil, whom he would read throughout his life. When Petrarch was fourteen, his father first sent him to the law school in Montpelier; two years later, he transferred Petrarch to Bologna, where he studied with his brother. While Bologna delighted Petrarch, law studies did not; he later recalled, "I was distressed to be seeking a profit from my talent" (*aegre ferebam lucrum ex ingenio meo quaeri*). His time in Bologna was by no means wasted, as he gained an informal education from his professors and friends and from the lively Bolognese literary culture. His formal studies were interrupted by a student uprising and a trip to Avignon, and in 1326 he and his brother finally left Bologna without graduating. They moved back to Avignon, where he began writing poetry to Laura (whose exact identity and existence are uncertain). Laura did not reciprocate his feelings but remained a source of inspiration (and torment) throughout her life and even after her death in the Plague.[12]

Having rejected a legal career, Petrarch entered ecclesiastical service and would hold various chaplaincies and canonries throughout his life. These positions gave him a livelihood and ample time for his own work. During the Avignon period, Petrarch studied classics and entered the service of Cardinal Giovanni Colonna, whose patronage would sustain him for many years. He made trips to Paris, Rome, and elsewhere, and in 1336 climbed Mont Ventoux with his brother. From the peak, it seemed to him that he could see not only France and Italy, but the past ten years of his life. He opened up Augustine's *Confessions* to a random page and read the sentence, "Men go to admire the heights of mountains and the mighty waves of the sea and the very wide flowing of rivers and the circuit of the ocean and the wheeling of the stars, and they leave themselves behind." In a letter, Petrarch describes the effect of these words on him: "I was stunned, I admit. Asking my brother, who was eager to hear more, not to bother me, I shut the book. I was angry with myself for admiring the things of this world, when I should have learned long since from the pagan philosophers themselves that nothing is admirable except the soul, beside which nothing is great."[13]

A year and a half after the Ventoux incident, Petrarch fled to the rural Fountain of Vaucluse, twenty miles from Avignon, in order to live in solitude. There is no single reason for his flight, nor did he necessarily know all the reasons; he wanted to distance himself from city life and from Laura, and to dedicate himself to literary studies and thought. It is possible that the Ventoux experience had spurred him to devote more attention to spiritual matters. According to Morris Bishop, this was a "sensational act" at the time; there had been hermits and cenobites (monks living communally), but no literary recluses. However, Petrarch was by no means a complete recluse in Vaucluse; Philippe de Cabasolles, bishop of Cavaillon, visited him frequently, and they became dear friends. Others visited him now and then; he also had contact with his servants and remained on the staff of Cardinal Colonna.[14]

Petrarch's relationship to solitude was ambivalent. He loved it but found that it sometimes gave full rein to his flaws: "for a soul obsessed with passions nothing is worse than leisured peace, nothing more hurtful than solitary freedom; for lascivious thoughts creep in and lewd imaginations, and fair-seeming evil, and the familiar curse of idle minds—love." He lived in Vaucluse from 1337 to 1341, with visits to Avignon. In 1341, in Rome, Petrarch was coronated as poet laureate (with a crown of laurels), after some skillful campaigning on his own behalf. He appeared at the ceremony in the robes of King Robert, who had examined him in Naples and deemed him worthy of the honor. He returned to Vaucluse in 1345 for another two years and continued to spend time there periodically until 1353, when he moved permanently to northern Italy. From then until his death in 1374, Petrarch undertook various political missions; wrote and revised volumes of letters, some written in verse and some addressed to Cicero, Seneca, Livy, and other personages of Roman antiquity; revised his poetry collection, the *Canzoniere*, as well as other works; enjoyed friendship and fame; responded eloquently to criticism and denunciation; wrote passionately about the importance of Rome and Italy; endured the deaths of friends, his son, and his beloved grandson Francesco; and assembled a magnificent collection of classical literature, which he bequeathed to Venice with the intent that it would become a public library.[15]

During the second stay in Vaucluse, in 1346, Petrarch began writing *De vita solitaria*, which he revised over the course of twenty years. Intended initially as a letter to Philippe de Cabasolles, the work expanded into a book; he would not let Philippe see it until it was complete. Philippe loved it so much that he often had it read aloud to him at dinner, the time when holy works were customarily read aloud. It is striking that a bishop would choose to have *De vita solitaria* read in place of a holy work—or perhaps as a holy work. In his introduction to the English translation, Zeitlin states that Petrarch departs from the traditional attitude toward contemplation, asserting instead "an ideal purely personal and private," and that he has more in common with Horace and Epicurus than with the mystics.[16] This is a bit of an overstatement; Petrarch draws extensively on the Christian contemplative and mystic traditions, not only in his examples but also in his rejection of the material world for things of the spirit. As the book progresses, Petrarch's own sense of solitude gradually diverges from the initial terms he establishes.

De vita solitaria consists of two books: the first an exploration of the nature, benefits, difficulties, and contradictions of solitude; the second a collection of examples of solitude. The first book contains a dedicatory foreword and six tractates. The first three tractates contrast the busy life with the solitary life, the fourth details the proper practices of solitude, the fifth refutes attacks on the solitary life, and the sixth once again praises solitude and decries the dullness and vanity of city life. The second book contains twelve tractates. Most of these are filled with examples of solitude: he tells of fathers of the Old

Testament, fathers (and some women) of the Christian faith, men outside the Christian faith, philosophers, poets, orators, emperors, legendary figures, and military leaders. There is also a long and fiery digression on the need to recover the Holy Land.

Petrarch acknowledges that, in addressing this book to his friend, he already has a sympathetic audience. "Nevertheless," he writes, "though I may not in speaking of a settled truth make the certainty greater, I may set it in a clearer light." This confidence also allows him informality: "I have neither scrutinized my books nor especially adorned my style, knowing that I am speaking to one who finds me pleasing even in an unpolished state." Though his intended audience clearly extends beyond Philippe de Cabasolles, the intimate dedication shuts out those who would be hostile from the start, those caught up in their own hubbub: "What gives the last touch to their madness is the pleasure they take in crowds and in noise. These are the men who carry their educated folly over the entire city like a vulgar and purchasable commodity."[17]

When contrasting the busy man with the solitary man, Petrarch suggests that solitude consists not in the absence of company, but in the absence of mental clutter and noise. The busy man and the solitary man may be two sides of Petrarch himself, or two sides of anyone. Bustle, not society, appears to be the main enemy. The busy man is surrounded by falsehood and deceit; the solitary man fills himself with humility and praise of God. At dinner, the busy man must bear with "a crowded array of flatterers" who "vie with one another in obsequiousness" while an ugly and opulent meal is served— "horrible beasts, unknown fishes, unheard-of birds, besmeared with costly spices and forgetful of their ancient home" (note the word play on *oblite* in the original: *fere horribiles, pisces incogniti, volucres inaudite, pulvere precioso oblite et oblite veteris patrie*). This gives him no real pleasure; "he perspires, he sniffs, he belches, he gapes, nibbling at everything and nauseated by all." The busy man belongs to a hostile and distant realm; the solitary man, to a nearby and familiar place. Petrarch writes of the latter, "In place of tumult he has peace, silence instead of clamor, himself instead of a crowd."[18]

The religious and secular aspects of Petrarch's treatise exist in close relation to one another. He seems at times to put religious life *on a level* with secular life: "I believe that a noble spirit will never find repose save in God, in whom is our end, or in himself and his private thoughts, or in some intellect united by a close sympathy with his own."[19] On the other hand, he describes the solitary life as preparation for heavenly life. Curiously, his vision of heaven has traits in common with the very city life he has fled; what distinguishes it from a city is its serenity (emphases added):

What a comfort and delight it is to enjoy the present and yet look forward to a better state, in place of a brief solitude from human society to partake of the *perpetual companionship* of the angels and the gaze of the divine countenance in which is the end of all holy longings and desires; instead of a few tears to have *laughter without end*, instead of earthly fasting *eternal feasting*, truest and inestimable *riches* in lieu of self-imposed poverty, the justice of the *ethereal city* in place of a forest habitation, the *starry palaces* of Christ in exchange for a smoky hut, the *choiring of angels* and the sweetness of celestial harmony in place of rustic silence, and, transcending all other melodies, to hear the voice of God as the most faithful, most trusted pledge of all these blessings when, after so many labors done, he calls his children to eternal rest![20]

This passage suggests Petrarch's ambivalence over solitude. It is as though solitude were an intermediary and even necessary state between burdensome society and celestial communion. Solitude has muted characteristics of a city: dim revelry, quiet community, simple and hearty meals; it sloughs off the noise of the city but hears the eternal chorus only in snatches.

The treatise is a work of ambling, questioning, and discovery, not of logical argument. Throughout the first book, Petrarch seems unsure why he loves solitude so much. He writes, "My love of a spot favorable to literary leisure springs no doubt from my love of books, or perhaps I seek to escape from the crowd because of an aversion arising from a discrepancy in our tastes, or it may even be that from a squeamishness of conscience I like to avoid a many-tongued witness of my life."[21] As the treatise continues, Petrarch hints at more aspects of solitude but does not bring them into a firm and final conclusion. He implies that solitude is open, not closed, and that a person learns about it slowly, through practice, thought, and observation.

Petrarch returns frequently to the idea that solitude exists in the mind. While he prefers serene places, his solitude does not depend entirely on location: "But when some need compels me to dwell in the city, I have learned to create a solitude among people and a haven of refuge in the midst of a tempest, using a device, not generally known, of so controlling the senses that they do not perceive what they perceive." He quotes Quintilian, who writes that "if we direct our attention, with our whole mental energy, to the work actually before us, nothing of all that strikes our eyes or ears will penetrate into the mind. . . . In the midst of a crowd, therefore, on a journey, and even at festive meetings, let thought secure for herself privacy."[22] He concludes the first book with the idea that we must tend to our internal lives, as the mind is battleground enough: "Let some govern the populous city and others rule the army. Our city is that of our mind, our army that of our cares: we are distraught with domestic and foreign wars.

Do we think that there is any government more restless than the state of the human mind?"[23]

In the second book, Petrarch illustrates the points he has made and brings up some new ideas and nuances. Zeitlin claims that the second book "contributes practically nothing to the growth of the thought"; this is not quite correct. It is in the second book that Petrarch draws attention to some of solitude's finer points. He refuses to spend time describing the lives commonly associated with solitude; instead, he examines "a few examples not so trite scattered through the more hidden parts of the scriptures" (*aliquot exempla minus trita, per secretiores scripturarum recessus sparsa*—a better translation of *trita* might be "worn out"). At the outset, Petrarch lists the many stories he will *not* tell, dramatic stories that have been told many times already. Which stories, then, will he tell? Surprisingly, many of his tales are of well-known figures, but he gives his own twists to their legends. He tells briefly of Adam, stating rather brusquely that he was happier in solitude than with a woman, and that this should be a warning to all. He tells of Isaac, who chose a field at sunset as the place for his meditation: "For no place is more favorable for the meditative man than a rustic solitude and no time of life than that tranquility of a more quiet life already verging toward the sunset of existence when youth's fervor has passed away and the hour of high noon, if I may use the phrase, has been left behind."[24]

Each story offers a different clue to the nature of solitude as Petrarch understands it. When describing the solitude of Jeremiah, Petrarch suggests its all-encompassing nature: "In short I am aware of all things being comprised within the single idea of solitude." Telling of Augustine, he brings in a striking quotation from his *Tractates on the Gospel of John*: "It is difficult to see Jesus in a crowd; a sort of solitude is necessary for the mind. God is seen in a kind of isolation of the attention. A crowd is a noisy thing; that vision calls for solitude" (*secretum*). With a tinge of embarrassment, he expresses admiration of the Brahmans, then drops the subject lest he "by chance mix up falsehoods with truth." He explains a contradiction in Demosthenes, who sometimes sought out places of complete tranquility and sometimes studied by the loud sea: "In one place he sharpened his talent, in the other he exercised his voice, but he did both in solitude." Of Hercules, Petrarch writes, "Although the fame of this man extends its branches high and wide, if you look for its roots your mind must turn back to solitude." One of his most complex examples is that of Cicero, who detested solitude and yet came to appreciate it over time.[25] Through the example of Cicero, for whom he had special affinity, Petrarch reveals some of his own ambivalence. He suggests, moreover, that those who love solitude may have resisted it at one time or may struggle with it even while treasuring it.

Toward the end of the second book, Petrarch returns to the ideas of leisure and friendship, explaining that not all kinds of leisure are beneficial. "I enjoin a holiday for the body, not for the mind," he writes; "I forbid the mind to be at rest in leisure, except on condition that it revives and becomes more fertile through a period of rest."[26] Moreover, this work of the intellect does not demand absolute isolation but in fact calls for company. He quotes Horace, who tells of how he rejoices at the arrival of a long-awaited guest, or a genial table companion in the rainy weather, when the day's work is done. Petrarch points out that such company is not welcome at all times; he himself does not like to attend banquets or to have his work interrupted frequently. When he meets with a friend, it seems to him that he is actually meeting with himself; such is the matching of temperaments and minds. Petrarch continues this thought into one of the most beautiful passages of the book: "Love knows how to make one from two, otherwise Pythagoras would command an impossible thing: that in friendship one happens out of many. From this it follows that any place which is capable of holding one person can hold two friends. No solitude is so profound, no house so small, no threshold so hindered that it does not open to a friend."[27]

Earlier in the book, Petrarch admits that friendship might be dearer to him than solitude, if he cannot have both: "If I had to do without one or the other, I should prefer to be deprived of solitude rather than of my friend."[28] Petrarch's solitude is a rejection not of humans but of false, distracting, or shallow associations. True friendship, by contrast, is not only essential to his solitude, but even more fundamental in some sense. It seems that for Petrarch, part of the point of solitude is to have more room for friends. Without friendship, such solitude would lose its life. What is this solitude, then?

Throughout the treatise, Petrarch uses the word "solitude" in different senses without distinguishing among them. In the second book, for the first time, he posits a triple solitude: "that of place, with which my present discourse is specially taken up; that of time, as in the night, when there is solitude and silence even in public squares; that of the mind, as in persons who, absorbed in deepest contemplation, in broad daylight and in a crowded market-place, are not aware of what is going on there and are alone whenever and wherever they wish." It is interesting that such an idea would occur so late in the work; this suggests that he is learning about solitude as he goes along. He illustrates the idea of internal solitude through the example of Saint Francis, who "traveled through wildernesses" and "often passed the night in half-ruined temples," yet whose mind, by day, "while his body was thrust hither and thither, in collision with men . . . remained fixed on heavenly thoughts."[29]

Near the end, Petrarch admits, "I intended to write a letter; I have written a book" (*Putabam enim epystolam scribere; librum scripsi*).[30] That sentence suggests the range of Petrarch's solitude: he is able to turn letters into books, yet they keep an intimate quality. The books are not written for an impersonal multitude; they are in some sense letters to friends. A work of solitude is an act of love and regard; like a book, it expands the original idea into something unexpected.

What makes *De vita solitaria* so compelling is the life of its language, the symmetries and rhythms of the sentences, the hidden play on words, the conversations with poets of the past. Petrarch does not simply lay out his ideas on solitude; he ruminates on the subject, wandering through literature and his own experience. He seems in his element. He starts out with sharp contrasts between the solitary life and busy life; by the end, he has mixed this with many subtle observations and inklings. Solitude occurs in more places than the reader (or even Petrarch) may originally have assumed; it holds variations and contradictions.

Petrarch leaves many questions open. Is solitude ours whether we want it or not, or do we will it in some way? Petrarch suggests that we find it through "fixity" of thought; but what do we find? Is it there to begin with, or do we create it? To pursue the question further, it is necessary to depart from Petrarch, just as he would have done. He writes, "For it is with a freer step, though perchance a less secure one, that I follow my mind rather than another's footsteps."[31] I suppose—and am glad—that there is no way to leave Petrarch behind, as the act of leaving him behind is partly a tribute to him.

SOLITUDE SHOWS US our best and worst. Like a wobbly chair loosing its legs, an unsteady thought comes apart in solitude. Among others, or in the midst of a hectic day, one is usually forced to put unpleasant, unfinished, messy thoughts aside; when those pressures or demands are removed, the thoughts come rolling out. But in solitude one is also able to gather oneself and to see more clearly. Such understanding, when it comes, is sturdier than our usual slipshod structures. The understanding is not complete, of course; we often want to know more than we can. We search for specific answers and receive only hints—or we receive answers that come at a skew, not in direct response to us, not on our terms. But, as in Robert Frost's poem "Take Something Like a Star," those hints and skews tilt our perspectives; they become part of our very minds.[32] Unlike appetizers or chess pieces, the things we take in solitude cannot be discarded, at least not easily.

Perhaps there are three layers of solitude. First, there is the deepest layer, the solitude that we carry at all times, that we cannot fully know. Then there is the layer that takes solitude, that decides at any moment to stand apart. Finally, there is the shaped layer, the result of standing apart and doing something with that separation. One could sum up the three layers as being, taking, and shaping. They are not always distinct; their rivulets run into each other. Solitude contains a vast range of human possibility, not all of it good. In solitude we have moments of transcendence, moments of bleakness, and much in between. We have laughter and clinking silverware; the sound of the foghorn; the late-night radio disc jockey, talking sleepily to his few owl-ish listeners; the drunk man collapsed on the park bench. Solitude can be cheerful, busy, lonely, wretched, and more. But no matter what form it takes, it holds a clearing for thought, if the mind is in good health.

What does it mean to honor solitude? It may mean nothing more or less than integrity: heeding and living out our differences from others. Solitude consists partly in our affinities: toward other individuals, toward nature or the city, toward human works—literature, art, science, mathematics, carpen-try, electronics, and other things. Solitude need not be taken in extremes, nor are any two solitudes identical. The greatest strength may lie in a flexible solitude, one that can bear with company and lack of company. In any case, it is not equivalent to a specific way of life. Solitude often brings to mind the monk and prisoner, but they do not represent solitude any more than others do.

The contemplative monk who lives in a monastery in the hills is not nec-essarily more solitary than the stockbroker. He has simply chosen a particular form of isolation as a road to a greater connection with God. He may relish chatter and gossip or rely on the approval of others; there is no guarantee that he takes up solitude in earnest. The twelfth-century mystic and theolo-gian William of Saint-Thierry wrote in his Golden Epistle (1145), "If anyone among you does not possess [piety] in his heart, display it in his life, practice it in his cell, he is to be called not a solitary but a man who is alone, and his cell is not a cell for him but a prison in which he is immured."[33] Similarly, a prisoner in a modern-day isolation cell may not be solitary in any spiritual sense. He is separated, but he may be longing for his cell phone so he can send a text message to his girlfriend. He may fret over his removal from the other prisoners. He may want nothing more than to get away from his thoughts. His seclusion itself does not increase his solitude unless he lets it do so.

In her speech "Solitude of Self" (1892), Elizabeth Cady Stanton describes solitude as "our inner being, which we call ourself"—something that is always with us, something that "no eye nor touch of man or angel has ever pierced." It is "more hidden than the caves of the gnome; the sacred adytum of the oracle; the hidden chamber of Eleusinian mystery, for to it only omniscience is permitted to enter." Stanton, who argued for the intellectual and spiritual independence of women, calls attention to solitude's deep privacy, its impenetrability, its presence in everything we do. Yet she takes care to point out that we cannot leave it untended. If, later in life, we do not have resources of the mind, we will have little life in us. Those who in old age "cannot find companionship in books," who "have no interest in the vital questions of the hour, no interest in watching the consummation of reforms, with which they might have been identified," will "soon pass into their dotage."[34] She implies that solitude can be active in the world, for it is our particular angle on the world that allows us to be involved meaningfully in it.

Any social activity has a degree of solitude. When gathered to listen to a speech, we are each alone with the words, experiencing them privately along with the others. In a church or temple, the faithful worship together, but they are also alone, and no one knows what another's faith is like. In a classroom, the teacher may lead a discussion, but each student has thoughts and questions that may or may not come forth. When we go hiking with others, we are sharing with them the sights and sounds, but there are moments when a member of the group falls behind, pauses to look over a cliff, or loses herself in branches and leaves and thoughts. While solitude is common to everyone and goes with us everywhere, in each individual it takes a particular shape. The woman on the train gazing out the window, the man who walks out to the balcony alone at a party, the college student who turns off the TV to read about the French Revolution or even wanders off in daydreams—all are showing something of their ongoing solitude. There is a current of solitude even in tedious committee meetings, at football games, or in an army.

Perhaps the opposite of solitude is not community but absolute currentness. There is nothing quite so dangerous as trying to be always up to date, for one simple reason: just moments after one becomes current, one falls behind. To keep from falling behind, one must stay alert to every update. To step back, to spend time on something not immediately relevant, is to risk "missing out," losing touch with the lickety-split relay of the latest, or so it seems. Even those caught up in the updates are not always sure why they need them. The *Los Angeles Times* book editor David L. Ulin comments, "Today, it seems it is not contemplation we seek but an odd sort of distraction masquerading as being in the know." To read books, Ulin notes, one must take time away from the noise, but distractions pull in the opposite direction, into the trivial demands of the moment. "What I'm struggling with," he writes, "is the encroachment of the buzz, the sense that there is something *out there* that merits my attention, when in fact it's mostly just a series of disconnected riffs and fragments that add up to the anxiety of the age."[35]

The pressure to keep up with the times not only distracts and dizzies us; it upsets and distorts our values. Once we subscribe to the "cutting edge," we lose the ability to judge it. We grab it, grab some opinions about it, and grab some more. What others are saying about the latest gadget or fashionable concept becomes more important than what we ourselves think. We are told that if we just get it now, or embrace it now, we will be at an advantage. Thus to think in any sort of depth, to judge things on our own, we must risk falling a little out of date, a little out of authority. We risk being judged as fools with nothing to say, just because we choose to keep certain thoughts to ourselves while they are in formation.

Part of grappling with solitude is learning what to keep to ourselves. We learn over time to calibrate our confidences. I have known the exhilaration of an intimate conversation with a friend; I have also known the letdown of saying too much or realizing that the other person didn't "get it" (or that I didn't understand what another was trying to tell me, or worse, that I wasn't listening). Without a sense of solitude, without the ability to hold things back, we would be continually disappointed by others. Here solitude overlaps with privacy. William of Saint-Thierry was referring to solitude when he wrote in his *Golden Epistle* that the spiritual man "should not entrust his treasures to men's mouths but conceal them in his cell and hide them away in his conscience, so as to have this inscription always in the forefront of his conscience and on the front of his cell: 'My secret is my own, my secret is my own.'"[36]

Is solitude pure, or is it mixed with our social nature? If it is mixed with our social nature, how do we distinguish it? If it is pure, why does it appear only in mitigated form? Some of this may be a question of semantics. If we declare solitude a pure state, then we must acknowledge that we never experience it in true form. If we consider it part of our social nature, then its purity is only relative. Or possibly, as Merton suggests, we experience the purity of solitude without even knowing it. We think of it as imperfect, yet the very possibility of solitude, the hope contained within it, is a perfect thing. The very lack of words may hold truth: "The solitary life, being silent, clears away the smokescreen of words that man has laid down between his mind and things." Perhaps the very word "solitude," repeated too many times, obstructs our understanding of it. Petrarch was wary of talking about solitude too much:

he worried that he might cause Philippe to regard it "as more infected even than cities with the disease of talkativeness."[37] At some point, one has to leave the explanations and definitions behind and set forth into the solitude, whatever it might be.

It may be impossible to know solitude fully. Presumably, one must be aware of one's solitude—even barely, even in flickers—for it to be solitude. But is the newborn baby aware of the separation from the womb? At the moment of death itself, does the dying person know that life is over? We have no way of knowing these things, because we cannot ask the baby or the person leaving the world. Thus in our two ultimate experiences of solitude, birth and death, we may be unaware of our state; our awareness may be possible only in between, during the span of our lives. We are thus confronted daily with conditions that touch the inchoate edges of life. There is adventure in solitude; we find ourselves winding our way through corridors, our passage interrupted here and there by the sound of a dog whining or the splash of sun and shadows on the floor. Solitude is filled with memory; when alone with our thoughts, we have room for things of the past. Solitude allows thoughts to verge on flesh and blood; in that sense it is the highest intimacy.

It should not come as a surprise, then, that solitude would be of great concern to writers, whose thoughts verge on flesh and blood. Just as literature requires solitude, solitude is made robust by literature. Petrarch wrote that "solitude without literature is exile, prison, and torture; supply literature, and it becomes your country, freedom, and delight."[38] If we forget literature, if we stop reading it closely and passing it on to others, we may well start to regard solitude as dreary and useless. Products, policies, and attitudes that push solitude aside tend to do the same to literature; the two end up in the same refuse heap, in the same corner of the room. The fourth chapter will look at literature and solitude together. But first: a word about distraction.

3

Distraction:
The Flip Side of Engagement

If something distracts us, it's the problem of distraction. It circles the room, buzzing victory and distress, confounding us all. We try to get at it with words. Book after book grapples with distraction in a technological era: Neil Postman's *Technopoly*, Mark Bauerlein's *Dumbest Generation*, Maggie Jackson's *Distracted*, Sherry Turkle's *Alone Together*, and rows and rows of psychology books and self-help manuals. Newspapers, magazines, and blogs tackle problems related to distraction: the dangers of driving while texting; the effects of multitasking on our reading and thinking; or the role of cell phones in the classroom. Researchers, parents, teachers argue over attention deficit disorder: Is it overdiagnosed or underdiagnosed? Overmedicated or undermedicated? Beneficial or destructive? Fabricated or real? No matter how much we discuss distraction, there is something bothersome beneath it, an itch we can't quite reach.

Often we mistake distraction for engagement. We think that if we are busy, we are focused. It is easy to get wrapped up in a project at the computer but to interrupt it every few minutes for other things: replying to email messages, reading news on websites, and so forth. Multitasking has become normal; a modest habit of checking email every few minutes seems nothing to get alarmed about. We can fool ourselves into thinking that it doesn't make a difference—that these little side activities don't distort or interrupt our thought. But the very word "multitasking" has something unsettling about it, a hint that not a whole lot of heart, thought, or soul goes into any of the tasks. It is hard to reckon with this notion, precisely because of the distraction; it is much easier to point at those other people who are so much more distracted, or to confess (now and then) to a problem of distraction and get it off our chests and minds.

Distraction means the pulling away of something; all depends on from what and toward what we are pulled. Sometimes distraction makes us aware of things we would not have noticed otherwise. One day, in San Francisco, I was walking home in a downcast mood, looking down at the sidewalk and barely seeing where I was going. I had no desire to talk to anyone; my eyes were blurry and my thoughts gloomy. Of course, just at that moment, a woman with a French accent approached me for directions. She began to tell me how much she admired the architecture of the neighborhood (pronouncing "architecture" as one would in French). I looked up and saw that the houses were indeed magnificent. I gave her directions, and she, without knowing it, gave me a way out of my state of mind.

Some distractions are necessary for survival, which, according to Maggie Jackson, "lies in the tricky push and pull between focusing and thus drawing meaning from the world, and staying alert to changes in our environment."[1] A parent must tend to the crying baby, sometimes getting up several times in the night. It is hard for parents of young children to find quiet time for much at all, unless they have a live-in nanny. Yet, difficult as this is, it is part of the endeavor of raising children, and as such it holds meaning. Likewise, any emergency worker must be on the alert, ready to rush to the next fire or accident, but must also concentrate on the situation at hand. The attention is always in danger of being broken, but this broken attention has a certain continuity: that of doing what needs to be done, on the spot, for someone's health or safety.

Some distractions can lead to a greater understanding of the original point or goal. Masters of digression, such as Laurence Sterne, Nikolai Gogol, and Herman Melville, know how to mix purpose with revelry, diversion with direction. Tristram Shandy, the narrator of Sterne's novel by the same name, gives a wonderful defense of digression:

> Could a historiographer drive on his history, as a muleteer drives on his mule,—straight forward;—for instance, from *Rome* all the way to *Loretto*, without ever once turning his head aside either to the right hand or to the left;—he might venture to foretell you to an hour when he should get to his journey's end;—but the thing is, morally speaking, impossible: For, if he is a man of the least spirit, he will have fifty deviations from a straight line to make with this or that party as he goes along, which he can no ways avoid.[2]

With grains of salt and specks of doubt, one might take this as a comment on life. Tristram tells us that it is "morally" impossible, not just scientifically impossible, for a historiographer to "foretell you to an hour when he should get to his journey's end." Why is it morally impossible? Because anyone of the "least spirit" will stray from the path many times. In other words, these unexpected directions form part of our existence, and we would do ourselves and others an injustice if we did not honor them. Of course, this is also Tristram's elaborate self-justification, told with spark and cunning. Sterne knew his narrator might drive the reader to the end of his wits, and that indeed may have been part of the plan. Following Tristram's story takes patience, spirit, and a sense of fun. *Tristram Shandy* shows us, over and over, that the straight line may not take us to the truth, and the goal may not be what we think it is at first. Such distraction, if it can be called that, is part of a greater focus; it takes us out of our limited view of life and into something intriguing, uproarious, and moving.

At its worst, distraction chops up our lyric and logic. When our thoughts get diced on the virtual cutting board, we lose the ability to test words and phrases for rhythm, sound, form, and sense. We ignore the structure of sense—the progression from one phrase or argument to the next, and the relation of each part to the whole. Worse, we fail to notice this loss, as there is little to hold us to a higher standard. We fall prey to what Susan Jacoby calls "junk thought": that which "uses the language of science and rationality to promote irrationality."[3] If our own reasoning skills are weak, or if we fail to take the time to exercise them well, we can fall for distortions and deceptions. We can mistake our own broken reasoning for true reasoning, our fleeting interests for sustained ones. We may put our lives at risk—talking on the phone while driving, or crossing a busy street while checking email. As we do so, we risk making the phone call or email cursory and thoughtless. Breaking our attention, we break the very activities.

Our newer technologies do not cause our distraction, but they may encourage and exacerbate it. Postman warned that "in every tool we create, an idea is embedded that goes beyond the function of the thing itself."[4] Our Internet may *contain* the idea of luring us away from wherever we are and whatever we are doing: animated advertisements crawling across the screen, a popup survey, a registration request, links that promise to fill the gaps in the blogs we read. There is very little on the Internet that encourages us to stay put and read something several times. Instead, we are pulled on to the next thing, to readers' brief comments on it, to comments on the comments, and to links from the comments to something else.

Our technology contains another idea: that of never-ending newness. Update upon update pushes itself on us; the anticipation of updates is part of our existence. We live in the presence of a hyped-up future. Or sometimes, instead of marching in with heralds and fanfare, the updates slink upon us by stealth. The desktop computer—which seems a rather tranquil place when we're not hopping all over the Web—receives new versions of this and that without our consent or knowledge, unless we diligently opt out of them (and this can take some effort). We're working on something, and suddenly the computer slows down to a crawl. Why? Only after the update is complete does it explain. Did we want or need it? The assumption is that we want the latest version of whatever it might be. We start to believe that we're better off with it than without it, that the latest is the best.

Those who complain of distraction often mean that they have trouble getting anything done—that is, they are pulled from important things to less important things, or to things of equal value, with inadequate focus on each one. Some have a persistent habit of "goofing off"—getting a snack, calling someone, checking email, playing a computer game, or doing some housecleaning that really doesn't need to be done right now. Some give in to every interruption: they answer the doorbell or phone, respond to messages immediately, and accept social invitations even if they had planned to do something else. In all of these examples there is very little filtering. The person does not weigh the importance of things; he succumbs to the pull, whatever it might be. Or he may know better but fall for it anyway. Turkle notes that "it is hard to maintain a sense of what matters in the din of constant communication."[5]

When we fail repeatedly to give our full attention to something that matters, we eventually conclude that it doesn't matter all that much. If we do not spend time alone with our writing, we may decide that it is really the blogs, tweets, and texts that count—after all, they are reaching people and making it out into the wide world. If, instead of listening to an entire album, we flip from one selection to another on the iPod, we may lose a sense of what makes a piece of music worth the listening. Our ear for language and music changes; we hear, in addition to the thing itself, the rather messy clamor of opinion, and the little voice that tells us that we can move on if we don't like something right away. We have the opportunity to sample far more albums and books than we could in the past, but with that, we have grown accustomed to the sampling mentality.

Distraction results in a scattering of intentions; to end distraction, one must gather oneself in some way; one must be willing to give something priority for a while. That is not a cure, of course; one does not overcome distraction just by granting importance to something. But this granting of importance is a start. This includes having dinner with a friend without checking the handheld gadget during conversation. It includes staying with a book long enough to enter its story, arguments, and rhythms. It includes practicing an instrument attentively and regularly enough to become fluent on it. To do any of this, one must be willing to dedicate oneself to something. To what? One must dare to decide. There is another side to this as well: one must be willing to play and ruminate a little, to be a little uncertain, to risk spending time on the wrong thing.

This allotting of importance is not arrogant; to the contrary, it takes humility to give one's attention to something for a while, no matter what the gains or losses. It has grown increasingly difficult to do so, partly because we expect feedback for our actions (we want to know, right away, whether a given course of action is successful), and partly because being "in the mix" *feels* more egalitarian than being alone. Many know the slight guilt that comes with turning down a party invitation for no reason other than a desire to spend the evening at home. It is even harder to turn down the all-present and ever-casual invitation into online life. It would seem that stepping out of it (turning off the handheld device for the evening, for instance) should not perturb us at all; the device will still be there, after all, when we come back. Nonetheless, it takes some willpower and can trigger anxiety.

Why is distraction, even in mild forms, so difficult to overcome? Many find that when they allow themselves to focus fully on something, the difference from the usual state is profound. The body relaxes; the mind entrusts itself to the task or thought at hand. If one wants to get the gist of a book, one skims it. If one wants to know the book, one gives oneself over to it for a while. Skimming and close reading are two different lives, two different ways of seeing the world. Of course, some skimming is inevitable; we cannot select books properly unless we allow ourselves to glance through them. There are some books, moreover, that we read for specific purposes; we may need to consult only a part of them. But if skimming becomes all that we do, then we look for books that help us skim: books with headings, bullet points, and straightforward purposes. Books less quickly grasped will be set aside for another time that may never come.

It seems obvious that schools should help students learn to read and work thoughtfully, to develop a life of the mind. Instead, there is a growing emphasis on visible activity and productivity. What isn't visible or tangible seems threatening, because it could be anything or nothing. How do we know that students are learning if we can't see signs of it here and now? How do we know that the class has accomplished anything if there isn't a product to put on the wall? Richard Hofstadter famously states that the meaning of intellectual life lies "not in the possession of truth but in the quest for new uncertainties."[6] Yet many education reformers seize certainties as though they were torches and spears.

EDUCATORS ACROSS THE ideological and pedagogical spectrum agree that students should be engaged in their learning. But what does engagement mean? Does it mean that students take their studies seriously and work toward better understanding and mastery? Or does it mean that students show certain external behaviors—such as sitting up, looking up, taking notes, participating in groups, and never being idle? The internal and external forms of engagement are not necessarily at odds with each other. But when the emphasis is overwhelmingly on the external, students have no letup. They must show activity and results whether these have meaning or not. They must respond instantly to directions and stay on the mark at all times. Dreaminess and lingering questions have no place.

To a great extent, American schools encourage students to rely on external stimuli and external results. The schools themselves, especially struggling schools, are in constant turmoil, so it is difficult to be still with anything. Year after year, they change their curricula, schedules, classroom setups, paperwork, pedagogical approaches, administrative structures, and more. Teachers learn to expect last-minute program switches; a teacher who had her own classroom may suddenly be asked to "team-teach," and a fifth-grade teacher may be assigned midyear to second grade. Fads are presented as the final word. Suddenly red pens are forbidden (too intimidating); the next year, it is forbidden for teachers to write on student work (too invasive). A curriculum that seemed to be working well is tossed out for something new (or old, as the case may be). Consultants come and go, some making more money per day than three or four teachers combined. Isaac Leon Kandel captured some of the absurdity in his satirical story "Alice in Cloud-Cuckoo Land" (1933), where Alice, well schooled in the new ways of education, praises "units of work" that "arise out of situations and remake the learner and the situation."[7] The jargon has changed somewhat, but the worship of change has persisted. It's like watching TV or playing a video game; things are always moving, yet we stay unmoved. Schools are under pressure to do something visible and measurable, whether well considered or not. They put similar pressure on students.

One of the most widespread fads affecting teachers and students alike has to do with multiple intelligences and learning styles. In his famous *Frames of Mind* (1983), Howard Gardner identifies seven domains of intelligence: linguistic, logical-mathematical, spatial, musical, bodily-kinesthetic, interpersonal, and intrapersonal. His primary point is that a number of distinct intelligences exist, each one related to specific content and influenced by the surrounding context and culture. Learning styles theories, which have existed for decades, are not quite the same as Gardner's theory. When educators bring up "learning styles," they usually refer to the popular theory, or group of theories, that each individual has a preferred style, be it visual, auditory, or kinesthetic, and that he or she learns best through this style, no matter what the subject. Gardner seems ambivalent over the relation of "multiple intelligences" to the concept of learning styles. On the one hand, he has made clear that his theory was not intended as an education model; on the other, he has suggested that individualized instruction, based on learning styles and intelligences, is the most viable pedagogical approach today.[8]

Education leaders and policy makers often conflate Gardner's theory with learning styles theories, insisting that teachers should match the lesson to students' specific intelligences and styles. The terms "learning styles" and "multiple intelligences" are bandied about so often that the ideas and research behind them disappear. People frequently mention these theories without really knowing what they entail or whether they stand up to scrutiny. Analyzing the research on learning styles, cognitive scientist Daniel T. Willingham finds no conclusive evidence that students learn best in their own style or modality. What the research does show, says Willingham, is that students learn best when the material is presented in the modality best suited to the *content*.[9] Yet many districts and schools require teachers to base lessons on students' preferred modes of learning. While intended to boost student involvement and motivation, such a requirement can easily turn into a distraction for students and teachers alike. It provokes a Saint Vitus' dance of methods and modalities; the teacher, trying to address all students' needs, may bring in visuals where imagination would have been better; sounds where silence might have been needed; and movement where the topic requires some stillness.

The District of Columbia Public Schools' (DCPS') teacher examination guidelines include the expectation that teachers will give students "multiple ways to engage with content" in response to students' needs and the demands of the lesson. While steering clear of the claim that *all* lessons should address *all* individual needs (the previous version required teachers to target three learning styles in the thirty-minute observation period), the guidelines retain vestiges of the learning styles idea. They state that the teacher may receive credit for targeting different "modalities" or "intelligences," for giving students different ways of engaging with the material within the same modality or intelligence, or for doing something else effective, whatever it might be. But the teacher receives no credit unless the students pay attention:

> For a teacher to receive credit for providing students a way of engaging with content, students must be engaged in that part of the lesson. For example, a teacher should not receive credit for providing a way of engaging with content if the teacher shows a visual illustration but most students are not paying attention, or if the teacher asks students to model parallel and perpendicular lines with their arms but most students do not participate.[10]

The problem with this statement is subtle. Clearly students must be paying attention in order for a lesson to be effective, and clearly the teacher should know how to command attention. Yet there is something puzzling about the idea that a teacher should not receive "credit" unless the students are responding in acceptable ways. There is a fine difference between the quality of a teacher's presentation and the students' response to it. The teacher may be using modalities that are entirely appropriate to the lesson, yet the students may be inattentive anyway. Certainly, the teacher should address this problem, but to deny the teacher "credit" is to equate the merit of a lesson with its instant appeal. Under such circumstances, how are schools supposed to teach students the difference between popularity and virtue, or fame and excellence? Students and teachers alike receive the message that what doesn't evoke an instantaneous and unanimous response is inferior to what does.

To keep students visibly involved in the lesson, educators take measures to prevent boredom or impatience. In *Teach Like a Champion*, Doug Lemov, managing director at the charter network Uncommon Schools, recommends changing the activities every ten to fifteen minutes. He refers to the "Age Plus Two Rule": that a student's optimal attention span, in minutes, is his age plus two.[11] Thus a ten-year-old might focus on a single activity for twelve minutes, and an eighteen-year-old for twenty minutes. To his credit, Lemov emphasizes that all activities should relate to the same topic so that the lesson does not become scattered. Still, the idea is problematic; if students expect a change of activity every fifteen minutes or so, they will be ill prepared for seminars and lectures or even for studying at home. They will be uncomfortable with topics and assignments that they cannot quickly grasp and finish. This is not to say that students should be expected to concentrate on one topic or activity for hours on end. But students need to develop more mental endurance than schools currently expect of them.

Lemov's book is full of valuable suggestions for teachers—concrete things they can do to improve their craft. Its main flaw is its assumption that children must always be productive and certain of the lesson's purpose. He advises teachers, "Students should never have to ask themselves, 'What am I supposed to be doing?' when they enter your classroom, nor should they be able to claim not to know what they should be doing. You want students to know what to do and to know there is no ambiguity here." He suggests that the teacher give them a Do Now, a short activity that leads into the lesson. "The activity should require putting a pencil to paper," he writes; "that is, there should be a written product from it." With such an activity, "they are both productive during every minute and ready for instruction as soon as you start."[12]

The Do Now is no novel or radical suggestion; it has existed for years and is required in many districts. It can be helpful as a way of warming students up for the lesson, but it can also become a crutch: students come to depend on concrete tasks and flail when they have nothing to do. Why not expect students to sit still and collect their thoughts for a minute or two? Lemov does not even raise this possibility that students could do such a thing or that it might be valuable. We hear much about the achievement gap, but there is also a "thinking gap" in education: between those who can sit still with thoughts and uncertainties, even momentarily, and those who cannot. Lemov seems to assume that all or most students fall in the latter category and that this cannot be changed.

Elsewhere in the book, Lemov reminds teachers to keep class discussion strictly focused and to bring students back on track whenever they go astray. He gives the example of a teacher who read a story about a girl and asked the students to identify the character trait that most accurately described her, from among several similar possibilities. A student offered a different trait; the teacher reminded him that "their goal was to decide from among the similar traits they'd identified at the outset."[13] This principle, observed too strictly, reduces the insights that can come out of a discussion. A teacher should keep the discussion on track but should not be afraid of the comment or question that falls outside its immediate domain. In this case, the teacher might have said, "Hold on to your idea; let's address this question first." Paradoxically, the insistence on "sticking to the point" can create a kind of distraction, as students and teachers may become intolerant of anything that is not immediately and directly relevant. Relevance can be deceptive. When reading literature, philosophy, and history, one can miss the point by sticking rigidly to the point, as many of the important points come through obliquely.

By no means does Lemov oppose thoughtfulness; his ultimate goal is to bring students to the stage where they can grapple with complex material. Yet he does not seem to consider the gaps and pauses that are necessary for such grappling. In his discussion of the technique Everybody Writes, he describes a teacher leading a discussion of Tim O'Brien's story "The Man I Killed," set in the Vietnam War. The teacher asks, "Why would someone write a story about not being able to talk about what he did, and in so doing, talk about it? Why would he talk about not being able to talk about it?" The students seem interested; they look at her blankly but eagerly, as though on the verge of answering. She responds by giving a summary of her own ideas on the matter.

Lemov is disappointed in the outcome; he calls it "a watershed moment," as the teacher has asked "exactly the kind of question that pushes students beyond their current understanding and knowledge of literature." The teacher missed the opportunity to get students to think about the question; she gave them an answer when they could have tackled the question themselves. All good points, so far. What does he recommend that a teacher do instead? Have everybody write, so that they may "wrestle" their thoughts into words.[14] There is nothing wrong with that idea. But why not let the students think a little longer, given their interest in the question? The difference between these two approaches is minor but significant; Lemov prefers to have the students *do* something, whereas many students might learn even more from holding the ideas in their minds. Lemov is right that the teacher didn't wait long enough for the students to answer, but he himself shows some impatience with the long pause and apparent nothingness.

When students must show constant activity, the subject itself may be oversimplified. A fast-paced teaching model known as Whole Brain Teaching (formerly called Power Teaching) emphasizes rapid interactions. The model has been growing in popularity; according to the Whole Brain Teaching website, over twenty thousand teachers have attended conferences or taken online training in the techniques.[15] Developed by Chris Biffle and others, Whole Brain Teaching consists of call-and-response between teacher and class. The teacher's brief presentations are interspersed with "teach" segments, where the students turn to their partners and teach the concept that they just learned. During the call-and-response portion, the teacher tells the students exactly how to respond. During the teach portion, the whole room is filled with talk: the silent partner mirrors the speaking partner, imitating every gesture. But what do the students learn?

In his video demonstration of a college philosophy course, Biffle calls the class to attention and announces that he will be teaching about Aristotle's four causes. He then commands, "Teach!" The students respond, "OK!" and turn to their partners to explain the four causes, making gestures as they speak. The partners mimic the movements. Biffle then calls the class back to attention, names one of the students, shows her a plastic triangle ruler, and explains that, "according to Aristotle, one of its causes is the matter it's made out of. It's made out of plastic." He asks the class for an "ah," which he receives. He goes on to say that the second cause "is where it comes from. It comes from the plastic-triangle-making factory." He asks for an "oh." He gets a unanimous "oh." He gives the triangle to the student and asks her to repeat the explanation; the other students mimic her gestures as she does this. He tells the class to give her a ten-finger "woo," which they give, then tells the students to teach the same explanation to each other. He gives the command, "Teach!" and the students turn to their partners again. In a similar manner, he presents the third and fourth causes. The third cause, he says, is the object's essence, "what it is," and the fourth is "what it's used for." Now, for extra credit, he has the students give each other a "high-energy" explanation of all four causes. From there, the lesson continues in a similar vein.[16]

Biffle's explanation of the four causes isn't quite correct. He skips over the idea of form, a key aspect of the third cause (which appears as the second cause in Aristotle's *Physics* and as the first or second cause in his *Metaphysics*). The fourth cause isn't only what the object is "used for"; it is also its end or goal. Moreover, the very concept of "causes" has subtleties that Biffle neither explains nor discusses with the students.[17] Biffle apparently presumes that college students lack the patience or ability to read Aristotle carefully, participate in thoughtful discussion, or listen to a lecture. Granted, it is possible that the lesson was supposed to be a brisk review, not an exposition of the topic. Even so, if the review distorts the topic, it is hard to see its value. One wonders why college students would need something frenetic like this. One wonders, moreover, whether students who went through the Whole Brain Teaching method in their K–12 years would be prepared for anything but continuation of the same.

What is the rationale for this model? According to the Whole Brain Teaching website, students who learn through this method are "engaging in all four learning modes: seeing, saying, hearing, and doing." The website explains, "Twenty years of education research tells us that the most effective learning takes place when a student engages the brain's primary cortices— visual, auditory, language production and motor—at the same time."[18] One should always be suspicious of vague references to "research"; the statement borders on the ridiculous. Does a piano student need to talk while playing? Does a student reading Faulkner need to look at pictures in order to grasp the meaning of *The Sound and the Fury*? Most learning naturally makes use of more than one brain function—but this need not be forced.

It is not difficult to see why Whole Brain Teaching might have appeal. It leaves no room for doubt; students are continually involved and know exactly how to respond. When asked for an "ooh," they give an "ooh." When asked to turn and teach, they do so; when asked to stop, they stop. But what is the point, and what are the consequences? Among other things, students come to expect unremitting activity. Thus they learn shortened, oversimplified, even erroneous versions of topics.

Whole Brain Teaching may be an egregious example, but it is part of a larger tendency. Schools, colleges, and universities have been changing the format and content of lessons to ensure that students understand the material on the spot. One controversial example is the adoption of the "personal response clicker." Initially developed for physics classes, the clicker has spread to other subjects and into K–12 education (and is perhaps inspired by changes in K–12 education). With the clicker, the student can answer multiple-choice questions in class, and the instructor can gauge whether the students understand the lesson. The concept sounds reasonable, but it has losses and pitfalls.

In 2001, Massachusetts Institute of Technology (MIT) introduced Technology Enhanced Active Learning (TEAL), which replaced introductory physics lectures with workshops and made use of the clicker and other technology. The clickers themselves had a clear rationale: instructors needed to know whether students understood the concepts, and clickers offered instantaneous feedback. The clicker is only one component of the program, which aims to make physics instruction interactive and hands-on. Students sit at circular tables where they collaborate with others on "table problems." Students are supposed to show signs of collaboration during class: for instance, by solving a problem together on a whiteboard. Every now and then, the instructor tosses out a multiple-choice question, and the students click. One student complained in an opinion piece, "This is MIT; contrary to the apparent beliefs of TEAL advocates, we are capable of solving problems without militant intervention." In 2003, students petitioned against TEAL on the grounds that it did not provide them with "the intellectual challenge and stimulation that can be expected from a course at MIT"; TEAL staff responded by creating focus groups and promising to address some of the students' concerns. TEAL stayed at MIT, despite students' objections; in 2008, it became a permanent part of the physics program.[19]

There is no mystery to the clicker or the software. The clicker sends the student's response to the computer, and the software tabulates the results, which may be displayed on a screen. Thus students receive real-time statistics on their collective performance. If many students entered a wrong answer, the instructor might explain it again or have the students explain it to each other. Then the students are given another chance with the question. The technology is transparent; it reports numbers but does not interpret them. Nor does it require a workshop format. I recently audited a physics lecture course where the professor used clickers sparingly. I expected to dislike the clicker; instead, I found it unobtrusive and at times informative. While I, as an auditor, did not have a clicker, I participated silently by answering for myself the questions that the professor posed.

The most obvious drawback to the clicker approach is that it breaks up the instruction into manageable bits (many would see this as an advantage). The bits may not be that manageable after all, precisely because they are bits. Often a student needs to take the new concept taught in class and ponder it, read about it in the text, and practice it by solving problems. Also, a student's immediate response to a question may not reflect how much he or she understands, especially while the lesson is in progress. When students turn and talk to each other about a question that some answered incorrectly, the ones who know the answer may simply tell it to the ones who don't, or they may explain it in a cursory manner. Usually, when the students tackle the same question again, the percentage of correct responses soars. This does not necessarily reflect learning. In addition, the multiple-choice format does not always measure students' understanding accurately, as it is often easy to eliminate one or two of the options. One may select the correct answer but be unable to explain it.

A still more irksome problem is that once you have the clickers and have gone to the trouble to set them up, you are under some obligation to use them; this in turn influences how you teach. Sometimes the clickers come bundled with a philosophy or attitude; professors may be urged to change their teaching methods. You may be the rare physics professor who uses clickers sparingly (as did the one whose course I audited), or you may feel obliged to transform your teaching to meet the supposed demands of the new age. The latter, it appears, is the aspiration of TEAL. The clickers serve not only to inform the instructor, but also to drive a workshop approach to physics. Such an approach may keep students on track who would otherwise slip, but it may also slow down, fragment, or trivialize the lessons. In TEAL, wrote MIT student Arun Agarwal in 2003, "the presentations don't hold a candle to a lecture, because they simply highlight issues from the reading, through quick board work and some PowerPoint. They are mainly there to make quick clarifications before we do the experiments and workshops." Agarwal identifies one of the contradictions of TEAL: it assumes that students will learn on their own, yet removes the explanatory lecture that is essential to such learning.[20]

Proponents of the TEAL program cite average normalized learning gains under the program. They argue, moreover, that TEAL promotes interactivity, gives instructors instant feedback, and gathers useful data for education research. But Agarwal and others note that the studies have been conducted by the TEAL staff members themselves and that TEAL is driven by commercial interests.[21] In any case, champions of clickers fail to address their pressing problems: first, that students are left on their own to struggle with the more difficult material outside of class; and second, that the real-time instruction is downgraded so that students can solve problems quickly in class. The uninterrupted lecture, for all its imperfections, offers more information, insight, and coherence than a workshop can. The lecture makes both contemplation and thoroughness possible and is usually supplemented with discussion sections and labs. By mixing discussion, lecture, and lab together in the same session, the workshop format may limit how much can be conveyed in a single lesson and overall.

Clickers may become even more distracting over time. Whereas the early clickers simply enabled students to answer multiple-choice questions, the next generation will likely allow for text messaging and exchanges of multimedia between students and the professor. This seems detrimental to the study of physics or anything else; it would be difficult, with so many messages flying back and forth, to follow a problem from start to finish or to prevent web surfing and socializing. Yet Eric Mazur, a professor of physics at Harvard University and a lead developer of TEAL, has no worries about this development. If this means that students will be surfing the Internet in class, "the teacher just has to be more interesting than YouTube."[22] It is a strange era where a teacher must compete with other forms of entertainment; it suggests an end not only of concentration but also of respect and wisdom. There is respect in turning the gadgets off and listening to the professor; there is wisdom in waiting to see what the lesson holds. A professor should not have to compete with YouTube at all. If toned down and kept within limits, the clicker might have some uses. But when it is taken beyond its limits, when we must ride it willy-nilly into the future, there is every reason to raise a hue and cry.

By 2010, more than half a million students were using clickers in classes on several thousand college campuses; many K–12 classes were using them as well. Professors and teachers now use clickers to monitor students' attendance and give quizzes. In some ways this may lead to an increase in student attention: students no longer have the opportunity to skip lecture or take naps during class (without hurting their grades). Still, it is telling that schools would have to go this far to keep the students involved. At the K–12 level, this means even more emphasis on multiple-choice questions; at the college level, it means that students may focus more on the minute requirements than on the larger demands of the subject. While supposedly being held accountable, they may come to ignore their greater responsibilities: to make their way into adulthood and to start taking their education into their own hands. In all the discussion of raising academic standards, one rarely hears about the need to demand *much* more listening, effort, focus, and perseverance from students. Instead, it is assumed that teachers should keep students interested, doing "whatever it takes" to keep them in the loop.[23]

The preceding examples—the DCPS teacher evaluation guidelines, Doug Lemov's suggested techniques, Whole Brain Teaching, and the ubiquitous clicker—have different sources, forms, and ends; indeed, in Aristotle's terms, they differ in all of their four causes. Yet, to varying degrees, all involve shaping the lessons according to the attention spans of the least patient students, as though there were no other way. Thus, in the name of engagement, students may be prevented from engaging deeply in anything. In the fifth chapter, I discuss yet another example of this tendency: the "workshop model," which in 2003 was mandated throughout the New York City public schools and remains the dominant model in many schools today.

What are the consequences of the emphasis on short-term engagement? First, students expect to be entertained; if the lesson does not seize them right away, they turn their gaze downward to their cell phones and other devices. Second, students who desire more challenge must reconcile themselves with something less. Third, teachers are faulted for students' lapses of attention; if the entire class is not engaged, the teacher is presumably doing something wrong. Fourth, the very curriculum is affected by this problem. If students depend on constant stimulus and activity in class, the very subjects and topics will be altered to accommodate their dependency. We will lose many of the difficulties and subtleties of the subjects, entrusting ourselves instead to quick answers and flickering real-time data.

WHY IS IT so difficult to tackle distraction in schools? Does it have some kind of appeal for the adults as well as the children? Or is it just so daunting that we give into it? One possibility, brought up earlier in the chapter, is that distraction masquerades as focus. When children are kept active with one fast-paced project after another, they don't have a chance to fall out of line. Nor do they have to do anything particularly difficult. It looks as though the class is functioning well; administrators observing the class take note of the teacher's control and the students' participation. When the tests are not particularly challenging, the test scores, too, may indicate success. Many argue that the ends justify the means: if test scores are going up and discipline is good, the method must be working. But we must ask in what sense it is working.

A more disturbing possibility is that we have paid too much homage to quick, visible results, no matter what their underlying value. We have become what Martin Buber described in 1923 as the "capricious man," who "only knows the feverish world out there and his feverish desire to use it."[24] Such heat over external things, such rush and scramble, is despondency inverted. Any substantial learning requires faith—not in a higher being necessarily, but in the value of things that cannot be grasped right away. The violin student perseveres despite scratchy notes, knowing that the music is worth the hours of practice. The physics student struggles with a proof, knowing that eventually the solution will come clear. The student of a language stares at the bewildering text until a few familiar forms come through, and then more and more. Without this kind of faith, one might as well be distracted. What is there other than the moment or the next step? Who cares about anything beyond the here and now (or there and definite)? So long as I pass the test and get to the next stage, who cares if I text in class?

The "who cares" attitude fizzles, though, as soon as one stands up for something, as soon as one calls out trivial things for what they are. It is not only older generations who do this; many teenagers realize that their lives have become too crowded and their contacts superficial. Many young people long and push for something else. But it is often adults who remember a different way of life. Even if the memories are somewhat distorted, even if we tend to glorify the old days of reading in the attic, hearing the robins at daybreak, having long conversations with a friend, tinkering with light bulbs and batteries, or taking long bike rides around the neighborhood, this awareness of another way of life gives dimension to the present. It is still possible here. We see through the latest rage, be it an education fad or a social network.

Someone might say, "We don't have time for loftier goals; those are elitist illusions. Outcomes are what we need. We have to press forward in order to succeed in the world, individually and as a nation. If we don't, other countries will." Such an attitude feeds on distraction and brings about distraction. It seems focused but is so dependent on the definite that it grabs whatever stimulus comes its way. Of course, to some degree, such an attitude is understandable. There is despair underlying it, and plenty of reasons for such despair: a bad economy, threats of terrorism, racial tension and violence, the pressure of global competition, urban poverty, and more. In the face of such dejection, a practical approach seems to offer the only true hope. Insofar as it points the way to concrete achievements, it seems enlightened, even wise. But ultimately it is a wall, and walls are only sometimes wise. It easily mutates into a negative view: that nothing beyond the tangible and visible can be trusted.

In his epic poem *The Changing Light at Sandover*, James Merrill relates, in terza rima (the rhyme scheme used by Dante), his encounter with his fictional—or, rather, versified—nephew Wendell. They run into each other in Venice, and eat together at a trattoria, where Wendell shows his uncle his sketchbook of portraits, the subjects afflicted by "pain, panic and old age." When asked about this, Wendell explains, "I guess that's sort of how I see mankind. . . . Doomed, sick, selfish, dumb as shit." Soon they part, and Merrill (that is, the narrator) takes a long walk around the city. Only after walking alone does he have a reply for Wendell, a suggestion of a larger perspective, in which time, space, and language turn around:

> I lose touch with the sublime.
> Yet in these sunset years hardly propose
>
> Mending my ways, breaking myself of rhyme
> To speak to multitudes and make it matter.
> Late here could mean, moreover, In Good Time
>
> Elsewhere; for near turns far, and former latter
> —Syntax reversing her binoculars—
> Now early light sweeps under a pink scatter
>
> Rug of cloud the solemn, diehard stars.[25]

Indifference and cynicism, even disillusionment with the world, have a seductive glow. When mixed with talent, as in Wendell's case, they can be quite persuasive indeed; they seem to be on the side of truth, bucking clichés and trends. Yet they are trendy in a sense, caught up in anger at the world, distracted by the here and now, oblivious to the longer term. Wendell has keen perception; his drawings are strangely realistic. Yet there is something he does not see: a gesture tossed across the centuries, a mischievous twinkle in things, the wordplay that is part of all words. Diehard stars—the two words alone explode into meanings: the stars that don't die easily; the stars hard as dice, tilting our luck; the stars hiding under the rug; the stars that outlast us; the ardent stars.

Distraction turns out to be more complex and ambivalent than it appears. We need some degree of it, just as we need to be able to resist it. I would never subscribe to a plan, however focused, that forbade daydreaming or walking around a city and thinking, even if it seemed to some a waste of time. To understand the proper relationship of distraction and focus, we must consider what we are trying to do. There would be no reason to resist distraction if we did not long for anything beyond ourselves or if there were nothing beyond appetites, sensations, and concrete gains.

This idea may seem to contradict the initial premise of the chapter. If distraction comes from susceptibility to outside stimuli, then how can awareness of something beyond ourselves help us out of distraction? The contradiction is only on the surface; one outside world is immediate, the other not. One outside world offers us quick gratification; the other offers us a long challenge (with delights strewn in). The former keeps our attention moving and darting; the latter demands stillness while drawing us out of ourselves. The worlds overlap at times, but the principle remains: to do anything substantial, one must be able to detach oneself from instant responses and results; one must sink into the work, at least for a while. But work is by no means all that we do or all that matters. There should also be room for frolic and whimsy and nothing at all. There should be room, in all of this, for an ice-cream cone.

In the final chapter of *Distracted*, Jackson suggests that we may be on the brink of an attention renaissance. "We are on the cusp of an astonishing time," she writes, "and on the edge of darkness. *I score an average reaction time of 77 milliseconds on alerting and 52 on orienting, figures calculated from how well I refocus or react when tipped to a change. I can react to a shifting world*" (emphasis in original). Perhaps some kind of renaissance is in store—though I dread of the prospect of taking attention tests and learning how to improve my score. Jackson might worry about this as well; earlier in the book, she writes that "if we want to shape our own future, we must consider how we want to live and how we want to define progress, and as we do so, prepare to welcome to our ranks the thinking person's most prickly yet necessary companion—doubt."[26] For a "renaissance of attention" to take place, we must renew the things worthy of attention. Sometimes we find ourselves mistaken in our choices, and we must regather our thoughts and judgments.

To fight distraction is to defend something that matters, something that requires devotion of the mind. This is part of the meaning of study: to honor

things through thought and longing. Many dismiss such yearning as imprac-
tical; we have enough on our hands, they say, with the daily scramble and the
demands of the age. But yearning can pull us out of the scramble; it can calm
the scramble itself. The teacher who longs to read about Chinese history will
set aside time for it in the evenings. The boy who longs to see a falling star
will stay up late, looking up at the sky for hours. In *Moby-Dick*, it is the *Ra-
chel*, returning from a vain search for the captain's lost sons, that ultimately
rescues Ishmael from the water near the sunken *Pequod* and makes the story
possible. If we abandon such yearning and seeking, if we defer to the petty
demon of "getting it now," then nothing will be left but our vicissitudes, and
we will have no will or thought but to follow them.

4

~

Antigone:
Literature as "Thinking Apart"

L iterature furls and unfurls itself; it mixes with the world and draws
away. So, too, with its creators. Writers differ in their habits but tend
to need a mixture of aloneness and fellowship. Some need a quiet and
sequestered existence, away from the bustle. Yet in this seclusion, the writing
becomes a romance and conversation with an unknown reader, who knots
the eyebrows, sputters, pauses, swallows away a lump, falls asleep, or pounds
a fist on the table. For others, the city ruckus is their grist; they spend time
in bars, cafes, parks, and flea markets, picking up voices and stories, sometimes chiming in. Yet part of them remains separate, assembling words and
ideas, finding rhythms, making fun and reverence of what they hear. There
are still others who spend most of their days at the office or in the shop, but
get up early or stay up late to write. Whatever the way of life, some part of it
must remain apart from others. Without the ability to think separately and
to shape words into forms, writers would have little to write beyond lists,
memos, instructions, and maybe the contents of a Venn diagram.

A sense of solitude (and an ear and eye for it, and a mind to shape it) sets
literature apart from other forms of speech and writing. Solitude may have
marked literature from its beginnings; one finds distinct references to solitude in Sumerian texts, which are among the oldest known works of written
literature. In a version of the *Death of Gilgamesh* that may date as far back as
the third millennium BC, the hero is told,

You must have been told that this is what the cutting of your umbilical cord involved. The darkest day of humans awaits you now. The solitary place of humans awaits you now. The unstoppable flood-wave awaits you now. The unavoidable battle awaits you now. The unequal struggle awaits you now. The skirmish from which there is no escape awaits you now. But you should not go to the underworld with heart knotted in anger.[1]

Another Sumerian work, the tale of *Inana and Šu-kale-tuda*, has a description of a "solitary ghost": "He saw a solitary ghost. He recognised a solitary god by her appearance. He saw someone who fully possesses the divine powers. He was looking at someone whose destiny was decided by the gods."[2]

In both texts, the word translated as "solitary" is *dili*, "single, unique, sole, alone." The word occurs in other Sumerian works, including the *Uruk Lament*, and is often used in an emphatic sense, in reference to heroes, gods, or unusual things.[3]

Without solitude, there are hardly stories to tell. What would the Talmud or the Old Testament be without Moses or Job? What would the *Iliad* be without Achilles, who removed himself from battle? Or *Moby-Dick* without Ishmael, or *Wise Blood* without Hazel Motes? Or *As I Lay Dying* without Darl, or *Rhinoceros* without Bérenger? Of course, literature also brings people together; it has been handed down from one generation to another; it has figured large in education, cultural events, ceremony, rites of passage, and shared daily life. Even there, it needs an element of solitude in order to cling. Any striking or beautiful language bears the mark of independent thought. Likewise, the listening that occurs in a group is in some ways solitary; each of us takes in the work alone while listening with others.

But literature is also a melding of writer and reader, of writer and language, of language and reader. If solitude is present in all of it, the reader rarely notices it, as he or she becomes part of that solitude. When asked whether the individuality of the writer was not important, William Faulkner replied, "Very important to himself. Everybody else should be too busy with the work to care about the individuality."[4] It is important not to let the idea of individuality or solitude eclipse the literature. The solitude of literature should become second nature, as when we take time with a book or when a school honors literature in its curriculum.

What does it mean to honor literature in schools? It takes a willingness to teach excellent works in the first place, and to quiet down enough to take them in. Many works would serve as examples here: I have chosen Sophocles' *Antigone* because it has retained its vitality for twenty-five centuries; because one could read it twenty times, understanding more each time; and because it offers an intriguing perspective on solitude. The play concerns Antigone, daughter of Oedipus, who defies the law and risks her life in order to give honorable burial to her brother, Polyneices. Antigone is many things, but her bravery, moral clarity, and aloneness are striking from the start. She is not immune to error, even deep error, yet she stands luminous, enclosed, and faithful, not bending her words or principles to please others.

I have read the play many times over the years; one day, not long ago, I was struck by line 510. When a guard catches Antigone burying her brother and brings her before Creon, the king, a swift argument ensues. Creon tells Antigone that she is the only one in Thebes who thinks the way she does. Antigone replies that the others see things the same way but hold their tongues. Creon then asks her, "Are you not ashamed to think apart from these men?" (*su d'ouk epaidēi, tōnde chōris ei phroneis*).[5] "Thinking apart" is essential to Antigone's character, the conflicts between the characters, and the poetry of the play. The concept cannot be broached lightly, nor is it an unequivocal good. Thinking apart may be essential to wisdom, art, and science; taken to extremes, it can also lead us far astray. I decided to follow this idea of thinking apart in the play; it took me by surprise and led to various surprises.

Before this foray began, I taught *Antigone* (among many other works) to eighth-grade English-language learners in a public school in Brooklyn. *Antigone* was not included in the curriculum; in fact, there was no literature curriculum at all, only a literacy curriculum, which focused on reading strategies such as summarizing, visualizing, predicting, and making inferences. *Antigone* was an unlikely choice for a middle school class, not to mention a class in English as a Second Language (ESL), but I thought my students would take to it and learn from it. I was not disappointed. Students loved it; some were so moved by the play and fascinated by its ideas that they wrote additional essays voluntarily. We focused on *Antigone* itself; I did not treat it as a vehicle for a skill, though skills came into play. I enjoy driving, but *Antigone* is more than a car or truck.

One day, in my second year of teaching, we were discussing the dialogue in which Creon's son Haimon tells his father that he needs to listen more to others—in particular, to their advice that he release Antigone. Creon responds angrily that he is in charge of the city and must be obeyed. I asked my students which of the two characters was right. Most took the side of Haimon. Then one girl raised her hand. Beckoning me, she said quietly, "I think Creon is right." I asked her why. She explained, "People always tell me I do what other people tell me to do. They say I should stick up for myself. Creon is the king. If he doesn't stick up for himself, the people will take advantage." This set off a passionate argument between two students. The next day, I structured the argument as a class debate. The two sides tied at the end; it became clear to the students that both Haimon and Creon were partly right and that it was a complex matter.

Educators often encourage students to make connections between the subject and their own lives—in educational jargon, to make "text-to-self connections." This is both wise and misguided. Yes, it is important for students to relate what they read to their own experience, but the overt practice of making text-to-self connections can distract from the text itself. The closer and more careful the reading, the more meaningful the connection is likely to be. In this case, the student had a profound insight that drew on personal experience, but it was the immersion in the play that allowed this. Her thoughtfulness and willingness to differ from the others may well have been inspired by the play itself.

A work of literature does not take well to generic processes. When we read or recite a beautiful work, it is as though we were in a wood carver's hands, whittled through the reading. We may bring our own implements, but we may not make too much of them; the literature will fling them away. Literature stands up to anything: to critics and kings, to formulas and fads; to tired minds and broken hopes, to those who say they're just following the rules.

LET US NOW enter the play with an eye to line 510, in which Creon asks Antigone whether she is not ashamed to think apart from the men. First I will give some background on the play.

In a field on a hill, at night, a corpse lies covered in dust. Guards encircle him and brush the dust off of him. Satisfied that they have fulfilled the king's orders, they retreat to a sleeping place upwind, so that the stench won't reach them. They take turns watching the corpse, insulting each other to stay awake. The night passes; the sun lifts in the sky. Then a tornado hits, blowing dust around, thrashing the trees, and blackening the air. For some time they can see nothing at all. When the winds settle down, a strange scene plays out on the terrain. A young woman—Antigone—has come up to the corpse. She lets out a cry and curses the one who uncovered him. Quickly she covers the corpse with dirt again. She pours three libations from a bronze casket. The guards rush down from the hill and seize her. She does not resist.

This is the story that the Watchman tells Creon in Sophocles' *Antigone*. If a movie were to be made of the play, this could easily be the opening scene; we are used to being taken in with our eyes in the movie theater. But in the play, it is a "visual" only through language, and it occurs two scenes into the play. The play opens not with imagery, but with a clash of principles: Antigone inviting Ismene to join her in burying Polyneices, and Ismene raising objections and concerns. There is very little physical action in the play, aside from the dances of the Chorus; the main action happens offstage and is narrated by one of the characters. The audience must listen with full mind, imagination, and knowledge.

Antigone was first performed almost 2,500 years ago, around 441 BC, at the festival of Dionysus Eleuthereus, in Athens.[6] In terms of plot sequence, it is the final play of Sophocles' Oedipus trilogy, but he wrote it before *Oedipus Rex* and *Oedipus at Colonus*. The Athenian audience was well acquainted with the back story, to which Sophocles added some innovations.

According to myth, Antigone is one of the four children of Oedipus and Jocasta; Polyneices, Eteocles, and Ismene are the three others. Oedipus has unwittingly killed his father and married his mother, fulfilling a prophesy. When he learns the truth, he blinds himself and gives up the throne. Because Polyneices and Eteocles are too young to rule, their uncle Creon takes over as regent. Oedipus has cast a curse on his sons; as a result, they begin to quarrel over rights to the throne. Eteocles, the younger brother, drives Polyneices into exile. Enraged, Polyneices amasses an Argive army in order to wreak revenge and claim the throne. Before the play begins, Polyneices has led the Argives against the Thebans; he and Eteocles have killed each other in battle. Creon declares that Eteocles will be granted a full burial, while Polyneices will be left to rot in the open air.

The play opens with Antigone inviting her sister to join her in defying Creon's orders—that is, in burying Polyneices. In the first line, she addresses Ismene as her full sister, as one just like herself.[7] Upon hearing Antigone describe her plan, Ismene responds fearfully, protesting that this is against the law and against the proper codes for women. Antigone, who is far more concerned with the laws of the underworld than with those of rulers, declares Ismene an enemy and states that she will perform the burial on her own. Immediately the audience or reader is swept into a difficult moral conflict where neither side seems absolutely right.

When Creon learns that someone has defied his order and buried Polyneices, he declares that the man responsible will be put to death. He becomes enraged when he learns that it was not only a woman, but Antigone, whom his son Haimon had intended to marry. He orders guards to watch over Antigone and her sister, whom he wants to put to death as well. (Later, after entreaty from the Chorus leader, he decides that he will not kill Ismene after all.)

In a heated dialogue, Haimon entreats his father to listen to reason; Creon insists that he does not have to do so. Haimon leaves in a rage. Later the blind prophet Teiresias pleads with Creon, describing ill omens that have occurred and suggesting that Haimon may take violent action. Creon reacts angrily at first, but Teiresias's final words make an impression on him. At last, the Chorus persuades Creon to release Antigone and to build a tomb for Polyneices. By then it is too late. We learn the awful series of events from the Messenger, who relates it to Creon's wife, Eurydice: when Creon arrives at the cave, he sees that Antigone has hanged herself. Haimon is there, too, with his arms thrown around her. Upon hearing his father's voice, Haimon spits at him and draws his sword. Creon dodges the blow; Haimon then stabs himself before Creon's eyes, throws his arms around Antigone again, and dies.

When Eurydice hears the news, she walks away in silence; the Chorus finds this troubling, as "a silence so extreme / Is as dangerous as a flood of silly tears."[8] Minutes later, she is found dead. Creon is crushed with remorse and recognition of his wrong; he wishes only for a swift death. The Chorus ends the play with the conclusion that wisdom is essential to a happy life and that one learns it in old age, after suffering great blows.

Antigone has been interpreted, debated, and adapted over the centuries. It was invoked in many medieval and Renaissance writings, transformed into new plays or poems by writers such as Friedrich Hölderlin, Jean Anouilh, and Bertolt Brecht; rendered in opera and other music by Christoph Willibald Gluck, Niccolò Antonio Zingarelli, Felix Mendelssohn, Camille Saint-Saëns, Arthur Honegger, and Carl Orff; and analyzed by philosophers and critics such as Georg Wilhelm Friedrich Hegel, Søren Kierkegaard, Martin Heidegger, Jacques Lacan, George Steiner, and many others. It is stark and immediate; it concerns, on the face, a young woman who defies the state in order to follow her conscience. Aspects of it could apply to any place and time. The choral odes are stirring, strange, and complex.

Antigone follows a structure typical of ancient Greek tragedy: an alternation of dialogues and choral poetry. It begins with a prologue, or opening scene, followed by an opening ode, the *parodos*, sung and danced by the Chorus. This is followed by an alternation of scenes (*epeisodia*, singular *epeisodion*) and odes (*stasima*, singular *stasimon*). The last scene is followed by the closing, the *exodos*. The structure makes for an interplay of direct and oblique expression, the former predominating in the scenes, the latter in the odes.

The Chorus, representing the thoughts of the people, contrasts with the two solitary protagonists, Antigone and Creon. But in representing the people, the Chorus goes beyond majority opinion and beyond opinion altogether. Mark Griffith writes that these odes "must be counted among the most opaque—as well as the most adventurous—in all of Greek tragedy. Indeed, so rich and suggestive are they in their language, and so far-ranging and abstract in their subject matter, that it is often difficult to extract from them a particular opinion or definite interpretation."[9] If the Chorus in *Antigone* represents the voice of the crowd, it is not the voice of chatter or gossip.

Rather, the Chorus's odes convey common memory, layers of the psyche, and deep lyricism.

Most tragedies have one central hero; *Antigone* has two. Critics have grappled with the significance of this. Steiner writes, "Pondering the dual or 'broken-backed' architecture of Sophocles' dramaturgy, commentators have repeatedly suggested that 'Antigone and Creon' would be a more just title." Hegel sees the two protagonists as representatives of two legitimate and opposing philosophies, where the conflict is not between good and evil, but between two limited positions, each of which contains a portion of good.[10] The presence of two protagonists remains perplexing. At one level, they represent two truths and two sets of laws. Antigone's truth is that of family ties and the underworld; Creon's, that of government and the upper world (the earth and the gods that rule it). Both are stubborn, both defend what they believe, but their worlds are in some way mutually unrecognizable. In addition, there is a slight skew and imbalance that makes the oppositions inexact.

In his *Poetics*, Aristotle wrote that a tragedy had to result in recognition; the hero must undergo "a change from ignorance to knowledge." With two heroes, the play both follows and breaks this rule. Creon certainly undergoes such a change; he realizes at the end that his errors have led to the deaths of those dearest to him. Whether Antigone experiences recognition is open to debate. Some scholars have argued that Antigone is self-certain (*autognōtos*) and "a law unto herself" (*autonomos*), unable to cede to others or admit to any error. Others see a form of recognition in her final lament, where she recognizes that she is completely alone, even among the dead: "But I have no place with human beings, / Living or dead. No city is home to me." She also recognizes, in ways she did not before, that the family curse has been playing itself out; whereas, at the start of the play, she saw a succession of troubles, she now grieves for "all our fate" and declares that "from such people wretched me was born."[11]

But this insight does not lead Antigone to the conclusion that she was wrong, only that she is miserable and alone. Her action remains intact in her mind. Robert F. Goheen suggests that Antigone's intuitions are in some sense untouchable; her isolation manifests itself in many ways, including her very use of words. "In individual scenes," he observes, "a high degree of tension is created by having Antigone and Creon use the same or similar terms to mean radically different things."[12] Her separation is not only a choice but also a way of being, a trait she cannot change. "Thinking apart" is part of her beauty and destruction. It is Creon's, too, but in a different way.

When Creon asks Antigone whether she is not ashamed to think apart from the others, he touches on her very essence (and, in some ways, his own). The line has been translated in a variety of ways; some have taken bold liberties with it, some have cast interpretations on it, and some have rendered it as literally as possible. These are a few of the translations:

"Aren't you ashamed to talk / treason?" (Kelly Cherry)
"And you, aren't you ashamed to differ so from them? / So disloyal!" (Robert Fagles)
"Are you not ashamed to differ from such men?" (Paul Roche)
"Maybe. But you are guilty, and they are not." (Dudley Fitts and Robert Fitzgerald)
"You are not ashamed to be the only one who thinks this way?" (Nicholas Rudall)
"Aren't you ashamed of thinking differently from them?" (Ruby Blondell)
"Aren't you ashamed to think differently from all the others?" (Ruth Fainlight and Robert J. Littman)
"And you are not ashamed to think alone?" (Elizabeth Wyckoff)
"Aren't you ashamed to have a mind apart from theirs?" (Paul Woodruff)
"Are you not ashamed to think apart from these men?" (Wm. Blake Tyrrell and Larry J. Bennett).[13]

Some of the translations draw attention to the idea of thinking apart, while others do not. A few translators have opted for the verb "differ" or the phrase "think differently." Others have interpreted this as "talking treason" or "not following the lead" of the elders. The Fitts and Fitzgerald translation departs drastically from the sense of the original. Wyckoff balances the meaning of the original with the metrical demands of the translation; she drops the idea of thinking *apart* from others but keeps the idea of aloneness of thought. Woodruff and Tyrrell and Bennett translate the line fairly literally (insofar as there can be a literal translation of this line), with "have a mind apart" and "think apart." Both translations emphasize the concept of thinking separately (not necessarily differently) from the others.

"Thinking differently" may seem synonymous with "thinking apart," but there is an important distinction. To the modern speaker of English, "thinking differently" could mean simply disagreeing with others or perhaps having a different way of reasoning. "Thinking apart" is less colloquial, more striking, and in some ways more profound. It suggests an isolation, autonomy, and distance, or even a separate physical world. One could think very much along the same lines as others—that is, hold similar ideas—yet still stand separate, as Antigone does (after all, as she points out to Creon, the elders agree with her). Her difference goes far beyond opinion; it is difference of being. Goheen calls this "a certain separation of her thought from the plane on which most of the other characters move."[14] In other words, her mind works in its own way, to the point where no one (other than Ismene) tries to reach her.

Solitude is part of Antigone's being, her fate, and her understanding; she recognizes her own solitude and the solitude of others. At the outset of the play, she gives Ismene a choice, arguably an unfair one: to be one with her or severed from her; to join her in burying Polyneices or to be an enemy in her eyes. When Ismene expresses reluctance to break the law, Antigone breaks with her in turn, but she takes no other revenge, nor does she try to change Ismene's mind. "Be the way that seems right to you," she says (*all' isth' hopoia soi dokei*).[15] Of course, one must not underestimate the significance of that break; where Antigone recognizes no division between her two brothers, she insists on one between herself and her sister. Nonetheless, Antigone does not punish Ismene further or try to control what she does. She recognizes in Ismene a separate mind—an enemy mind, but a mind nonetheless.

Creon has no such sense of internal freedom; he does not recognize other minds. To him, the citizens exist to obey their ruler, who in turn offers justice in the name of Zeus and all the gods.[16] His intentions are benign and his approach to ruling logical (he wants to bring peace and order to the city), yet he makes no room for thoughts that differ from his own. Woodruff's translation (which I quote except where noted) reads,

Such is the character of my mind: Never, while I rule,
Will a criminal be honored higher than a man of justice.
But give me a true friend of this city
And I will pay him full honor, in death or life. (lines 207–10)[17]

Creon asks of the Chorus that they "not side with anybody who disobeys" his decree that Polyneices shall be left unburied (219). Not only does he demand obedience, but he impugns the integrity of those who disagree with him. When anyone challenges him, he concludes that the person must be insane or profiting from a bribe. As the play progresses, his denial of others' freedom (of thought and action) becomes fiercer and isolates him more.

It is this very denial of others' minds that brings Creon into confrontation, first with them, then with himself and his error. One by one, the others depart from him, first through overt disagreement, then through death. Although it is Teiresias who finally brings Creon around, Haimon's challenges have their effect as well. Haimon pulls out all the stops; his speech to his father begins respectfully but turns quickly into a criticism of his very mind. He shows his own mental prowess while calling Creon's thinking into question:

If a man believes that he alone has a sound mind,
And no one else can speak or think as well as he does,
Then, when people study him, they'll find an empty book.
But a wise man can learn a lot and never be ashamed;
He knows he does not have to be rigid and close-hauled. (707–11)

The word for "having a sound mind" is the aforementioned *phronein*, which also means "to reason, to have understanding, to be wise." Haimon points out the lack of *phronein* in Creon's thinking: Creon is too "close-hauled," too exclusive for true reason, and therefore incapable of wisdom (in his current state). Haimon illustrates this problem masterfully with the similes of a tree and boat:

You've seen trees tossed by a torrent in a flash flood:
If they bend, they're saved, and every twig survives,
But if they stiffen up, they're washed out from the roots.
It's the same in a boat: if a sailor keeps the footline taut,
If he doesn't give an inch, he'll capsize, and then—
He'll be sailing home with his benches down and his hull to the sky. (712–17)

When these attempts at persuasion fail, Haimon becomes angry; he tells Creon that if Antigone is put to death, someone else will die too (he does not say who, but Creon takes it as a threat). At the end of their argument Haimon swears that Creon will never look into his eyes again. The Chorus leader intercedes, warning Creon that impassioned youth can mean trouble. Creon responds, again using a form of *phronein*: "Let him go, him and his lofty ambitions!" (*dratō, phroneitō meizon ē kat' andr' iōn*; 768). But Creon himself is not using his head, and he will be punished for this.

Creon's isolation grows and grows—yet he cannot recognize reasoning outside of his own. He remains unmoved when the blind prophet Teiresias tells him of an omen: "And I heard a voice I've never known from a bird: / Wild screeching, enraged, utterly meaningless" (1001–2). Teiresias goes on to tell of a sacrifice melting on the altar, not bright with the flame of Hephaestus, but "spitting and sputtering in clouds of smoke," with bladders "bursting open, spraying bile into the sky" (1009–10). Creon scoffs at the omen, accusing Teiresias of loving gold and profit.

But something changes over the course of the dialogue. Teiresias gives a gory forecast: that Creon will "make a trade" with his "own boy's corpse," that mutilators lie in ambush for him, and that he will be "tangled in the net" of his "own crimes." Teiresias finishes with the warning that Creon cannot outrun the sting of the arrows he has shot at him (*tōn su thalpos oukh hupekdramēi*) (1066, 1076, 1086). Shaken, Creon asks the advice of the Chorus leader, who counsels him to release Antigone and build a tomb for Polyneices. Creon agrees to do so, but his change of heart comes too late. It seems that Creon's final understanding, his *phronein*, had to coincide with his complete isolation and crushing grief. But is that isolation solitude? And is it even isolation, or is it a return to a community?

There is a paradox and endlessness to Creon's solitude; he is both alone and not alone throughout. In the first part of the play, he is mentally alone in that only his will counts, yet he tries to join the others' will to his. In the latter part, where he concedes his error, he is physically alone, confronted with deaths. He tells the servants to lead him away, as he is now "worth less than a nobody" (1325). Yet, in being led away, he finally finds himself in concord with the people; submitting to their judgment and acknowledging his wrong, he sinks into their society. The play ends with the Chorus, who use the word *phronein* in the final line (*gērai to phronein edidaxan*). The ending words suggest that Creon's boasting has ended and that he has joined in common wisdom, as soul-breaking as it is. The word *phronein* here could mean reason, practical wisdom, or good thinking. The final lines have been translated in many ways; I offer my own here:

Wisdom is by far the foremost part
Of happiness, and one must not be impious
Toward the gods. Great words,
Paying for the great blows of the overproud,
Teach one, in old age, to be wise. (1348–1353)[18]

Antigone's solitude is likewise paradoxical and endless; unlike Creon, she has not struggled against it. She has willingly given up the company of the living for the company of her dead brothers and the gods. She believes that she will be reunited with her brothers, but she has no knowledge of the realm of the dead, beyond a sense of its laws. Later she senses what she has risked; she sees that she may be entirely alone, without the support of anyone on earth or below. She asks, "How can I expect a god to help me in my misery? / To whom should I pray now? Do you see? / They are counting all my reverence to be / Irreverence" (922–25). By "they" she means the people, not the gods, yet she fears that the gods and the people may blame her alike. Nonetheless, even in complete isolation, she affirms, in the translation of Tyrrell and Bennett, that she has suffered unjustly, "having piously rendered piety" (*tēn eusebian sebisasa*).[19] She has no human company, but perhaps she retains the company of principle: the sense of having done right. The scene is troubling and inconclusive; it is possible that she has lost her one community, that of the underworld, at least in her mind. Unlike Creon, she does not see error in herself, but she sees it in the family line and has lost some of her certainty.

Both Antigone and Creon think apart from others in some way, but what is the nature of this thinking? Much has been written about the importance of *phronein* and other words related to thinking in the play.[20] Sound thinking and distorted thinking are sometimes hard to tell apart; what seems sane to one is insane to another. The play's core tragedy is that the good minds cannot meet; Creon and Antigone both have good reasons for what they do but cannot see each other's reasons. The Chorus's odes reflect this mystery and enclosedness of mind.

Known as the "Ode to Man," the first ode (after the *parodos*) is grand and sonorous; it reads like trumpets, sun, and storm. It is thrilling to listen to it in the original Greek; even the best translations cannot convey the symmetries, rhythms, and wordplay. Yet much of the glory does survive in English (Fagles's translation here):

> Numberless wonders
> terrible wonders walk the world but none the match for man—
> that great wonder crossing the heaving gray sea—
> driven on by the blasts of winter
> on through breakers crashing left and right,
> holds his steady course
> and the oldest of the gods he wears away—
> the Earth, the immortal, the inexhaustible—
> as his plows go back and forth, year in, year out
> with the breed of stallions turning up the furrows.[21]

Goheen draws attention to the repetition in *deina* and *deinoteron* ("wonders" and "more wondrous") and the meanings the two words open up: "fearsome and marvelous, potent and strange, mighty and resourceful, wonderful but also terrifying." A few lines later, the Chorus presents a remarkable image and idea: that man works the oldest of the gods (in the Greek, *hupertatan* means both "eldest" and "highest"), "the immortal, the inexhaustible" (*the n / te tan hupertatan, Gan / aphthiton akamatan apotruetai*). In other words, man is in physical contact with the first of the gods and thus all the gods, who are tireless but affected by humans. Victor Bers, a Hellenist at Yale, points out that this ode shows man inventing everything he needs for physical life and for the social order, *not* getting these gifts from the gods.[22]

The ode contains a hint of irony; while it glorifies humans, it may cast their virtues in doubt. In the previous scene, the Watchman takes pains to tell Creon that he did not commit the crime, whatever it is. He is an example of man with less-than-wonderful qualities, as his first priority is to save his own skin (239–40).[23] Given this context, the words of the Chorus carry a tinge of mockery, but only a tinge. After all, in the scene following the ode, Antigone shows great bravery when she is brought before Creon and says, "I did it. I won't deny anything" (443). We are left with the sense that the Chorus is right—that there is something wondrous in humanity, not undone by the petty behavior of the Watchman. Even so, the words *deina* and *deinoteron* seem slightly precarious, as does the entire ode.

The ode consists of two strophes (stanzas) alternating with antistrophes; each antistrophe echoes the complex meter and answers the ideas of the strophe before it. When one reads the ode aloud in Greek, one starts to hear how one pattern leads into another. There is something moving and mysterious about the lines, *kai phthegma kai anemoen / phronēma* (in Woodruff's translation, "Language and a mind swift as the wind"; 354).[24] The Chorus marvels at language and makes the listener marvel in turn. Some of the juxtapositions cannot be translated well into English. The opposition of *pantoporos* and *aporos* ("all-resourceful" and "resourceless") and of *hupsipolis* and *apolis* (approximately "lofty of city" and "having no city"—understood to modify man) suggest that the characters may be on the brink of glory or disaster.[25] The end of the second strophe reads (with Greek words added to Woodruff's translation):

> He has the means to handle every need, [*pantoporos*]
> Never steps toward the future without the means. [*aporos*]
> Except for Death. He's got himself no relief from that,
> Though he puts every mind to seeking cures
> For plagues that are hopeless. (360–64)

The end of the second antistrophe states that if he "honors the law of the land / And the oath-bound justice of the gods,"

> Then his city shall stand high. [*hupsipolis*]
> But no city for him [*apolis*] if he turns shameless out of daring.
> He will be no guest of mine,
> He will never share my thoughts [*mēt' ison phronōn*],
> If he goes wrong. (371–75)

In the original, the word *aporos* occurs immediately after *pantoporos*, and *apolis* immediately after *hupsipolis*, creating a sense of tottering between extremes, a sense of danger. There is something scintillating and ominous here: whatever is highest in man may come crashing down. The declaration

"He will never share my thoughts" (literally, "May he never think equally with me" or "May he never make common cause with me") could apply to Creon as well as to Antigone.[26] Antigone breaks the law of the land, but Creon violates a law of the gods, in dishonoring the body of Polyneices. This precariousness has much to do with solitude; going out on a limb and being solitary are in some ways one and the same.

The poet and critic Vyacheslav Ivanov writes about the role of infringement in tragedy: the tragic hero, confined by his limited view but compelled to act on it, infringes on the cosmic order or on the rules of society. He cannot do otherwise, as he "bears within his inmost core his own autonomous law."[27] For Ivanov (who was writing about Dostoevsky), there is a deep relationship between solitude and crime. But such solitude carries integrity and dignity as well; the hero does what he or she must do, according to his or her understanding and principles. What perplexes us, even today, is the sympathy we feel for the erring hero, the need we have for such error, such aloneness.

I first read Antigone in ninth grade. I have returned to it many times since then. Only in the past year did I memorize the first ode, in Greek. I found myself reciting it every day, enjoying the sounds and rhythms, and lingering on certain phrases and words. Although it is sung by a group representing the city's elders, it has a private and mysterious quality. I came to it from line 510, which is blatantly about solitude, and found that the ode perhaps contained the greater solitude. Now, after all this time, I feel like a true beginner with *Antigone*, ready to read it slowly in Greek, pausing as often as I need to pause, thinking as much as I need to think, and finding my interpretations sometimes wrong.

Like man tilling the earth in the first ode, I would teach *Antigone* year after year, if I could. Not all students would love it, but many would remember it later. Some would find themselves thinking about it; some would watch performances and listen to recordings; some would find a way to pass it on.[28] Whether alone with it or in a class or audience, they would take in something of its solitude—the solitude that moves through voices, dances, and crowds, over the revolving waves, through the rain, through the city, through the mind, and into singular action.

WHY IS *ANTIGONE* not part of the usual public high school curriculum? The short answer is that there is no usual public high school curriculum. A 2010 study led by scholar Sandra Stotsky showed that public high school literature curricula in the United States are inconsistent and that even the standard classics are taught in a small percentage of courses. Of the 773 high school literature courses considered in the study (both standard and honors courses), only 44 teach *Antigone*. The most commonly taught work, *Romeo and Juliet*, is taught in 173 of the 773 courses.[29] Thus it appears that there is no set of literary works that most students read in high school and not even a strong likelihood that students will read any particular text.

Many schools and districts expect English teachers to emphasize themes and skills, not literary works. In *Creating Literacy-Rich Schools for Adolescents*, education professors Gay Ivey and Douglas Fisher recommend organizing lessons around "a theme, a big idea, or an essential question" and selecting texts that will "engage the adolescent learner." It will not do to have all students reading *Romeo and Juliet*, they say, since a whole-class approach does not "respond to the unique needs, strengths, or interests of adolescents." Rather, texts should be suited to students' interests and levels. "If it sounds as though we hate Shakespeare," they write, "that isn't the case. Shakespeare and other works from the canon of great literature can and should be part of the English curriculum. We just know that the texts have to be matched to students. We have a hard time imagining a ninth grade class of thirty-six students all reading, and willing to read, the same book at the same time." The National Council of Teachers of English (NCTE) similarly recommends strategy instruction, diverse texts, and student choice of texts as ways to motivate adolescents to read.[30] The great drawback of such an approach is that it sacrifices the study of specific literature; literature class is no longer about the works themselves but about the operations to be performed on them.

Most state standards across the United States do not specify any literature that students should read. In New York State, for instance, one of the standards specifies that students in middle school will

> read and view texts and performances from a wide range of authors, subjects, and genres; understand and identify the distinguishing features of the major genres and use them to aid their interpretation and discussion of literature; identify significant literary elements (including metaphor, symbolism, foreshadowing, dialect, rhyme, meter, irony, climax) and use those elements to interpret the work; recognize different levels of meaning; read aloud with expression, conveying the meaning and mood of a work; and evaluate literary merit based on an understanding of the genre and the literary elements.[31]

These are fine goals, but they emphasize skills, not literary works. There is no indication in these standards that any particular literary works are inherently valuable—that students should read such authors as Homer, Sophocles, Shakespeare, Donne, Hugo, Melville, Dickinson, or Chekhov. New York

State is no anomaly; most state standards in English language arts focus on skills, not on actual works of literature or categories of works. The new Common Core State Standards emphasize the importance of high-quality literary texts, particularly Shakespeare and American foundational documents, but they leave the selection of specific texts to curriculum makers.[32] It remains to be seen what shape these curricula will take.

In many school districts across the United States, including New York City and San Diego, elementary and middle schools follow the Balanced Literacy program, which focuses on strategies. Balanced Literacy uses the "Reader's Workshop" and "Writer's Workshop" formats, which hail from Teachers College, Columbia University. In a typical Reader's Workshop lesson, a teacher gathers the students on the rug, explains the point of the lesson (for instance, to learn about making predictions), and proceeds to read a story or poem aloud. During the "read-aloud," the teacher pauses at some point in order to perform a "think-aloud" in which she models the intended strategy. For instance, if teaching about predictions, she might say, "Hmm . . . I wonder whether Paul will knock on the door of that house. Let me look for some clues." Having shown how she makes a prediction, she resumes reading. When it comes time for a new prediction, she might ask students to "turn and talk" to their partners about what they think will happen next. Having practiced this a few times, the students go to their groups to practice the strategy on the books they are reading. The teacher circulates to confer with groups and individuals. At the end of the lesson, the students briefly discuss what they have learned.

The main problem with strategy instruction is that it elevates the strategy above the literature. It is one thing to teach strategies; it is quite another to make the strategies the very point of instruction, lesson after lesson, day after day. They are a weak common thread, compared with literature itself. A given strategy does not apply equally well to all texts, and one must be skillful and discerning when applying it. Predictions, for instance, are sometimes most useful when wrong. Authors frequently break patterns and expectations on purpose. One can learn much from observing, for instance, how Elizabeth Bishop breaks and sustains the pattern of the villanelle in "One Art." To make predictions properly, one must be alert to the nature of the work itself; one becomes alert through reading and listening. The cognitive psychologist Daniel T. Willingham argues that strategies (i.e., the common versions of them) are essentially tricks, not skills, and can be taught briefly.[33] The more complex kinds develop over time, through close reading.

Unfortunately, strategies have come to occupy the center of the lesson and have spread throughout the grades. Some elementary and middle school teachers try to move toward literature instruction, but there are numerous obstacles. Schools may not have class sets of literary works, and they may have few classics. Officials conducting walk-through observations may want to see students completing charts, talking in groups, and reading books that match their individual levels. Balanced Literacy consultants and coaches ensure that teachers are complying with the program, from the structure of the lesson to the lists on the wall. Many students enter high school without having read a serious work of literature. Moreover, since the literacy blocks take up a good portion of the day, students may not be learning other subjects either. History, science, and even arts are subordinated to reading strategies.

In high school, literature instruction becomes visibly stratified and strategized. Those who lack preparation end up in remedial classes (sometimes called "genre studies") that use methods like those of Balanced Literacy and that emphasize personal responses to text. Other students may take standard required courses; the most advanced students may take honors and Advanced Placement courses. Thus many students graduate high school with minimal exposure to complex or layered literature. They have not been immersed in the thought and writing of an author, time period, or culture. They have a collection of strategies but no idea that certain works are untouchable by strategies.

Some proponents of strategy instruction have recognized its possible pitfalls but not the losses inherent in it. Stephanie Harvey and Anne Goudvis note, for instance, that students should learn to make meaningful connections, not just any connection at all.[34] Yet they defend the practice of making connections deliberately and consciously, as a focus of lessons and a general reading practice. Similarly, in a 1987 article, educators P. David Pearson and Janice A. Dole considered the possibility that excessive emphasis on strategies could "turn relatively simple and intuitively obvious tasks into introspective nightmares." Like Harvey and Goudvis, they saw some of the drawbacks of strategies, but concluded that "they should not prevent researchers from continuing efforts to understand what constitutes effective comprehension instruction and to persuade teachers and administrators to consider these instructional techniques as they develop reading programs."[35] Even the most cautious proponents of strategy instruction ignore one of its key weaknesses: strategies cannot hold a candle to literature itself.

The usual reading strategies are entirely inadequate for an understanding of *Antigone*. One could summarize the plot, but then one must consider why the plot is so important and how it is shaped. One could predict whether or not Creon will change his mind, but such a prediction would do little to illuminate the play, unless one paid close attention to subtle details and understood the importance of being wrong. One could make an inference about Haimon's cryptic words or Eurydice's silence, but this is best done through close attention to the details of the play. One could "visualize" one of the vivid scenes—but it is more important to see how the language makes it vivid, and how images and ideas alternate. Any strategy held too high will distract from the beauty of the play: the fierce and soulful poetry, the taut rhythm, the moral conflicts, the ambiguity of good sense and delusion, the characters' integrity, and the many meanings of words.

Someone might respond, "Such literary study is fine for advanced students, but what about students who can barely read? Don't they need some basic reading skills before they can do the kinds of sophisticated things described here?" Yes, but strategies are not the skills they need. They need vocabulary and grammar; they need to hear, read, and discuss excellent literature, so that it becomes part of their consciousness. In addition, they need to study history, science, and other subjects, in order to build knowledge and gain perspective on what they read. Then, when they enter high school, they should be ready for literature courses. Students who can barely read should be given intensive remedial help—outside of literature class. At the same time, they should read literature in literature class, struggling with it if need be. A text that seems daunting will often come clear to the student who perseveres with it. Moreover, literature exists at many levels simultaneously. Within the same class, there may be many kinds and degrees of understanding; the students may learn from each other and from the teacher's expert guidance of the discussion. Schools should protect the study of literature and help students as needed.

The Chorus in *Antigone* says that he who honors the laws of the land and the justice of the gods will be *hupsipolis*, that is, he will have a great city. One could say this about literature: if students learn to enter it and honor it, they will have the makings of a rich life. They will also have an opening to true difference; by immersing themselves in the sole voice of another, they will start to hear their own voice, assenting, questioning, disputing, singing along, starting a new poem or song. Much of this literature is difficult for readers today; the ideas may seem distant, the words obscure, or the sentences long and complex. It is the teacher's duty to help the student enter the work, and this takes time and care. It cannot be done when students in a given class are reading many different works at the same time. It requires a certain reverence—not the reverence of calling an author "great" just because everyone else does, but the reverence of treating the work, for a little while, as the most important thing in the room and mind.

To understand literature, one must draw on knowledge, but one must also be willing to leave the known behind. It makes eccentrics of all of us. When we memorize a poem, we spend hours with its words, sounds, and shapes. When we read a novel, we inhale its air and trudge through its towns. We do not easily rejoin the world when we are done. But in an atmosphere of constant activity and glib conversation, we have no such places, and no one quite knows what to do when the hubbub stops. To set our individual course, or have any say in our culture, we must have room to know, contemplate, and protect what we love.

We? But how can we do any of this together, when it involves thinking apart? Oddly, there is community in the apartness. When singing in a chorus, you do not chat or whisper, or at least you shouldn't; you are in the music and in some way alone with it. Yet you hear the many voices and belong to them. The swell is yours, as is the fading. So, too, it may happen that you are reciting a poem, alone, on the edge of a lake. A word or line makes you shiver, and you know the shiver is not yours alone, but a rhythm passed from mind to mind, a passing ghost, a frisky gust, the tug of something wrong in the world, a cadence of water and pebbles.

5

$\sim$

The Workshop Model
in New York City

In January 2003, the New York City Department of Education announced its new reform plan, Children First, which would include a reading program (Balanced Literacy) and mathematics program (Everyday Mathematics and Impact Mathematics). All but some two hundred high-performing elementary and middle schools would be required to implement these programs in the fall. Then came a separate, informal announcement, conveyed through regional superintendents and school administrators, that teachers throughout the grades, including high school, would now be required to follow the "workshop model," a generalized version of the Reader's and Writer's Workshops of Balanced Literacy. Each class period was to consist of three parts. First, there was the mini-lesson, ten to fifteen minutes long, in which the teacher presented the topic, usually a skill or strategy. This was followed by thirty-some minutes of group or independent work on the skill or strategy. In the final minutes of the lesson, students would come together to "share" what they had learned. In at least one region of New York City, teachers were given stopwatches so that their mini-lesson would not exceed the allotted time.[1]

Teachers throughout the city were dismayed; a workshop model may be appropriate for certain lessons and topics but not for others. It was not suitable for presentation of a mathematical proof or for discussion of literature. It was not right for lessons that required extended instruction or an ongoing exchange between teacher and students. One high school social studies teacher protested, "How do you explain the causes of World War I or the rise of fascism in Europe in 10 minutes?" It was an "impossible task," he answered. Another high school teacher observed that "the Constitution does not explain itself" and that "it requires a master teacher to navigate students through the complexities."[2]

The workshop model came bundled with a set of assumptions about teaching and education; it was often held up in contrast with traditional classrooms of the past. Students' desks were arranged in groups of four or five so that students could interact with each other easily. The blackboard, though tolerated, carried stigma; at some schools, teachers were required to cover it and use a whiteboard or chart paper instead. The workshop was supposed to transform the teacher's role; a teacher was no longer a "sage on the stage" but a "guide on the side." Teachers were supposed to spend most of the class time circulating from group to group, assisting students, and taking notes on their progress.[3]

To a large degree, the workshop model set the curriculum. Class sets of literary classics were sent back to the storage room (whole-class reading of literature would generally be limited to brief "shared readings"). Each classroom had its own library filled with chapter books, teen novels, a few classics, and books on sundry topics. Each classroom was supposed to have specific items on the walls—materials specified by the Department of Education and written out by the teachers—and student work was to be on display at all times. Teachers were supposed to maintain a "print-rich" environment, with charts, student work, and other written material covering the walls. Many teachers hung student work on clotheslines stretching from wall to wall, in order to make room for the required displays.

Though implementation varied from region to region and school to school, the workshop model seeped into every crack of school life. Administrators expected to see it in action when they conducted formal observations or peeked in the room. In professional development sessions, consultants told teachers to "teach the child, not the subject"; to have all students "engaged" in cooperative groups performing "hands-on activities"; and to produce "evidence of learning" in every lesson. "Evidence of learning" often consisted of "graphic organizers"—Venn diagrams, "mind maps," and other charts and diagrams. Students were supposed to take part in Accountable Talk, a form of discussion developed (and later trademarked) by the Institute for Learning at the University of Pittsburgh. The principle behind Accountable Talk was that students should respond to each other and use evidence to substantiate their points. In practice, the mechanics of Accountable Talk often took precedence over the substance. Observers expected to see students using "starter phrases": for instance, "I would like to challenge what José said." Whether the challenge had merit was hard for an outside observer to detect.[4]

Observation forms and checklists helped ensure that the model would be enforced. Principals and district officials conducted frequent "walkthroughs"; that is, they entered classrooms and checked off items and practices on a checklist. One "walkthrough checklist" used by principals in New York City's District 75 (a geographically noncontiguous district for students with autism and other severe disabilities) includes the following questions:

> Does student desks [sic] arrangement promote eye-to-eye conversation and inquiry? . . . Are writing centers/areas established in classrooms? . . . Does the teacher follow the 3 components of Readers Workshop? (Mini Lesson, Independent Reading/Conferencing, Share) . . . Are the 7 proficiencies of good readers being shared and practiced? . . . Are students applying strategies from the mini lesson? . . . Is student writing celebrated and displayed in varying stages? . . . Have all students been assigned a talk partner? Are students given opportunities to talk during the interactive read aloud? Is talk encouraged?[5]

Even in this district, which serves students with especially high needs, teachers had little pedagogical authority.

In some cases, the workshop model suited the teachers' style and subject; in others, it replaced structures that would have been better suited to the lesson. Teachers who used it only out of obligation found themselves struggling with classroom discipline. Students sense when the teacher is not on secure footing and when the subject is being presented in a forced manner. If the teacher is acting according to her best thinking, this will come across. If she is trying to please the administration, if she is nervous about faces peering in, that, too, will be apparent. Teachers, students, and schools need structures of various kinds, but when the structures do not suit the lesson, students recognize that something is amiss.

WHAT IS TEACHING, and what matters in it? To gain some insight into the question, let us look into Plato's *Symposium*, written around 360 BC. It tells about education obliquely, like a poem or riddle, challenging and teasing the reader just as the characters within it challenge and tease each other. An account of a subdued but lively drinking party, the *Symposium* combines speeches and dialogue, philosophy and comedy. The toned-down atmosphere allows the ideas to take over, yet there is revelry in the air. It is an evening of many intermediaries.

The *Symposium* is framed as a story told by Aristodemus (who witnessed the event) to Apollodorus and related by Apollodorus to his companions. In addition, it contains two more retellings: that of Plato, who tells the entire story, and that of Socrates, who relates what his teacher, Diotima, taught him. Thus the speeches, teachings, and conversations have been memorized and passed on several times. This suggests how important and enjoyable the story was to the listeners and tellers at various stages. Apollodorus acknowledges that he has forgotten parts of what Aristodemus related to him, yet what he remembers is substantial.

In the story, Agathon the poet has invited people over in honor of his victory in a dramatic competition. Socrates arrives late, when the feast is half over; in the meantime he has been standing outside, absorbed in thought. After Socrates enters and eats dinner, Eryximachus proposes that each person give a speech in praise of Love.[6] Having agreed to this, they begin without further ado. Each participant—Phaedrus, Pausanias, Eryximachus, Aristophanes, Agathon, and Socrates—offers a different perspective on Love; each tries to outdo the speakers before him. Yet each, until Socrates, describes Love as a god or as something divine.

The Symposium is bawdy and jocular, sometimes outrageous, strewn with light and rough teasing: for instance, when Eryximachus advises Aristophanes on how to get rid of his hiccup, and when Alcibiades, who comes in drunk after the speeches have concluded, delivers a coarse yet admiring eulogy of Socrates himself. Yet the speakers approach the topic with intensity; each speech has a unique character, and each one tries to seize upon the nature of Love. Agathon's speech appears to be the pinnacle: instead of praising the effects of Love on humans, he praises the god himself for his beauty and goodness. He finishes with a eulogy that includes two lines of poetry: "Peace among men, and stillness of sea and wind; / Bedtime of winds, and slumber in our pain."[7]

Then comes Socrates' turn. One suspects that he will shake things up in some way, and indeed he does. First, he challenges the assumption that Love is divine. He subjects Agathon to a series of questions, culminating in a stumper: if Love is love of something in particular, and if it is love of something that it lacks, and if that thing is beauty, then how can Love be called beautiful, when it longs for the beauty it lacks? Agathon has no answer. Socrates then tells what he learned from his own teacher, Diotima, who introduced him to the idea of Love as mediator between the divine and human worlds. According to Diotima, humans move from a love of specific beauties to a love of the essence of beauty; this movement from the specific to the essential is movement toward wisdom. Such wisdom is desired not by the wise, who already have it, or by the ignorant, who have no sense of it, but by those in between, and their very desire is Love.[8] So Love is in motion between two states of being.

By telling the story of how he himself was taught by Diotima, Socrates hints at a metaphor. He suggests that the teacher, too, is a mediator between two worlds: that of ignorance and that of illumination. Teaching and love are thus kindred, by implication; both are messengers and mediators. As Socrates came to Diotima with specific questions and ended up with a greater understanding than he had before, so his companions at Agathon's feast are learning from him now. They come to understand their own speeches and the subject of Love in a new light.

How does the teacher mediate between ignorance and illumination, according to Plato? The method seems less important than the spirit in which it is done. Socrates teaches largely through questioning, Diotima through telling (with some questioning as well), but both are able to make sense of a complex subject and bring their students to a new level of understanding. The *Symposium* suggests, indirectly, that such mediation depends on solitude. The educator David Coleman observes, "The *Symposium* at once portrays the vitality of sharing ideas in conversation and the essential role of solitary concentration. . . . Socrates resists the pressure of war, the pleasure of company, and the demands of courtesy to spend time thinking alone."[9] The time spent alone allows Socrates to bring illuminating ideas to Agathon's party. He has not abandoned the group; rather, he is a fuller participant than he might otherwise have been.

Back in the modern-day classroom: if the teacher is mediator, then she should determine the lesson structure, within reason; the lesson structure is part of her translation of the subject for the students. In some cases, the teacher needs a combination of structures and approaches. In other situations, one particular structure serves for an entire course; a literature course may be conducted entirely as a seminar, for instance, and a beginning language course may consist mostly of drill and conversation. It is essential that the structure or method not become an obstacle but instead convey the subject, at the appropriate level, as fully as possible.

If the participants in the *Symposium* had been required to follow a workshop model, no one would have been allowed to talk or listen for very long. The entire discussion would have lasted about fifteen minutes. It is unlikely that anyone would be reading the *Symposium* today, as nothing in the discussion would have been worth memorizing and passing on. To create something memorable, one must be capable of holding many ideas and details in the mind. One must be able to think through an idea on one's own and present it to others in its entirety. Teachers and students alike should have room for sustained thought. Discussions should refine and challenge the thought, not limit it.

∼

WHY DID New York City school officials mandate a single model for all grades and subjects? It is not simply that officials thought this model would work; they were also in search of a "big idea" that would serve as catalyst for other changes. The workshop seemed to make way for student autonomy and initiative, practical application of learning, and more. By having students *do* things in every lesson, by having them talk with each other and take charge of their learning, the schools would raise their achievement, or so officials hoped.

The workshop model has many antecedents. It derives immediately from the Teachers College Reader's Workshop and Writer's Workshop, the two main components of Balanced Literacy, which in turn derives from creative writing workshops and various strands of progressive education. In addition, the quest for an all-purpose model has roots in various "comprehensive" reforms of the twentieth century.

Balanced Literacy was influenced in its early stages by the work of Donald Graves, who criticized the "imbalance between sending and receiving" in education (where the teacher sends and the student receives). Such an imbalance, he said, "should be anathema in a democracy."[10] In an ideal Balanced Literacy world, children direct their own learning, and the teacher gently guides them along, functioning as a coach more than a repository of knowledge. This creates a dilemma: if the teacher is not supposed to teach anything substantial, at least not directly, how are the students supposed to reach a point where they can direct their own learning?

A lesson plan published by the New York City Department of Education illustrates this conundrum. In this lesson, first-grade students learn to identify unknown words by looking at the picture. The teacher begins by gathering the students on the rug, complimenting them on their work, and explaining the purpose of the lesson. Then she reads aloud to them from a book such as *Two Little Dogs* by June Melser. The lesson plan spells out what the teacher is to do and say:

> Read the title *Two Little Dogs* and look at the cover. Open the leveled book and begin to read. Read to page 5. "*They ran after a . . . .*" Struggle with the unknown word "bird." Act like a struggling reader and model trying out a previously taught print strategy. Try to stretch out the beginning sound "b-b-b-i-i." You may say, "I'm still not sure! Maybe the picture can help me."[11]

The teacher then looks at the picture and guesses that the word is "bird." After this demonstration, she gives students another example of an unknown word and has them talk to their partners about what it might be. Once they have done this, she brings them back together and says something like "I overheard such great thinking. I heard partners say that they thought it was a door, but they looked closer at the picture then said maybe it's a gate. Wow, what great readers!" Students then practice the strategy alone and with partners. At the end of class, they come together again to share what they have learned.[12]

This lesson plan has serious problems. First, it is a highly unreliable way of identifying words; it evades the necessary skill of decoding (converting letters into sounds and sounds into words). It assumes the illustrations will be closely connected with the text; this is not always the case. It forces the teacher to pretend to be less intelligent than she is by mimicking a struggle with a word. It has her praise the students for being "great readers" when all they did was use a picture to identify a word. In sum, the lesson encourages students to look *away* from the text. The actual contents of the book are irrelevant to the lesson; the teacher is entirely focused on a strategy. That is precisely the point: to arm students with this strategy so that they can then apply it on their own in the remainder of the class time. But what if the strategy doesn't apply to what they are reading? The students will be lost, as they lack the actual knowledge they need (in this case, decoding) to make sense of their books.

Let us consider another example: a lesson for middle school English-language learners, also published by the New York City Department of Education. Titled "Everyone Is a Poet," the lesson begins with the premise that poets write about "every day [sic] events, every day things and feelings." To illustrate this principle, the teacher reads aloud "Poem" by Langston Hughes ("I loved my friend"). Then she models a "feeling" poem, which follows the following format:

Line 1: Name an emotion
Line 2: "Smells like . . ."
Line 3: "Tastes like . . ."
Line 4: "Feels like . . ."
Line 5: Repeat the emotion.

In independent work time, students write their own "feeling poem," following the pattern provided. Then they form groups of three to read their poems to each other.[13]

This lesson plan misses the point of the Hughes poem. What makes it remarkable is not its expression of feeling (though there is intense feeling there) but its way of conveying meaning through reserve and brevity. The very structure suggests a person's opening and closing. Students could begin by considering why the poem continues after saying that there's nothing more to say. They could compare it with Edwin Arlington Robinson's villanelle "The House on the Hill," which states, in the third line, "There is nothing more to say," and then continues for sixteen more lines.[14] This would be a whole-class discussion, or series of discussions, led by the teacher. By contrast, having students write a "feeling" poem (which isn't a poem at all) shortchanges both the Hughes poem and the act of writing poetry. Students should have the experience of writing poetry, but they should be given the sense of what that actually means. It is much more than the expression of feelings, much more than figurative language alone. There is form and sound to it; there are tensions that push past the immediate meaning. Students may not be able to accomplish all of this at once, but they can become aware of it.

Balanced Literacy proponents maintain that children will perform like experts if treated like experts. Lucy Calkins, one of the originators of Balanced Literacy, recommends referring to children as "professional writers." She writes, "One effective strategy for buoying a writer's identity is to tell the child he or she has written just like a professional writer often does." She advises teachers to say, "You're trying to do something you've seen another author do! That's so professional of you!" There is a contradiction here: while appearing to treat children as original writers, she praises them for imitating others. Granted, writing, like any art or craft, involves a degree of imitation. But to call a child "professional," simply because he or she has imitated an author in some way, is to suggest that professional writing is tantamount to conformity. To the contrary, it is during *apprenticeship* that imitation plays an especially important role. As apprentices gain practice, as they work, play, and experiment, they begin to develop their distinctive voice and style. (One might also think of students as "amateurs"; Rafael Heller makes a compelling case for this.)[15] To call children professional writers is to suggest that they have already arrived. Arrival, when it means being just like the others, seems a bit dreary.

The Teachers College Reader's Workshop and Writer's Workshop were influenced by creative writing workshops and various strands of progressive education. The creative writing workshop, which dates back to the 1880s, encouraged students to believe that anyone can be an expert—in this case, a writer. Writers' workshops and creative writing courses have always had a somewhat tense if not antagonistic relationship with academia. According to scholar D. G. Myers, the field of creative writing "owes its existence to an anti-scholarly animus that was originally directed against philology" and is "forever defined by its opposition to literary scholarship." Where philology strove to make the study of literature systematic, creative writing programs asserted that students learn about literature by making it. In the words of

Norman Foerster, founder of the School for Letters at the University of Iowa, this allowed them to "study it from the inside."[16]

The creative writing workshop thrived outside of academic institutions and on their periphery as well as within them. The Bread Loaf Writers' Conference in Vermont, founded in 1926, inspired the creation of many writing conferences; by 1977 there were ninety summer conferences for writers of all walks of life. Today there are about 150 creative-writing MFA programs, in addition to numerous conferences, retreats, and informal workshops. While they vary in rigor and method, they share the assumption that students benefit from group interaction and that they come to understand literature by participating in it. (Nancie Atwell, one of the leading developers of Balanced Literacy, reports that her teacher at Bread Loaf "persisted in inviting me to become *my own resource*, to learn about writing firsthand by becoming a writer and researcher.") Some workshops encourage students to learn from each other; others are taught in lecture style. Some are for students who have never written a poem or story, others for published writers who seek structure and feedback.[17]

Creative writing programs have been condemned and extolled. Their critics charge that they produce authors who write and think alike; their champions credit them with transforming the humanities themselves. Louis Menand writes that "creative-writing programs are designed on the theory that students who have never published a poem can teach other students who have never published a poem how to write a publishable poem"; yet he affirms that "in spite of all the reasons that they shouldn't, workshops work." Michael Loyd Gray has criticized the "fiction by committee" approach, in which the participants' assessments of others' work "are often based, unfortunately, on the latest trendy 'stories' students have read, which all too often are little more than barren sketches." Some see a positive influence on academia; Theodore Weiss writes that poetry writing workshops have helped the university become "a major patron of the arts—the chief sanctuary for poets already well on their way." Some find that the workshops do best when wary of their own pitfalls. Mary Oliver warns against letting the workshop tame the writing; there is the danger that a writer will give up "some rough but unusual fashioning of lines" that does not find favor with the group. She holds that no matter how helpful the workshop, the poem requires "a patch of profound and unbroken solitude."[18]

Not only the creative writing movement, but a number of strands of twentieth-century progressive education influenced the workshop model. Of these, the child-centered movement, the activity-school movement, and the efficiency movement stand out as the strongest influences. Drawing on the theories of Jean-Jacques Rousseau, Johann Heinrich Pestalozzi, and others, child-centered schools allowed children to choose their own activities and direct their own learning (to varying degrees). They reached their apex in the early decades of the twentieth century; by the 1920s and 1930s, even their proponents were restless with their excesses. In extreme cases, each day's instruction was completely spontaneous; in more moderate cases, teachers planned units and lessons in consultation with the students, or took the students' interests into account.[19] The workshop model, too, relies on the premise that the child should direct his or her own learning to some extent. The teacher provides a variety of tasks or activities to meet the students' needs; in education jargon, she "differentiates" instruction. Different groups may be working on entirely different material, students may be grouped according to their level of advancement, or students within a group may be assigned different roles or tasks.

The workshop model has many traits in common with activity schools, which were initiated in Europe near the end of the nineteenth century and emulated in the United States. According to Michael John Demiashkevich, an activity school did one or more of several things: emphasized manual training, prepared students to contribute to national productivity, or combined physical and mental activity in order "to promote normal development of the child." The third variant took hold in American elementary schools in the 1930s; schools across the country encouraged activities based on children's desires and interests. Some schools integrated the activities with an academic curriculum; others pursued activities for activities' sake. In 1935, New York City initiated an activity program in sixty-nine public elementary schools; after six years, the board of education recommended that all elementary schools adopt it (it is not clear how many actually did, and the results of the initiative were mixed).[20] Like the activity schools, the workshop model emphasizes tangible, visible work over abstract mental work. Workshop model proponents frequently refer to the virtues of "learning by doing"; they take pride in the fact that the students end up with a product.

The connection between the workshop model and the efficiency movement is subtle but strong. With the rise of industry and the popularization of business language at the start of the twentieth century, schools began applying business concepts, particularly concepts of efficiency, to every aspect of their operations, from budgeting to scheduling to curriculum. The mechanical engineer Frederick Winslow Taylor, author of *Principles of Scientific Management* (1911), believed there was one best way to get a job done and that it could be scientifically determined. In Taylor's view, workers should not be thinkers; the management should plan the work, and the workers should carry it out. Influenced by his methods and principles, schools began measuring teachers, students, and subjects, in hopes of maximizing output; they adopted methods that showed greatest results at the least cost and discarded those that did not. They laid out productivity standards, such as the number of multiplications that students should be able to perform per minute. In a fascinating study of the efficiency movement, Raymond E. Callahan draws attention to "the extent, not only of the power of the business-industrial groups, but of the strength of the business ideology in the American culture on the one hand and the extreme weakness and vulnerability of schoolmen, especially school administrators, on the other."[21]

The workshop model similarly employs business concepts, particularly those of consistency and productivity; teachers are supposed to follow the model exactly, keeping their mini-lessons within limits and including the same components in every lesson. It is a curious blend of what Wesley Null describes as "systematic curriculum" and "existentialist curriculum." It is systematic in that teachers are supposed to implement the model without questioning it; it is existentialist in that it supposedly gives priority to students' interests and needs. In this sense, the workshop model is an example of what Diane Ravitch has called a "left-right strategy"; during its heyday, it pleased both the pedagogical left and business-minded reformers such as Alan Bersin and Joel Klein.[22] It seemed to promise both efficiency and creativity, making classes both productive and fulfilling.

Why would anyone consider the workshop model efficient? Officials believed that it epitomized cooperative learning, which supposedly had been proved superior to other modes of instruction. In education policy, the lethal phrase "research has shown" tends to put an end to discussion, unless people are wise to it. In this case, the research is incomplete. There have been numerous studies of cooperative learning, beginning in the 1970s, but very little analysis of the premises underlying such studies. Whenever one considers the effect of a particular model on achievement, one should ask, "achievement of what?" Achievement in the abstract means nothing. Unless one considers what education should entail, one cannot assess the virtues of cooperative learning or any other model.

In 1981, David W. Johnson, Robert Johnson, and others conducted a meta-analysis of cooperative, competitive, and individualistic approaches to classroom learning. They found that "cooperation is considerably more effective than interpersonal competition and individualistic efforts"; that "cooperation with intergroup competition is also superior to interpersonal competition and individualistic efforts"; and that "there is no significant difference between interpersonal competitive and individualistic efforts." In other words, according to their analysis, cooperative learning, with or without competition, was superior to other social structures in the classroom. In this meta-study they did not consider subject matter; they found that it did not have a significant effect on the outcome. The tasks fell into the following categories: concept attainment, verbal problem solving, categorization, spatial problem solving, retention and memory, motor, guessing-judging-predicting, and rote decoding and correcting. When considering how the type of task affected the results, they found that rote decoding and correction tasks were the only ones that did not favor cooperation. Thus, they considered two categories of tasks: rote decoding and correcting and all the others.[23] They (and the studies they considered) made a curious assumption that lessons focus on a "task." With the exception of the task of "concept attainment," such emphasis excludes lessons in which students discuss a question or listen to an extended presentation by the teacher. In other words, the studies focus on topics and lesson formats that lend themselves to cooperative structures in the first place.

A year earlier, educator Robert E. Slavin (cofounder of the Success for All program, along with his wife, Nancy) had reached different and subtler conclusions. Slavin proposed a "new model of classroom instruction based on cooperation as a dominant instructional mode." Citing numerous studies conducted in the 1970s, he found that cooperative learning had a positive effect on student achievement, race relations, and mutual concern among students, especially the latter two. Noting that "lack of concrete understanding of what constitutes 'achievement' may explain contradictory outcomes in different studies," he found that the effect on achievement was the weakest. In social studies, the effects were especially weak; he suggested that this might be due to incongruity between the classroom activities and the tested knowledge and skills. Overall, the cooperative activities with the greatest effect on achievement were those with group rewards based on the demonstrated learning of all of the members. Moreover, according to Slavin, highly structured cooperative learning techniques tended to be more effective for "low level learning outcomes," and less structured techniques for "high level cognitive learning outcomes." Thus, the optimal lesson structure depended largely on the type of lesson. Despite these observations, which seem to point toward varied instruction, Slavin concluded that cooperative learning, planned and executed properly, had advantages over other types of instruction.[24]

As the calls for cooperative learning grew louder, some of the complexities in the arguments dropped out of the picture. Education professor Steven T. Bossert pointed out in 1988 that "the cooperative learning movement has taken on an imperialistic quality"; that more group work is not necessarily better, and that children should learn how to work in cooperative, competitive, and individualistic settings. But such a measured perspective was rare among cooperative learning supporters. Policy makers repeatedly claim that research has shown the superiority of cooperative learning. In its *Education Research Consumer Guide*, the U.S. Department of Education defined "cooperative learning" vaguely as a "successful teaching strategy in which small teams, each with students of different levels of ability, use a variety of learning activities to improve their understanding of a subject." One of the "earliest and strongest findings," according to the newsletter, was "that students who cooperate with each other like each other."[25]

If education is supposed to make people *like* each other, then cooperative learning is a reasonable means to that end. But liking can be bland; respect and appreciation have more substance. What about the other effects of cooperative learning? The newsletter stated that it had a "consistently positive" effect on achievement when "two necessary key elements—*group goals* and *individual accountability*—are used together." While this makes a degree of sense, it does not address what the students are supposed to achieve and what might be lost in group work. Instead, the newsletter points to cooperative learning's potential to "develop and use critical thinking skills and teamwork; promote positive relations among different ethnic groups; implement peer coaching; establish environments where academic accomplishments are valued; and even cooperatively manage schools."[26] The goals and supposed benefits sound impressive, but there is no counterbalance here; the newsletter does not question its emphasis on social goals or consider that group work might interfere with good ideas. It is as though children were put in a playpen together and asked to make a tower out of blue cubes—and then praised and heralded for doing so together. But what if the playpen activity were not so good for building an arch, bridge, or dome? In a world enraptured with the playpen activity, what would happen to the things that had no place inside it? Would one stop thinking about arches and fix one's thoughts on blue towers that could easily be toppled?

PEDAGOGICAL MODELS ARE immortal yet worldly; that is their double convenience. They wriggle through criticism yet demand compliance. When teachers protested the rigid implementation of the workshop model, Deputy Chancellor Carmen Fariña responded that many of the problems had already been addressed and resolved—that is, the *real* workshop model was not so bad. Schools chancellor Joel Klein claimed that he had never meant the model to be a rigid mandate.[27] But checklists, observation forms, rubrics, handouts, and other materials suggested otherwise. Professional development sessions emphasized and followed the workshop model. Consultants visited schools to make sure teachers were using it. Literacy and mathematics coaches showed teachers how to implement it. Its language was ubiquitous, its paperwork pressing; to depart from it, a teacher needed skill, guile, and confidence.

The workshop model relies on a caricature of its supposed opposite, "traditional" teaching. In *Teaching the Best Practice Way*, Harvey Daniels and Marilyn Bizar describe the traditional and workshop classroom as opposites: "When the workshop starts to work, it turns the traditional transmission-model classroom upside down; students become active, responsible, self-motivating, and self-evaluating learners, while the teacher drops the talking-head role in favor of more powerful functions as model, coach, and collaborator." Yet traditional teaching cannot be reduced to a single method, nor should "transmission" have a negative connotation. Traditional teaching has included lectures, discussions, laboratory work, and many combinations of them. Describing existing methods in 1983, Slavin acknowledged that "most teachers use some combination of lectures, discussions, individual seatwork, small homogeneous groups working with the teacher, and individual tests."[28] Nonetheless, proponents of the workshop have often characterized traditional classrooms as monolithic settings where the teacher talked and the students took notes. Such a confining description of traditional teaching confines the workshop model as well.

Insofar as it was mandated for all classrooms, the workshop model has much in common with other "comprehensive" reforms. From the curricular reform movements of the 1930s onward, reformers have tried to bring change to entire districts. In many cases, as Diane Ravitch has pointed out, no one really knew what "comprehensive" change was, and "saying that a project would be comprehensive did not make it so." It was a word of convenience, she writes, "a buzz-word, a word that local officials learned to invoke at the right time if they wanted federal funds." More recently—for instance, in San Diego at the turn of the twenty-first century—leaders pushed a set of reforms, specifically Balanced Literacy, onto the school system and fired those who questioned or resisted them.[29] The desire for a grand solution in education has many possible sources: distrust of partial, incremental, or piecemeal reform; a desire for a quick fix or "big idea"; a desire to look good; and impatience with things that take time.

The very insistence on an overarching model or "big idea" creates problems in education. Big ideas tend to undo themselves; their very grandness precludes the kind of discernment essential to good teaching. Taken down from the pedestal, the workshop model has a place among other kinds of lessons. If an eighth-grade class is studying the Renaissance, for instance, a teacher may plan a combination of lectures, discussions, and projects. The lessons may focus on history or literature, but there may be some special lessons as well. One lesson might be devoted to the work of Galileo; another might be devoted to the city-state. In one lesson, students might learn a Renaissance madrigal; in another, they might listen to a Petrarch sonnet in Italian and in various translations. Students might perform scenes from A Midsummer Night's Dream or learn about the concept of divine proportion. The structure of the lesson would correspond with what the students were learning.

The workshop model has some unwieldy features. In some ways, the small group may be the most distracting of structures. One of the most common complaints about small-group work is that some group members do all the work and some make all the decisions. It is not always the most able or thoughtful students who do this; some groups are dominated by "take-charge" personalities who lack the patience to hear out the more hesitant members or to probe a complex idea. There are many other problems. Small-group discussion can easily become frenetic, with some members steamrolling and others trying to get a word in (or just dropping out). The noise of many groups working at the same time can make it difficult for anyone to think. To ensure that everyone is accountable and productive, teachers often end up reducing the task to something everyone can handle and dividing tasks among group members. The students at the lowest levels may be given the task of keeping time or writing down what the others say. Ironically, this can turn into a miniature society of leaders and laborers.

But the greatest problem with the workshop model is that it forces group work onto subjects that are at least part solitary. It allows for some independent work, but the overwhelming emphasis is on small-group work. Thus students lose the sense of thinking and working alone and steadily, apart from others. Sadly, without such apartness, it is difficult to learn the fundamentals, go far into the subject, or even come together in a meaningful way.

What of the virtues of the workshop model? Certain lessons lend themselves to it well. Suppose advanced English-language learners (at the seventh-grade level, say) were reading Agatha Christie's mystery story "The Adventure of Johnnie Waverly." The students might be assigned to work in detective teams, each team looking at the evidence surrounding one of the primary suspects (Mr. Waverly, Mrs. Waverly, Miss Collins, and Tredwell). The class would already have read the beginning of the story. During class, each team would read the middle of the story, focusing on a particular suspect, and decide whether this suspect was guilty or innocent. Then the class could come together, pool its findings, try to solve the mystery, and read the end of the story, in which Poirot reveals the solution.

Or suppose students were reading *Romeo and Juliet*. For one of the lessons, students might work in groups to block out the fight in the first scene—that is, to determine the actors' positions and movements. This fight displays the hierarchy of characters, progressing from an exchange of insults among servants to an intervention from the prince. As they analyzed this scene and figured out how to stage it, students would gain a sense of the language and conflicts of the play. The groups would demonstrate their blocking in front of the whole class and would explain the rationale for their decisions. In this example and the preceding one, the group work is appropriate for the topic at hand and need not take up every lesson.[30]

Sometimes a workshop can serve as the culminating activity of a unit. One of my most rewarding workshop lessons was a mock Senate session, which came at the end of a unit on the Constitution and the Bill of Rights. I had taught my students about the three branches of government and the principle of checks and balances. I had explained to them, in basic terms, how a bill becomes a law. Many had memorized the Preamble. All of this took place over the course of two weeks. Then I explained to them that they would have a chance to act as senators. For homework, each student would write a bill. In class, they would take up their bills in their committees (small groups) and amend them as needed. Each committee would present the revised bills to the Senate (the whole class). The Senate would debate the merits and drawbacks of each bill and would vote on it. At the end, we would come back together as a class and comment on what had taken place. While this departed somewhat from the standard workshop format, it had all the components.

When the day arrived, the students were ready and eager to begin. Each student chose a state to represent; one chose Alaska, another California, and so forth. The committees vigorously revised the bills; by the time it came time to debate and vote on them, they had given them some thought. To my surprise, after a heated discussion, they voted down a bill requiring parents to give money to their children. One student said, "My parents work hard. They come home sometimes at midnight. Why they [sic] give money to children for nothing?" Others agreed, adding that children should help their parents, not ask for more from them. By the end of the class period, students had tried their hand at lawmaking (in highly simplified form); revised each other's writing in the committees; debated interesting subjects as a class; and related all of this to what they had been learning about the Constitution. None of this would have been possible if I had adhered strictly to a workshop model every day. I was fortunate that administrators trusted me to plan and execute my lessons—but I worried that at some point I might get in trouble for not adhering to the workshop model all the time.

In my first two years of teaching, I sometimes made the mistake of planning workshop lessons for the sake of having a workshop. Some of these failed miserably. In one workshop lesson, I had students write step-by-step guides (known as "narrative procedures") explaining how to make a dodecahedron out of marshmallows and toothpicks. Needless to say, their attention went to the marshmallows. There were many things wrong with this lesson, but most of it (besides the marshmallows themselves) was the use of the workshop for something as complex as this. This would have worked better as a series of lessons on geometrical shapes, their definitions, and their names—by no means out of the realm of English as a Second Language, which is supposed to include academic vocabulary. Once students mastered the necessary concepts, vocabulary, and grammar, they could explain how to make a dodecahedron. At that point, it would be instructive and enjoyable to make an actual dodecahedron in class or at home (without marshmallows); this would give them a chance to test their instructions for errors or omissions.

To find the right kind of lesson for a topic, a teacher must do what Socrates did in the *Symposium*: stand outside alone and think. She must spend time on the topic itself, finding her own way into it, considering ways to present it, and anticipating questions that might come up. She should not sacrifice the topic to a model, if the model does not fit. It is not that the teacher must find a unique method for each lesson or draw from an enormous grab bag; rather, she should be probing and exacting. She should come to the lesson with a grasp of what she is to teach and the freedom to teach it in the best way possible. That is as important for a lesson on verbs as it is for a lesson on the Bolshevik Revolution or the solar system.

A teacher shows students how to strive toward something beyond their immediate capacity—how to learn it, spend time alone with it, make it part of themselves, and see beyond it. This requires not only knowledge, but good sense: identifying what one is trying to do and looking for the best way to do it. Good sense repels nonsense by nature; it builds on itself instead of undoing itself. For these reasons it should exist in policy as well as in the mind. Teachers cannot make all decisions on their own; they need certain structures and guidelines. But the structures must encourage good work, allow for reasonable variation, and come from sound thinking about the subjects. The last, though often neglected, is fundamental. To understand what good teaching entails, one must delve into the things to be learned. Through such immersion, one comes to know the subjects' shapes. In these shapes, over time, one starts to see ways of teaching; in a tilt of a polyhedron, one starts to see a lesson plan.

6

~

The Folly of the "Big Idea"

One evening in 2003, I was conversing with a lawyer-writer and his friend, also a lawyer. I had corresponded with one of them about music and fiction; this was our first meeting in person. They took this opportunity to put me to the test. With a mischievous twinkle, the first one asked me, "Do you think inside the box or outside the box?"

I had to give it some thought. I wasn't familiar with the expression. Was it possible to think outside the box, whatever the box might be? It seemed to me that there would be another box outside it, and then another, somewhat like Matryoshka dolls. Also, it seemed it would be a lot more interesting to think inside the box; I would get to know its contents. I took a deep breath, leapt over the mental puddle, and replied, "Inside the box." They clapped; I had passed the test. We discussed it and agreed that thinking "outside the box" was an improbable and silly proposition. Ironically, we were thinking outside the box about the very subject of thinking outside the box, which, I suppose, put us "inside the box."

Now that I was aware of this expression, I started hearing it all over the place. People used it blithely at work meetings conducted around cubicles where people swung around on their ergonomic swivel armchairs. I noticed it in company mission statements, read it on blogs, overheard it in cafes. No one seemed to question the premises of the expression. There seemed to be broad consensus that you could step outside the broad consensus, just like that—by getting your mind outside that dastardly box. If you just dared to ask, "What if—?" even without finishing the sentence, the rest would follow.

Grammar didn't matter. Outside the box, you didn't need to know. You just needed to wonder.

This starry-eyed conception of innovation has some basis, of course. Inventors, thinkers, and artists differ in their thinking from those around them, but much of this difference comes from the rigors of their work. Paradoxically, it is that time spent in a room, on a particular subject, that leads them to stretch or break through the subject's structures. Sometimes an idea does seem to come out of the cracks in the floor or the feathers in the sky. But more often than not, those who discover or create things are caught up in the meshes of their work and thoughts. Their ideas may look big or small; how they look to others is not the point. There is enough right there before them, in the study, on the easel, in the book, under the microscope.

Educators claim that children have long been drilled in dry, disconnected facts and that they need to be exposed to the realm of big ideas. Yet, taken out of context, a "big idea" is no better than a disconnected fact. In fact, big ideas and tidbits of information get dull quickly. To give life to ideas, one must ground them in the details of a subject, observing how one idea leads into another and raising questions along the way. This is true even in abstract branches of philosophy, for one must be precise with the abstractions. Similarly, historical tidbits, those dreaded "names and dates," become interesting when related to other facts and to something larger. In this chapter, I will argue in favor of "medium-order" thinking, which draws on details and points to larger concepts. In particular, I will show that a single Newton theorem, drawing on centuries of mathematics and pointing in a new direction, holds more ideas than a focus on "big ideas" possibly could.

But first let us take this idea of big ideas seriously, in order to locate the problem with it. There is nothing new in the notion that schools should encourage students to generate their own ideas; it has a long legacy, in traditional as well as progressive education. It is part of our culture and history: the hope of finding new answers to problems by looking within ourselves (as a group) and breaking from the constraints of the past. There is reason for such hope; it takes introspection and daring to come up with new ideas, and people with gumption have done it. But one must also be immersed in a problem, aware of its origins and implications, in order to have insights into it. It is this sense of motion—the grasp of an idea's direction—that brings about discovery. It consists of the understanding that "If x is true, either y or z is possible," or "Having solved y, we must now call x into question." With few exceptions, it is impossible to engage in any kind of advanced thought without having something to think about, something one understands well and can see from many angles. This point has been made so many times that it hardly bears repeating. What, then, is the fuss about? Why the continued cry for bigger ideas in the classroom? Isn't it obvious that the big ideas come out of working within the subject?

It is partly a problem of jargon. Some proponents of big ideas in the classroom have no intention of discounting the specifics and arrangement of subject matter—but by the time their ideas have been passed on several times, the particulars are lost. Other proponents of big ideas have nothing more concrete in mind at all. They start with vagueness and end with vagueness; what they have in mind is not a particular subject but some nebulous scenario where students criticize, compare, create, synthesize, evaluate, and so forth. Just what they should criticize, it is not clear, but it hardly matters, so long as they are doing it. Sometimes the jargon of big ideas is put forth wisely, sometimes foolishly—and without specifics, it is hard to tell the good and bad ideas apart. Jargon is the bane of education policy; it suggests a desire for sweeping, all-purpose concepts. Diane Ravitch has written in many books about "our national infatuation with fads, movements, and reforms"; our infatuation with big ideas is part of this blush and crush.[1]

Until we establish what the words mean, they will play tricks on us. Two schools could claim to encourage "critical thinking," and the quality of their instruction might differ drastically. In fact, the worst thing for the teaching of important ideas is vague talk about teaching higher-order thinking, big ideas, and so on. It is better to look at the subject matter itself and see where ideas come into play. Quite often, they appear right next to those old-fashioned facts. When one learns a language, for instance, it is often the minute grammatical details that lead to larger insights. A student who learns Latin declensions will start to see traces of declensions in English and recognize differences between inflected and noninflected languages. One who learns the fundamentals of harmony and counterpoint is in a position to notice when a composer introduces an unusual progression or chord.

Certainly there is a problem when instruction does not touch on ideas at all. But the difference between idea-rich and idea-bereft instruction can be subtle; it may not be apparent to the outside observer. Suppose, for instance, that a class were studying William Shakespeare's famous Sonnet 130 ("My mistress' eyes are nothing like the sun"). One rather bland approach would be to have students read the poem and talk about the theme of love: what it means to love someone, and how it involves appreciating a person's imperfections. The students might consider how Shakespeare (or the speaker) loved his mistress even though her eyes were not like the sun, her lips not truly red, and so forth, and they might consider how that applied to their lives. Such discussion may appear to involve big ideas of love and imperfection, but it does not require a close reading of the poem, nor is it particularly enlightening. Unless it were a probing philosophical discussion (more appropriate for a philosophy class than for a lesson on a sonnet), it would likely result in the facile conclusion that people's imperfections endear them to others, or something similar. It would likely result in discussions of students' own relationships—a potentially volatile subject that may take them away from the poem. There is nothing wrong with considering how a poem relates to one's life—after one has read it carefully.

A more promising approach would be to consider how each of the mistress's attributes is put forth in a different way. The first is a negative comparison: her eyes are "nothing like the sun." (The very "nothing" bears pondering.) The second comparison is trickier: "Coral is far more red than her lips red." This implies, on the one hand, that her lips may be *somewhat* red (as the difference is one of degree), and on the other, that they can-not really be red at all (as coral is pink at most, and still "far more red" than the mistress's lips). The next comparison has an if-then structure: "If snow be white, why then her breasts are dun"; this involves a witty twist-ing of the factual (snow *is* white) into the hypothetical (if snow *be* white). Each comparison in the poem has a slightly different logical structure, and yet the repetition of comparisons suggests a pattern. What might be the meaning of the logical variations? What is wriggling in here, what life is pushing through? If students consider this question, they will start to see a relationship not only between form and meaning, but between various parts and internal structures of this sonnet. As students become aware of the poem's logic and rhythms, they will start to hear subtleties in it; they may notice words and phrases (such as "damasked") that did not strike them the first time.

The preceding lesson examples convey two distinct approaches to big ideas. In one, students identify and discuss a theme, drawing on their own experience. In the other, they look closely at the internal workings of the poem and consider their meaning. The latter is much more likely than the former to teach them something about the poem, the ideas within it, and the sonnet in general. The former masquerades as critical thinking but reduces the poem to something less than it is. Relating a given theme to personal experience takes no expertise and often leads nowhere. Students discussing the poem in this manner may point to details in the poem, but they are not looking at how the details fit together. The poem hardly affects the discussion; it serves as a springboard and not much more. In the latter example, the students are immersed in the poem and start to grasp larger principles of poetry.

The difference is between big ungrounded concepts, on the one hand, and details that form larger shapes and patterns, on the other. Alfred North Whitehead's 1917 essay "The Aims of Education" sheds some light on this distinction. Whitehead argues that the teaching of "inert ideas" leads to "mental dryrot." What are these "inert ideas"? They are ideas that students learn out of context and leave untouched; they are not "utilised, or tested, or thrown into fresh combinations." To combat inert ideas, Whitehead suggests that the key ideas taught in school be "few and important" and that they be "thrown into every combination possible." This way, the student will play with them, "make them his own," and start to see their possibilities.[2]

Big ideas on their own are inert ideas; there is nothing much to do with them. One can speculate about them, fumble with them sloppily, or confuse them with other ideas. To do something interesting with an idea, one needs to see where it comes from and where it might lead; one must understand its precise meaning or meanings in relation to a particular subject; and one must consider it from different angles. "What we should aim at producing," writes Whitehead, "is men who possess both culture and expert knowledge in some special direction." The education leading to this is "a patient process of the mastery of details, minute by minute, hour by hour, day by day," as "there is no royal road to learning through an airy path of brilliant generalisations." The point of study, Whitehead argues, is to develop, over time, "that eye for the whole chess-board, for the bearing of one set of ideas on another."[3] From this perspective, it is the kinetic quality of a subject—the movement from facts to ideas and from one idea to another—that makes the instruction both solid and intriguing.

This kinetic quality has nothing to do with hopping from topic to topic or turning instruction into a dazzling show of multimedia. It has everything to do with the close study of a subject. In the *Nicomachean Ethics*, Aristotle warns that "we must not look for equal exactness in all departments of study, but only such as belongs to the subject matter of each, and in such a degree as is appropriate to the particular line of enquiry." For instance, he explains, a carpenter and a geometrician look for different kinds of precision when seeking a right angle: "the former is content with that approximation to it which satisfies the purpose of his work; the latter, being a student of truth, looks for its essence or essential attributes."[4] One might take this to mean that some fields are more exact than others, but that does not seem to be the point. Rather, Aristotle implies that each field has a particular kind of exactness. Ask a carpenter and a geometrician to build a wooden box, and the carpenter's right angles might be more precise, as far as physical objects go. Yet the carpenter's box might not serve the geometrician's purposes, beyond approximate illustration. The geometrician might need a perfect right angle, in the abstract realm, even if his imprecise box served the purposes of illustration. Thus, general terms take on different meanings from one field to another.

Why is this not a given? Part of the problem is due to the corruption of ideas as they spread. Educators have held that advanced thinking (known as higher-order thinking) can be both identified and encouraged in the classroom. The term "higher-order thinking" is commonly attributed to Benjamin Samuel Bloom, who in 1956 published the *Taxonomy of Educational Objectives* (commonly known as Bloom's Taxonomy) with his colleagues. However, the *Taxonomy* does not use the term "higher-order thinking" at all, and the phrase "higher order" occurs just once. The authors seek to classify different kinds of thinking that may occur in the classroom, not to rank them according to their importance or worth. That is, they describe a progression from simple to complex cognitive processes, but take pains to emphasize that the latter requires and includes the former. "Problem solving or thinking cannot be carried on in a vacuum," they write, "but must be based upon knowledge of some of the 'realities.' The intellectual abilities represented in the taxonomy assume knowledge as a prerequisite." There is no way to skip over knowledge:

> One may take the Gestalt point of view that the complex behavior is more than the sum of the simpler behaviors, or one may view the complex behavior as being completely analyzable into simpler components. But either way, so long as the simpler behaviors may be viewed as components of the more complex behaviors, we can view the educational process as one of building on the simpler behavior.[5]

Despite their efforts, Bloom and colleagues were unable to prevent the distortion of their points. Over time, "higher-order thinking" became a catchphrase and mantra. Education leaders insist that there must be more of it, that factual knowledge is inferior to ideas; that disadvantaged students have been confined to factual learning; and that students should be encouraged to think in higher ways whenever possible, no matter what the topic or their level. E. D. Hirsch Jr. points to the erroneous judgment implicit in the term. "It is mere prejudice," he writes, "to assert that the strategies associated with using domain-specific information are of a 'higher order' than the knowledge itself."[6] Many educators recognize that basic knowledge is essential to higher-order thinking and that one cannot teach good thinking in the abstract. Nonetheless, the clamor for higher-order thinking has grown louder and more confused.

In 1984, Larry Cuban wrote that the area of "thinking skills, reasoning, critical thought, and problem solving" had become a "conceptual swamp"; the swamp has only grown murkier, as it is now mixed with calls for more emphasis on technology, career preparation, global literacy, social-emotional skills, and other assorted means and ends. In 1990, the Council of Chief State School Officers (CCSSO) pointed to the need to stress "higher order learning for all in order to enable our populace to make necessary civic decisions." To this end, schools were to design curricula to "support higher order learning" in a manner that was responsive to "students' developmental needs and differences," including cultural and gender differences. Thus, schools were to take on the elusive and enormous task of making higher-order learning both universal and individual.[7]

Over the past decade, the demand for higher-order thinking has coincided with loud calls for instruction in "21st century skills." The 21st century skills movement consists of a loose association of educators, policy makers, government leaders, business and technology firms, and others. Citing changes in the global economy and national job market, they propose an emphasis on 21st century skills at all levels of education, from elementary school through college. These skills (which have always been needed in some form) include broad concepts such as creativity, innovation, problem solving, communication, collaboration, teamwork, and critical thinking, as well as media and technology literacy, financial literacy, health literacy, and global literacy. At the forefront has been a coalition called the Partnership for 21st Century Skills (P21), whose membership organizations include Adobe Systems, Apple, Dell, Hewlett-Packard, Microsoft, and Verizon. P21 argues that "every aspect of our education system . . . must be aligned to prepare citizens with the 21st century skills they need to compete." Accordingly, it offers schools, districts, and states "tools and resources to help facilitate and drive change."[8]

Technology has a prominent place in the 21st century skills movement, but this is not simply a drive to get more computers into classrooms. P21's overriding argument is that traditional subject matter should be "infused" with technology and 21st century skills. The danger is that the very insistence on these skills can disrupt and distort what is taught. Many of the projects suggested by P21 show meager understanding of the subjects. One eighth-grade English project involves having students contribute images to an online slideshow that illustrates a social issue such as "prosperity, justice, integrity, peace, or security." A twelfth-grade English project has students follow Twitter logs of newspapers and compare them with the corresponding news articles.[9] A description of an eighth-grade arts project reads,

Students examine how composers, artists, choreographers, and playwrights use the arts to communicate particular ideas, themes, or concepts (such as relationships, overcoming obstacles, optimism vs. pessimism), and to evoke particular emotions or feelings (joy, sadness, tension, relaxation) in the listener or viewer. They analyze and compare these devices and develop multimedia presentations illustrating how such communication occurs through each of the arts disciplines.[10]

The description is too general to mean much. Beyond that, the premises of the project do not hold up under scrutiny. Composers, arts, and others do not "use" the arts to communicate ideas and evoke feelings. Certainly they convey ideas and feelings through an artistic work, but the work is its own entity with its own meanings. The way of conveying something is inseparable from what is said; the message is a complex interplay of form and sense. Yes, at the outset of the *Iliad*, Homer calls on the muse of epic poetry to sing of the wrath of Achilles, but this is no ordinary wrath, nor can it be separated from the epic. The *Iliad* creates this particular wrath, just as the wrath fills the *Iliad*. It is by reading the *Iliad* that one comes to understand what this wrath means. It would take an extraordinary presentation—multimedia or otherwise—to convey any of this in a few minutes. In most cases, a multimedia presentation on the expressions of feelings through the arts would likely take the form, "Here's sadness in *Swan Lake*, here's sadness in *Romeo and Juliet*, and here's sadness in a Dégas painting." Even a more sophisticated presentation—showing how certain movements and colors evoke sadness—would miss the point, since the work may transform the very sadness that it evokes.

It is a little too easy to find fault with P21. Some might complain that P21 is a straw man, not representative of the 21st century skills movement. But the organization has considerable influence; not only does it include representatives from leading technology companies, but it has recently formed a "strategic management relationship" with the CCSSO. Beyond that, the flaws in P21's proposals point to a widespread problem: a misguided notion that "content" is important but more or less arbitrary, serving as a filler for instruction in the skills. P21's "skills maps" read like collages or pastiches, each project disconnected from the others, each piece of "content" unrelated to those around it. Thus, while calling for more connections, P21 actually encourages fragmentation. One sees similar tendencies in the proposed Model Core Teaching Standards created by CCSSO's Interstate Teacher Assessment and Support Consortium; they state, for instance, that "the teacher develops and implements projects that guide students in analyzing the complexities of an issue or question using perspectives from varied disciplines and cross-disciplinary skills (e.g., a water quality study that draws upon biology and chemistry to look at factual information and social studies to examine policy implications)."[11] There is a nervous, restless resistance to focusing on a single subject.

Political leaders, education policy makers, and media commentators call for the same bundle over and over again: creativity, innovation, collaboration, critical thinking, and problem solving. They rarely take time to define each one or to consider what each one means in context. In March 2009, in a speech to the Hispanic Chamber of Commerce, President Obama said, "I'm calling on our nation's governors and state education chiefs to develop standards and assessments that don't simply measure whether students can fill in a bubble on a test, but whether they possess 21st century skills like problem-solving and critical thinking and entrepreneurship and creativity." The *New York Times* columnist Thomas Friedman, praising the potential of integrated study, named his favorite integrated subject, "rainforest math." He explained, "There's so much one can learn from the laws of nature—not just biology, but Einstein, Newton, physics. And you drive both environmentalism and you drive math. So it's those kinds of intersections that are going to produce the most innovative students."[12] Expecting students to learn biology, Einstein, Newton, and physics through rainforest math is no more realistic than expecting assessments to measure students' creativity and problem solving (and entrepreneurship and all those other desired things).

But President Obama brings up a real problem: filling in a bubble is not good education. It has its place, but this place has been exaggerated. Unfortunately, part of this is due to the very emphasis on general skills and so-called higher-order thinking. What makes standardized tests so perplexing is their lack of specific content, especially in English language arts. Students are tested on general reading skills; even the multiple-choice questions are designed, supposedly, to test their ability to summarize, find the main idea, make inferences, and so forth. Yet they are not expected to know any particular poem, story, or essay; the tests measure reading comprehension, not literary knowledge. Ironically, because these skills are not grounded in specific literature, schools end up drilling students in skills, including skills that supposedly belong to an exalted order. If policy makers wish to encourage students to think deeply about problems, they should pay more attention to the actual stuff of learning, the subject matter itself. That would lead to tests that were more substantial on the one hand and less domineering on the other. What kinds of curricula will prepare and inspire students to contribute to various fields and to society? What kinds would gird students with knowledge, expose them to significant works, and allow them to play with ideas in the context of a field? These are the questions that should be asked.

To show how a specific problem in a specific subject can draw on the history of the field and lead to new insights, I will give an example from Newton's *Philosophiæ Naturalis Principia Mathematica* (commonly known as the *Principia*). First published in 1687, the *Principia* lays out principles of time, force, and motion, using mathematical methods suggestive of calculus. A monumental and difficult work, the *Principia* is rarely read in full, yet anyone with a strong high school mathematics background can grasp at least some of it. What makes the work particularly challenging (and enjoyable) is Newton's tendency to make leaps in his argument, relying on the reader to see the intermediate steps. Once the reader does grasp those steps, he or she has gained other insights along the way. This is an excellent example of "medium-order" thinking—grounded in details and rife with implications.

Why bring a Newton theorem into this discussion? I introduce it because it shows how much one can learn from studying a problem in action—that is, taking stock of its premises, working through it carefully, and considering its implications. Taken at face value, it proves Johannes Kepler's second law of planetary motion: namely, that "the velocity of a planet varies in such a way that a line joining the planet to the sun sweeps out equal areas in equal times."[13] If it were included in a high school geometry course, many students would be excited to find themselves capable of working through a Newton theorem. If students learned it well enough to explain it from scratch, they would bring it into themselves; it would be like a sonnet, something they could play out in their minds and consider in different ways. Later, in calculus and physics courses, they would remember the theorem and see it in a new light; they could translate it into more modern terms, using vectors. This goes beyond the generic practice of "problem solving"; this is the study of a particular problem for its internal workings and relation to the larger field. It is this kind of concrete study that helps students see how one theorem follows from another and how much can be found in simple shapes.

THE THEOREM TO be examined here is the first one in the *Principia*: book 1, proposition 1, theorem 1.[14] My explanation consists of three parts: a presentation of the theorem, a discussion of the prerequisites for understanding it, and an explanation of the proof. A reader with a basic grasp of geometry can understand it, with some patience and perseverance. To those who say, "Oh, this is math; it isn't for me," I suggest that they give it a serious try.

Newton's theorem reads, "The areas which bodies made to move in orbits describe by radii drawn to an unmoving center of forces lie in unmoving planes and are proportional to the times."[15] In other words, an orbiting body sweeps out equal areas in equal times in a single plane. What does this mean? Imagine, first of all, a body in orbit around a fixed point S. Think of the radius extending from S to the orbiting body at point A (figure 6.1).[16] Consider an interval of time and the area swept out by the orbiting body during this time. If, in this interval of time, the body travels from point A to point B, the area swept out will be the area enclosed by radius SA, curve AB, and radius SB. Newton says that for every equal time period, the area swept out will be the same.

How does Newton prove this? He begins by considering polygons then shows how the polygons approach a curve as the time intervals approach zero (figure 6.2).

There are several prerequisites for understanding Newton's proof. It relies on laws, corollaries, and lemmas (auxiliary propositions) previously established in the *Principia*: specifically, Newton's first law of motion, first corollary to the laws of motion, and fourth corollary to the third lemma.

The first law states that "every body perseveres in its state of being at rest or of moving uniformly straight forward, except insofar as it is compelled to change its state by forces impressed."[17] In other words, bodies in motion will persevere in motion, and bodies at rest will stay at rest, unless some force is applied to them.

The first corollary is a bit trickier and just as important to the argument. It states that "a body acted on by [two] forces acting jointly describes the

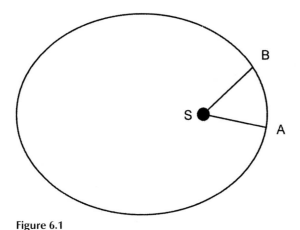

Figure 6.1

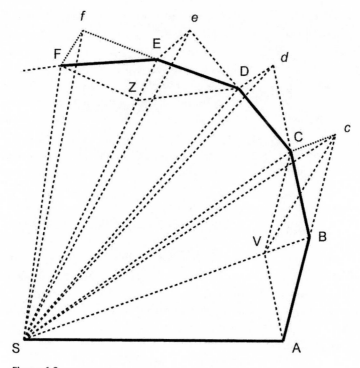

Figure 6.2

diagonal of a parallelogram in the same time in which it would describe the sides if the forces were acting separately."[18] In other words, if, in a given interval of time, one force causes a body to move from A to C, and if, in the same interval of time, another force causes the same body to move from A to B, then the combination of the forces, in the same interval of time, will take the body from A to D (figure 6.3).

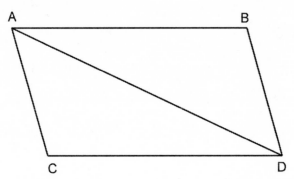

Figure 6.3

The lemmas have to do with limits. The basic premise is that if you have a curve, and parallelograms (in this case rectangles) inscribed above and below the curve, and the number of parallelograms increases indefinitely, then those above the curve and those below the curve will approach equality. The fourth corollary to the third lemma states that these "ultimate figures" are "not rectilinear, but curvilinear limits of rectilinear figures."[19] If you look at Newton's diagram (figure 6.4) and imagine the number of parallelograms increasing indefinitely, then you can imagine how they will approach "curvilinear limits." As their number increases indefinitely, the width of each will be narrower, and the area between them and the curve will approach zero.

Newton's theorem also presumes basic knowledge of Euclidean geometry. Specifically, it requires the knowledge that "triangles which are on equal bases and between the same parallels are equal to one another" (Euclid, *Elements*, postulate 38).[20] In other words, triangles with equal bases and heights are equal in area.

These are some of the prerequisites for understanding the proof. Now let us take a look at the proof itself.

First, Newton considers a body traveling from point A to point B. According to the first law of motion, if no force is impressed upon the body, it will

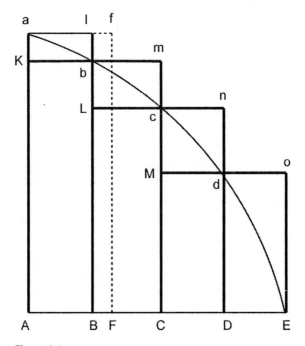

Figure 6.4

continue on the same line at the same velocity. Thus, in the time it takes to move from A to B, it will move from B to c, and segments AB and Bc will be of equal length. In the words of Newton, "Let the time be divided into equal parts, and in the first part of the time let a body by its inherent force describe the straight line AB. In the second part of the time, if nothing hindered it, this body would (by law 1) go straight on to c, describing line Bc equal to AB, so that—when radii AS, BS, and cS were drawn to the center—the equal areas ASB and BSc would be described" (figure 6.5).[21]

How do we know that the areas of ASB and BSc are equal? Newton does not explain this; the reader has to figure it out. Look at the bases AB and Bc. We already know that they are equal in length. We can see that the heights of these triangles are equal as well; we need only imagine a line running through S and parallel to AB. Since the two triangles both lie between the two parallels (the bases lying on one parallel and the opposite vertex touching the other), they are of equal height. Therefore, since their bases and heights are equal, they have the same area (see Euclid's postulate 38, mentioned earlier).

Now, suppose that a centripetal force (that is, a force pulling the body toward the fixed point S) were to act on the body at point B, causing it to deviate from its course and follow the line BC. The direction of that *force* (not the body itself) is parallel to SB, since the pull is directly toward S. The resulting path, BC, is the diagonal of the parallelogram described by Bc and cC (per the first corollary, mentioned earlier), and it lies on the same plane as the triangle ASB (figure 6.6). Newton writes,

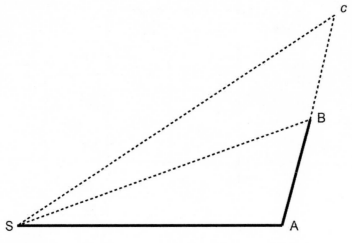

Figure 6.5

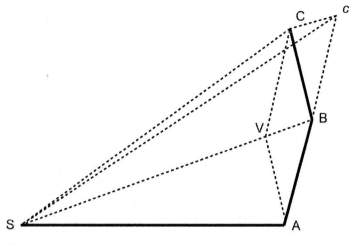

Figure 6.6

But when the body comes to B, let a centripetal force act with a single but great impulse and make the body deviate from the straight line B*c* and proceed in the straight line BC. Let *c*C be drawn parallel to BS and meet BC at C; then, when the second part of the time has been completed, the body (by corol. 1 of the laws) will be found at C in the same plane as triangle ASB.[22]

We know that it takes the same amount of time for the body to travel from A to B as from B to *c*, per the first law of motion. We know also, from the first corollary, that it takes the same amount of time to travel from B to *c* as from B to C. Newton continues, "Join SC; and because SB and C*c* are parallel, triangle SBC will be equal to triangle SB*c* and thus also to triangle SAB."[23] Again, the reader has to fill in some missing pieces in order to understand why triangles SBC, SB*c*, and SAB are equal in area. The implied logic is as follows: the areas of SBC and SB*c* are equal, since both have the same base (SB) and the same height (C*c* is parallel to SB, the base). Thus, the area of triangle SAB (which we already know is equal to the area of SB*c*) is equal to the area of SBC.

Newton goes on to say that if S continues to act at points C, D, E, in each of the equal time intervals, the resulting triangles will have the same area, and these lines will be in the same plane: "By a similar argument, if the centripetal force acts successively at C, D, E, . . . , making the body in each of the individual particles of time describe the individual straight lines CD, DE, EF, . . . , all these lines will lie in the same plane; and triangle SCD will be equal to triangle SBC, SDE to SCD, and SEF to SDE."[24] Again, we are left to figure something out: why are the triangles in the same plane? To understand this, refer back to figure 6.2. The triangle BC*c* clearly lies in the same plane as SAB, since B*c* is a continuation of AB, and *c*C is parallel to SB. From there, it is clear that triangles BC*c* and BVC lie in the same plane, as do BVC and SBC. Thus, SAB and SCB lie in the same plane. This will be true for the successive triangles as well.

Newton now returns to the original theorem: "Therefore, in equal times equal areas are described in an unmoving plane; and by composition [or *componendo*], any sums SADS and SAFS of the areas are to each other as the times of description."[25] In other words, when S acts on the body successively at equal time intervals, the areas of the resultant triangles will be equal, and they will lie in the same plane. Not only that, but if one takes any two combinations of triangles, their areas will be in the same proportion to each other as their times (figure 6.2).

So far, Newton has shown that when S acts on the body instantaneously at equal time intervals, the resulting triangles will be equal in area. But this is not sufficient for an understanding of orbit; a body in elliptical orbit follows a curved path, not a polygonal path. How do we get from the polygon to the curved line? Newton explains,

> Now let the number of triangles be increased and their width decreased indefinitely, and their ultimate perimeter ADF will (by lem. 3, corol. 4) be a curved line; and thus the centripetal force by which the body is continually drawn back from the tangent of this curve will act uninterruptedly, while any areas described, SADS and SAFS, which are always proportional to the times of description, will be proportional to those times in this case.[26]

In basic terms, the more triangles there are, the closer the body's path will come to a curve, and the closer the centripetal force will come to continuous action. The areas will remain proportional to the times; so what held true for the polygons will also hold true for the curve. The orbiting body will sweep out equal areas in equal amounts of time. Thus concludes the theorem.

This simple theorem is remarkably rich. It offers a glimpse into the history of mathematics, as it represents a movement from Euclidean geometry to limits (essentially integrals). It helps explain planetary orbit; it holds true when the path is elliptical as well as when it is circular. Thus it proves Kepler's second law, provided that orbital motion is indeed the limit of polygonal impulse motions.[27] Also, the leaps are as instructive as the method; this theorem relies on the reader's knowledge and presents some puzzles at first. It would be difficult to understand it without a grasp of Euclidean geometry and the laws, lemmas, and corollaries laid out earlier in the *Principia*. One must take time with the details; one must figure out why the various triangles are indeed equal in area, and why they lie in a single plane. Without this understanding, the bigger ideas remain elusive. This is just the first theorem, and one of the easiest to grasp; having worked through it, one starts to sense the vastness of the *Principia*.

What lively education discussions we would have, if we could bring theorems and sonnets to the table, as a matter of course, and if scholars, teachers, and members of the public took part. This would be not only enjoyable but enlightening, a refreshing contrast to vague rhetoric about thinking skills. Granted, it is not so easy for tired working people to assemble at the end of the day to discuss literature or mathematics. A public forum of this kind might be difficult to bring about or sustain. But even without going so far, even if we tilted education discussion toward the subjects themselves, many of the "conceptual swamps" would clear, and many "inert ideas"—to return to Whitehead—would either crumble or perk up.

INNOVATION REQUIRES NOT only knowledge, but fluency with that knowledge, often the result of many hours of working, practicing, and thinking. It is naive to suppose that we can simply innovate by releasing our creativity or by asking big questions. Computer engineers—today's role models of innovation—spend so much time tinkering with specific programs that the language becomes second nature. It may seem to an outsider that they are innovating out of the blue, but they are not; they are fluent in the codes, problems, and conventions of their field. Also, to be innovative, one need not go to the cutting edge of a field. Often we do not know what the cutting edge is until we sharpen it ourselves. It may not be recognized as a discovery for a long time.

Returning to Aristotle's point, just as each field of study has its own kind of exactness, so each field has its code. It takes some perseverance to make sense of it. Once we make our way into it, there are still more codes to crack, and after those, more still. Yes, it is a great thing to bring our findings back into the world, to make sense of them for others. But that is a meaningless endeavor unless we have something to bring. First we have to go far into the field and spend much time alone there. Most of the time, the thinking may not seem "higher order" at all. We are just learning our way around. Big thoughts do come, and at times they shake structures. But the modest thoughts are often more important than they appear.

Yet there is much to be said for toying with ideas, whatever their size. From the time they know how to speak, children start to pester their parents with questions, often stumping them. Such questions are at the root of both contemplation and action. E. B. White writes of "the haunting intimation (which I presume every child receives) of his mystical inner life; of God in man; of nature publishing herself thorough the 'I.'" He goes on to describe this experience:

> A boy, we'll say, sitting on the front steps on a summer night, thinking of nothing in particular, suddenly hearing as with a new perception and as though for the first time the pulsing sound of crickets, overwhelmed with the novel sense of identification with the natural company of insects and grass and night, conscious of a faint answering cry to the universal perplexing question: "What is 'I'?" Or a little girl, returning from the grave of a pet bird, leaning with her elbows on the windowsill, inhaling the unfamiliar draught of death, suddenly seeing herself as part of the complete story.[28]

The encounter with the universe, the sense of things beyond our comprehension yet close to us—that is part of childhood, part of adulthood, part of all life. A poem or mathematical proof pushes up against things we cannot fully comprehend. Newton's theorem reveals something of the workings of the solar system. To pretend that there is no wonder in our lives, to pretend that we have no truck with things great or tiny, that we must stick with our own size—such arrogance is as serious as the arrogance of pretending we can come up with great ideas out of the blue.

Nor does all our thinking have to be precise. In fact, some of our better thoughts may be messy, speculative, tentative, or whimsical. It would be dreary to limit our thoughts to those that logically and clearly followed from existing knowledge and thoughts. There is a place for dreams and wandering, for doing things without a purpose or plan.

In Anton Chekhov's story "At Home," the father, a public prosecutor, has tried to convince his seven-year-old boy that smoking is bad for him (the governess caught the boy smoking three times in the father's study). After trying to persuade him every which way and failing (delightfully—the boy is in a world of his own), he tells him a story that he makes up on the spot. It has the desired effect; the boy gazes at the dark window, shudders, and says that he won't smoke anymore. After the boy has gone to bed, the father finds himself ruminating on the relationship of truth and fiction:

> "They'll say that it was beauty and artistic form at work here," he reflected. "That may be so, but it isn't comforting. It's isn't a genuine means, all the same. . . Why must morals and truth never be presented in their raw form, but only with admixtures; why must they be sugared and gilded like pills? It isn't normal. . . Falsification, deception . . . tricks."

The story concludes, "He set to work, but lazy, homemade thoughts still wandered in his mind for a long time. Beyond the ceiling, the scales could no longer be heard, but the inhabitant of the second floor was still pacing from one corner to another."[29] Chekhov shows fondness for these thoughts, as scattered and inconclusive as they are; he recognizes that they complement the stricter modes of thinking. He also suggests their private nature. Perhaps the father is trapped in the language and logic of his profession; perhaps the evenings are the only time when his mind can wander freely. But the story's tone is not despondent; there is something warm, albeit melancholic, about the father's thoughts at home. It is a brief but untrammeled time, an enclosed time, except for the sounds from the floors above, which do not interfere.

Such privacy is largely absent from today's quest for big ideas. The talk about them may even prevent them from occurring; to find one's way to ideas, one must be willing to go into quiet, to bear with their tentative forms. There is some loneliness in pursuits that don't bear immediate results or that others don't understand. To study an ancient language, to practice scales and arpeggios, to spend hours on trigonometry problems, to listen to a piece of music with no one around, to experiment with an electronics kit, to look into a historical question, or to puzzle through a mathematical work that few will ever read, even to daydream—this requires a degree of isolation. Such activity is hard to convey to others. Often it seems that nothing will ever come of it. Then there is the little breakthrough—the musical passage that comes together, the problem solved, the verb figured out. What seemed insurmountably difficult becomes second nature. From there, new difficulties present themselves, and with them new ideas. Ultimately one's work turns into something that others may appreciate—a translation, a performance, a book, or a lesson. It may abound with ideas. Are they big ones? Are they innovations? We may not know right away.

Whitehead writes that all education must be for the present, which is "holy ground." This can be a stumbling block for those who, like myself, distrust the present a little, who believe that we lack sufficient perspective on the present to give it much credence. But what does Whitehead mean by "the present"? He does not mean the jittery kind—the anxiety over what is happening and what others are saying and doing. Rather, the present to which he refers "holds within itself the complete sum of existence, backwards and forwards, that whole amplitude of time, which is eternity."[30] This kind of present is a mystery and a contradiction. On the one hand, it simply isn't there; each present instant streams into the past, as each future instant streams toward us. On the other hand, there is everything to be found in this stream. We may find stillness in it, if we choose—not the stillness of "mental dryrot," but that of concentrating on something, following an idea, and resting on that very selection as outside events race by. This present allows us to move in all directions; to think back, look ahead, and turn a problem around and around. The nervous, unstable present imagines itself above and beyond the past when it is not; the steadfast kind makes room in itself for the past and future, for the full stretch of thought.

Some argue that the pressures of today are indeed the reality, that we face disaster unless we act fast. Workplaces, they insist, need quick thinkers with a sense of the here and now—people who can solve a pressing problem or create a popular product. They need people who can work on teams, who are social and flexible, who respond quickly to updates and stay ahead of the game. Well, such skills may well be needed for certain occupations, but not for all. We still need musicians who devote their lives to their instruments. We still need editors who read the manuscripts thoughtfully and understand what the author is doing. We still need historians to tell us how things came to be the way they are. We still need foresters to keep our parks alive and beautiful. We still need the religious, who see something beyond the immediate demands of the world but also respond to suffering. We still need carpenters who put care into every nail and measurement and tend to the damages of weather. We still need teachers, who must understand the lasting things of education as well as the changing things. Employers' demands do not stay still anyhow; in twenty years, the workplace trends may have shifted. The challenge is to discern the true forms of past, present, and future, and to hold them even when false forms dangle and sparkle around us.

7

~

The Cult of Success

In November 2002, Grigory Perelman astounded the mathematical world by posting an outline of his proof of the Poincaré conjecture on the Internet. The following April, he presented his proof at the Massachusetts Institute of Technology and, two weeks later, at the State University of New York at Stony Brook. His audiences of students and mathematicians sat in suspense. They recognized that if the proof had no errors or gaps, it could help determine the shape of the universe. "The atmosphere was tense," writes Donal O'Shea. "Everyone knew how delicate and subtle the speaker's arguments were, and how easy it was to go astray. Everyone wanted them to hold." The Stony Brook audience also included a few reporters who, unlike the mathematicians, were mainly interested in the question of the million-dollar Millennium Prize to be awarded by the U.S. Clay Mathematics Institute. What was Perelman's attitude toward the prize? Would he accept it?[1]

Perelman proved what Henri Poincaré posited in 1904 and earlier: that the three-dimensional sphere, or "three-sphere," is the only finite three-dimensional manifold that is "simply connected"—that is, in which every loop can be shrunk to a point.[2] Just as a two-dimensional sphere (such as the surface of the earth) can be thought of as two two-dimensional disks glued together along their boundaries (which are circles, or one-dimensional spheres), the three dimensional sphere can be thought of as two solid three-dimensional balls glued together along their boundaries (which are two-dimensional spheres). Like a two-sphere, a three-sphere is finite, but has no edge; one leaves one solid ball and immediately enters the other.[3] It is hard to conceive of such a shape, not to mention the possibility that this is the only possible finite, simply connected three-dimensional manifold—but even a glimmer of it might intrigue children and adults of many walks of life.

The Poincaré conjecture, now proven, helps narrow the possibilities for the shape of our universe. If we can determine that all loops in the universe shrink to a point, then we can be fairly certain that the universe is a three-sphere. The shape of the universe is still unknown, and experimental data do not all support the theory of a three-sphere, but Perelman's proof has at least shown that certain conditions would point to a three-sphere and nothing else.[4] Of course, it takes years of mathematical study to make sense of the implications. One must understand not only the mathematics but the place of the conjecture and the proof in history. Lacking this understanding, one may perhaps hope to gain it; lacking the desire or means to gain such understanding, one may acknowledge one's lack of it; lacking such acknowledgment, one is likely to latch on to peripheral matters (and to misunderstand even those).

In March 2010, some newspapers reported, under sensationalist headlines, that Perelman had turned down the million-dollar prize: "World's Cleverest Man Turns Down $1 Million Prize after Solving One of Mathematics' Greatest Puzzles"; "Strange Russian Genius Declines Million-Dollar Prize from U.S.A."; "Grigory Perelman, Reclusive Russian Math Genius, Refuses $1 Million Prize"; and more. Readers argued about whether he was a fool or a sage. Some called him selfish (he could have accepted the money for his mother's sake, after all); others called him noble. A reader, "Ana," from El Salvador quoted from the film version of *Doctor Zhivago*: "the kind of man that the world pretends to look up to and in fact despises." Few had anything to say about Perelman's discovery. Whether they praised him for his higher values or derided him for his lack of common sense, their focus was on the prize, not what it stood for, and on his mental state, not his intellectual work. Masha Gessen based her 2009 biography of Perelman, *Perfect Rigor*, on conversations with people other than Perelman, as she had no access to the mathematician himself. She became so intrigued with the idea that he might have Asperger's syndrome that she discussed his case with Simon Baron-Cohen, a leading researcher on autism. Baron-Cohen offered to evaluate Perelman, who did not take him up on the offer.[5]

The point is not that Perelman is just an ordinary man (he isn't) or that his decisions make complete sense to outsiders (they needn't). The point is that journalists and the public felt compelled to explain his actions. Heroic, eccentric, crazy, autistic, oblivious to the world, indifferent to fame—any of those adjectives would do. But no one will explain him correctly; he doesn't want such explanation. A writer of fiction might invent a character based on Perelman and might get *him* right—but it would be someone else, not Perelman. What would be wrong with simply leaving Perelman alone? Why so much chatter about his motives and mentality? What bothers people, it seems, is not Perelman, but rather his violation of the social codes of success. Or else, not knowing what to make of the proof itself, they latch onto pop psychology, which is easier to spout than mathematics.

SUCCESS HAS MEANT wealth, virtue, excellence, wisdom, personal content-ment, or any combination of these, but its definition has flattened over time, particularly in the past few decades. A combination of economic anxiety, aggressive advertising, ubiquitous ratings, and verbal vagueness has led to an emphasis on the external aspects of success—money, status, and appearance. Ranking is especially important. A "successful school" (in education discus-sion and reporting) is one that has raised test scores; a "successful teacher" or "successful reform" has done likewise. A "successful student" has earned high grades, landed a job with a high salary, or both. In research studies, newspaper articles, and general education discussions, there is far more talk of achievement than of the actual stuff that gets achieved. What strikes the listener is how blithely the term "success" is used, as though there were noth-ing wrong with it and nothing missing. In a *New York Times* article titled "Is Going to an Elite College Worth the Cost?" Jacques Steinberg asks, "Do their graduates make more money? Get into better professional programs? Make better connections? And are they more satisfied with their lives, or at least with their work?" He ignores the possibility that education might have benefits other than prestige, connections, earnings, or even personal satisfaction. William Deresiewicz, who sat on the Yale College admissions committee, described the recently admitted students as "great kids who had been trained to be world-class hoop jumpers."[6] Our society has come to wor-ship the god of blatant accomplishments and overt results.

Or is it a god of fantasy? The philosopher Luc Ferry argues that the con-temporary world "incites us to daydreams at every turn" (by "daydreams," *rêves éveillés*, Ferry means imitative fantasies). He writes, "Its impressive train of stars and spangles, its culture of servility in the face of the powerful, and its immoderate love of money tend to present daydreams as a *model* for life."[7] Indeed, our view of success includes an element of make-believe—the conjured notion that we can succeed *as others do* and that we deserve it. It also involves devotion to metrics: the modern "science" of measuring every-thing we do, in order to increase our chances and our profits. School districts measure teachers and schools according to the students' test score gains, regardless of what they mean. Amazon recommends books to purchasers on the basis of detected purchase patterns. Social networking sites announce how many friends or fans each person has and how many people liked the person's post or comment; such ratings are supposed to guide the Internet user through the morass. Employers administer multiple-choice personality tests to determine whether potential employees have the desired personal qualities. These measurements, disparate as they seem, all serve to rate performance, predict success, and prevent failure. Of course, these are decent aims, or can be, but the formulas rely on a false understanding of them. We don't always want books that others like us have liked. The curmudgeonly employee may prove brilliant and industrious. The person with few online "friends" may be beloved and admired elsewhere.

What does that strange word "success" mean? We don't know—and there's a chance that it doesn't mean much at all. In "The Fallacy of Success" (1909), G. K. Chesterton mocks the term for its sheer vapidity:

> There has appeared in our time a particular class of books and articles which I sincerely and solemnly think may be called the silliest ever known among men. They are much more wild than the wildest romances of chivalry and much more dull than the dullest religious tract. Moreover, the romances of chivalry were at least about chivalry; the religious tracts are about religion. But these things are about nothing; they are about what is called Success.[8]

Success is no accomplishment, Chesterton argues; it is only as good as the things we are and do: "To begin with, of course, there is no such thing as Success. Or, if you like to put it so, there is nothing that is not successful. That a thing is successful merely means that it is; a millionaire is successful in being a millionaire and a donkey in being a donkey." It is possible to succeed at something, but one does that by excelling in that particular area. To that end, we may seek out books about the subjects themselves: "You may want a book about jumping; you may want a book about whist; you may want a book about cheating at whist. But you cannot want a book about Success." Chesterton acknowledges that when people write about success in the abstract, they are usually referring to material gain: "It is not mere business; it is not even mere cynicism. It is mysticism; the horrible mysticism of money."[9]

It is mysticism indeed, wrapped up in elusive and dubious science. America has had a long history of efforts to predict success and failure. In *Born Losers: A History of Failure in America*, Scott A. Sandage tells how Lewis Tappan invented credit reporting, a highly coveted commodity after the panic of 1837. Compiling information from local informants around the country,

Tappan sold profiles of businessmen, with assessments of their character and practice. Essentially a surveillance system, his invention became an industry; the Mercantile Agency sold reports on ledgers that later evolved into type-written "red books," large red-edged quarto volumes. Laden with allusions to success and failure, these reports often took the form of prophesy. One report read, "The general opinion here is, that he is in a v[er]y critical & embarr[asse]d condition, and that there is a strong probability of his *failure*." Sandage notes that "in this context, 'probability' was a rhetorical, not a statistical, science."[10]

Sandage suggests that Walt Whitman's *Leaves of Grass* was influenced by the new "science of identity" practiced by Tappan and others. According to Sandage, Whitman "styled himself a surveillance agent, a voluminous cataloguer of intelligence." There is a paradox in Whitman's cataloging, Sandage notes; even as his poetry draws attention to a world beyond the ledgers, "the poet's distinctively omniscient tone recalled the enterprises of Broadway and Nassau Street." When Whitman writes, "You and your soul enclose all things, regardless of estimation," he criticizes the science of estimation while at the same time claiming to know the contents of his readers' souls.[11] Sandage's observations should provoke much thought and study; one can see grounds for them in lines like these (from the first edition of *Leaves of Grass*):

Have you reckoned a thousand acres much? Have you reckoned the earth
    much?
Have you practised so long to learn to read?
Have you felt so proud to get at the meaning of poems?

Or these:

Have you heard that it was good to gain the day?
I also say it is good to fall . . . battles are lost in the same spirit in which they
    are won.
I sound triumphal drums for the dead . . . I fling through my embouchures
    the loudest and gayest music to them,
Vivas to those who have failed, and to those whose war-vessels sank in the
    sea, and those themselves who sank in the sea,
And to all generals that lost engagements, and all overcome heroes, and the
    numberless unknown heroes equal to the greatest heroes known.[12]

Leaves of Grass is in many ways a song of unseen successes, the kinds that involve failure. Other works of American literature likewise play on the dream of success and point to its paradoxes. Tennessee Williams's play *The*

Glass Menagerie, set in the Great Depression, shows a family failing to realize its hopes. Amanda, the mother, wants her shy and withdrawn daughter, Laura, to find either employment or marriage, yet neither prospect seems likely. As it turns out, their very bravery is their victory; Laura, seemingly timid, shows her strength when the "gentleman caller" (coincidentally, her secret crush from her high school past) reveals, after kissing her, that he is not available after all. Her dignity is success, but it is shown as memory, in dreamlike form, not as the kind of success that pushes forth in the world and makes itself known.

Such success is dreamlike not only because it resides in memory but because it is so remote from what the world acknowledges. It shimmers like a separate life. Let us say, for instance, that a young man has been racking up a credit card debt because he wants to be like his friends, who can afford more luxuries than he. He wants a new corduroy jacket, though his jacket is just fine; he goes browsing in the stores, trying things on, but something is squirming in his stomach. He's on the brink of getting a two-hundred-dollar jacket—and then he hangs it back up, walks out into the wind, and enjoys the brisk air so much that he decides to take a long walk along the river, smoking a cigarette as he goes (no, he's not perfect). No one will applaud him; if they notice his light step and subdued grin, they'll assume he's having a good day. But it's more than a good day. He has figured out, for now, that he has what he needs and doesn't have to buy anything. This is more momentous for him than a promotion, as welcome as that might come, and more cherished than the jacket would have been, as much as he liked it. This kind of success exists in each of our lives, and it exists in stories; but it is not what people usually consider when they consider doing well in the world.

Perhaps we are losing our sense of Whitman and Williams, the words that separate themselves from success's screech and glare. Television has slowly tipped our consciousness and sensibilities toward the visual display. For decades, anyone with a public profile has had to pay some attention to looks—or be rebellious in not doing so. The author interviewed on the talk show has to dress well, wear makeup, speak clearly, make good eye contact, and appear relaxed; the presidential candidate has to look both dynamic and confident. Slowly wrought arguments must contend with the jingles of commercials. Today this pressure extends to all. The Internet and accompanying technology—handheld digital video cameras, the World Wide Web—make it even easier to craft a public persona, and with that ease comes obligation. College and job applicants bolster their applications with videos, photos, and animated slideshows. Colleges use videos to advertise themselves; in 2010 Yale University's admissions office released a musical video, *That's Why I*

Chose Yale, which gives the impression that Yale students are outgoing, hard working, beautiful, and fun loving.[13] Presenting yourself online has become an essential skill, not just for celebrities and institutions, but for job seekers, students, artists, freelancers, business owners, and scholars. Everyone can have a public self for the world to see. Even comments on blogs often come with an "avatar" (a cartoon figure or photo). It is common today to speak in terms of one's "personal brand"—the particular way that one presents and markets oneself.

Schools and universities, even school systems, have taken up self-advertising with fervor. Colleges and universities, seeking to improve their image, recruit aggressively so that they can both attract a more diverse student body (or, rather, a less eccentric one) and turn more students down. According to the *New York Times*, the University of Chicago has sought to break away from the stereotype of "a place for nerds and social misfits who shun sunlight and conversation." Whereas in the past, the university drew students who were attracted to its particular intellectual climate, in 2010 it received 19,347 applications, an increase of 43 percent over the 2009 total. It abandoned its unusual essay questions and joined the Common Application, which supposedly brings in more applicants. It hired the direct marketing firm Royall & Company to assist with its recruitment campaign. It put out a brochure showing University of Chicago students in a variety of group activities. When conducting outreach, admissions officers emphasized the university's pre-professional and career preparation opportunities.[14] As the University of Chicago joins a larger trend, it loses its identity as a university that stands outside of trends.

The trend toward advertising has affected K–12 education as well. There are essentially two kinds: advertising for political self-promotion and advertising for survival (with overlap between the two). Beginning in the fall of 2008, the Fund for Public Schools purchased subway advertisements proclaiming the successes of the New York City Department of Education. One advertisement read, "Because finishing is the start of a better future, New York City public high schools have increased graduation rates by more than 20% since 2002." Aaron Pallas, a professor of sociology and education at Columbia University's Teacher's College, noted that such advertisement was not common practice in cities and that the timing was strategic, given the upcoming vote on mayoral control and the mayoral election. It seemed likely, in other words, that these ads were intended to promote Mayor Bloomberg himself. In any case, when the very Department of Education advertises itself, it sets the tone for schools, teachers, and students. It becomes difficult to escape the spin. Public schools find that they must advertise themselves in order to compete with charter schools for students and stay afloat; principals have to spend time devising brochures, pitches, and recruitment plans.[15]

Of course, presenting oneself well in public is neither novel nor offensive; it is a necessity. The danger is that one can start to live in and for one's public image; one can forget the value of the things one does not show. In his 1947 essay "The Catastrophe of Success," written in response to the wildly enthusiastic reception of *The Glass Menagerie*, Tennessee Williams comments on the nature of the public image:

> You know, then, that the public Somebody you are when you "have a name" is a fiction created with mirrors and that the only somebody worth being is the solitary and unseen you that existed from your first breath and which is the sum of your actions and so is constantly in a state of becoming under your own volition—and knowing these things, you can even survive the catastrophe of Success![16]

If one takes Williams's words to heart—if one grants that "the only somebody worth being is the solitary and unseen you"—then one is left wondering what remains of that "somebody" today. To the degree that even our private lives have become public (through Facebook, ubiquitous video cameras, and so forth), we have little that is unseen by others and little room to tend to it. There is little room for the thoughts that course this way and that through our minds, the persistent questions, the recurring troubles and delights, the most difficult decisions, the phrases that change in meaning over time, the people who die, the stubborn fact that things often do not go the way we want.

If success consists of image and material acquisition, how does one attain it? It seems to require a combination of self-esteem and metrics: believing in oneself on the one hand and, on the other, measuring one's achievements and doing what it takes to raise the numbers. The culture of self-esteem dates back to early-twentieth-century "New Thought," a cultivated mental state that was supposed to lead to success. Practitioners referred to it as a science of the mind. In 1911, Frank Channing Haddock recommended reciting a daily affirmation that begins,

I, IN MY DYNAMIC POWER, AS A THINKER, COMMAND THAT PHASE OF MYSELF WHICH RESTS ON AND NEAREST THE INFINITE, AS THE LOTUS RESTS ON THE SURFACE OF THE NILE, TO DRAW FORTH FROM THE DEPTH AND VASTNESS OF LIFE, NEW POWER, NEW THOUGHT, NEW PLANS AND METHODS FOR MY BUSINESS AND MY SUCCESS.[17]

The historian Richard Weiss notes a "tone of plaintiveness" in the mind-power writings of the time; despite their insistence on the power of the mind, they "lack the ring of full conviction, somewhat in the manner of an individual trying to believe in spite of himself." Such insistence characterizes later success writings as well—for instance, Norman Vincent Peale's formula "(1) PRAYERIZE, (2) PICTURIZE, (3) ACTUALIZE."[18] The very suffix -IZE leaves one suspicious, as it seems forced, unwieldy, and funnier than it was meant to be.

Besides the affective route to success, there are formulas, which often carry a tinge of magic. Economists have long worked on calculating the profitability of individuals and organizations, in business, medicine, transportation, and other fields. In education, this has taken the form of value-added assessment: algorithms that calculate teachers' effectiveness, or added "value," on the basis of their students' test scores. Originally developed by the statistician William Sanders at the University of Tennessee, value-added assessments number among the key reforms promoted by think tanks and the federal government. While many scholars caution against the use of value-added assessment in high-stakes decisions, others insist that they should be used precisely in that manner. The economist Eric Hanushek states that if we could just replace the bottom 5 to 10 percent of teachers with average teachers, our schools' performance could rise to a level near the top internationally. The *Los Angeles Times* caused a furor in August 2010 when it published the names and ratings of some six thousand public school teachers; Secretary of Education Arne Duncan approved the action and urged other districts to follow suit.[19]

While it makes sense to look at students' performance on tests when evaluating teachers, there is something strange about the idea that the sheer act of ranking and replacing teachers will cause *student* performance to soar. It is as though students had no say in their own performance—as though their very mental workings could be controlled by an outside force. There is something equally strange about placing so much trust in the test scores themselves, without regard for the nature of the subject, the material tested, the quality of the tests, the relation of the tests to the curriculum, the other things taught, and much more.

Attempts to reduce failure through formulas abound. Teach for America has been seeking to identify effective teachers before they even begin teaching, by finding correlations between personality traits and increased test scores. Their findings have been inconsistent and inconclusive; their most robust conclusion is that teachers who in college pursued measurable goals such as GPA and "leadership achievement" were likelier to bring about test score increases. Similarly, districts across the country administer the Haberman Educational Foundation's Star Teacher Pre-Screener, a multiple-choice test intended to predict whether prospective teachers have the necessary qualities for raising student achievement.[20] Such formulas seem scientific but actually rest on faith that if we could only tweak things right, achievement would rise to desired levels. The problem—and not a trivial one—is that even if one could identify a "type" of teacher likely to bring up test scores, that type would not necessarily be the best kind of teacher in all ways. Students need different kinds of role models—not only go-getters, but people who take deep interest in something, whether or not it carries status, high pay, or visible marks of achievement. By treating test scores as the main measure of a teacher's worth, these initiatives could keep many fine teachers out of the field and narrow the very idea of education.

In a similar manner, psychologists have been trying to identify personality and behavior traits associated with student success. According to Paul R. Sackett, professor of psychology at the University of Minnesota in Minneapolis, the greatest predictors of student success, as far as student behaviors go, are conscientiousness (e.g., work ethic, dependability, and perseverance), agreeableness (teamwork, emotional stability), various kinds of extroversion, and openness to new experiences. Roger P. Weissberg, an education and psychology professor at the University of Illinois at Chicago, is developing "common-core standards for social-emotional learning," while others are working on programs for the teaching and assessment of emotional skills.[21] As with the Teach for America formula and the Star Teacher Pre-Screener, this research seems biased in favor of a particular kind of success and the kinds of personalities likely to attain it. Many thoughtful and capable students dislike working on teams, enjoy thinking on their own, and are not necessarily agreeable. If "common-core standards for social-emotional learning" do indeed catch on, they may cast eccentric, dreamy, and reclusive individuals as deficient.

School programs are filled with success stories and success talk, yet their conception of success is often limited. In Chicago, the organization Strategic Learning Initiatives brought its "turnaround" program to ten struggling schools; much of the reform was aimed at preparing students specifically for the kind of questions they would encounter on the test. Every day, the students received "success time" devoted to the practice of skills. They learned to identify "clue words" in test questions so that they would know which skill to apply. Success came up as a theme as well; when the students learned about Wilbur and Orville Wright in history class, the teacher asked the students to identify the character traits that made the brothers successful. But are character traits the deciding factor here? In *How We Reason*, Princeton psychology professor Philip N. Johnson-Laird demonstrates that it was in fact their exceptional reasoning, not their perseverance or other qualities, that set the Wright brothers apart from their rivals.[22] That is, they made sense of a succession of failures; they not only persisted through failure, but learned how to interpret it correctly. To understand how they made their discovery, one must look closely at their work all along the way. This is much more interesting and complex than platitudes about their character traits; sadly, the standardized tests are more likely to have a question about character traits than a question about the Wright brothers' actual work.

The quest for a success formula sometimes takes surprising turns. Malcolm Gladwell's *Outliers* posits that success is a matter both of intensive practice (amounting to some ten thousand hours, regardless of the field) and circumstance; it actually matters, in many cases, where one was born and in what year. Ability is not enough; even hard work is not enough, he demonstrates. One must also be in the right place at the right time, and one must seize this advantage. His argument is appealing and hard to dismiss. Yet he misses one of his own crucial points. When describing the success of attorney Joe Flom, he notes, "Think of how similar this is to the stories of Bill Joy and Bill Gates. Both of them toiled away in a relatively obscure field without any great hopes for worldly success. But then—boom!—the personal computer revolution happened, and they had their ten thousand hours in. They were ready."[23] Gladwell observes that Joy and Gates were not thinking of worldly success, but he fails to acknowledge the importance of this. Their immersion in the work itself, without thoughts of great success, may have had a great deal to do with their accomplishments. Moreover, such immersion is often inherently rewarding; a person need not end up like Gates to deem the hours of work worthwhile. Gladwell's limited definition of success weakens his otherwise intriguing observations.

In this quest for a formula for success, we lose the gradation between the unseen and the seen, between the visible and invisible. The armies of the visible and invisible rage at each other, and the invisible loses. When we argue that some of the most important things in life cannot be seen or measured, we set ourselves up for defeat, because the invisible is just that: invisible. A stronger argument is that we need a mixture of the visible and invisible, the measurable and unmeasurable—and that the former sometimes gives us a glimpse of the latter. It is through contemplating imperfect geometric figures that we can imagine Plato's ideal forms; it is through making sense of a sonnet that we glean something beyond its overt logic and rhyme. Some believe with fervor that the most important things are the tangible, measurable ones;

others believe with equal fervor in the unseen. But the mixture is essential to the understanding of both the seen and the unseen.

This grasp of the mixture of the visible and invisible, the measurable and immeasurable, was at one point a central aspect of liberal education, part of every study and part of the spirit of study. In mathematics, one wrestled with abstract concepts that did not translate immediately into practical examples; in literature, one tried to grasp what made a passage particularly beautiful. Such efforts varied, of course, from school to school, teacher to teacher, and student to student, but learning went far beyond the literal and immediately applicable. Teachers and professors delighted in the students who pursued subjects out of interest, not just for a grade. A lecturer could make artful use of a digression, and at least some students would listen for the connections and the meaning. Today the teacher who digresses is frowned upon; everything in a lesson is supposed to move toward a specific measurable goal. Teachers are supposed to announce the objective at the start of the lesson, remind students of the objective throughout the lesson, and demonstrate attainment of the objective at the end.

Such a utilitarian view of education has a long history, but in recent years it has overtaken education discourse. It can be attributed to the loss of a literary culture, the introduction of business language and models into education, and the resultant streamlining of language. Schools and industries have become less concerned with the possible meanings of words, their allusions and nuances, than with buzzwords that proclaim to funders and inspectors that the approved things are being done—goal setting, "targeted" professional development, identification of "best practices," and so forth. Thus we lose the means to question and criticize the narrow conceptions of success that have so much power in our lives. We speak the same language that the success promoters do, more or less. I myself write about "narrow conceptions of success" when I could put it, say, in terms of a bike shop that is called a success because it sells to a champion cyclist, or a nest that is called a success because the chicks that hatched in it ended up catching many worms. The phrase "narrow conception of success" is as limited as the success it criticizes.

In his oft-quoted 1906 letter to H. G. Wells, William James (who, ironically, had some sympathy for the New Thought of Haddock and others) complained about "the moral flabbiness born of the exclusive worship of the bitch-goddess SUCCESS." He continued, "That—with the squalid cash interpretation put on the word success—is our national disease."[24] Today's criticisms are less vivid. "Has the aversion to failure in our society gone too far?" asks the Canadian economist Todd Hirsch. "We've become so intolerant of mistakes and errors that we go to enormous extents to either hide them or pass them off as success in disguise." He explains the problem succinctly, yet the very language shows symptoms of the problem. Today's language of success (even the language of its critics) lacks bristle. Even if newspaper articles acknowledge the limitations of material success, they are likely to call them limitations, nothing more interesting than that. The generic vocabulary of the social sciences clangs around us. We lose the words of Ishmael and their surrounding sense: "Doubts of all things earthly, and intuitions of some things heavenly; this combination makes neither believer nor infidel, but makes a man who regards them both with equal eye."[25]

JUST AS WE dream of attaining success, we dream of obliterating failure. In *Facing Up to the American Dream* (1995), Jennifer Hochschild writes, "Because success is so central to Americans' self-image, and because they expect as well as hope to achieve, Americans are not gracious about failure. Others' failure reminds them that the dream may be just that—a dream, to be distinguished from waking reality."[26] Many believe that, in order to attain success, they must somehow distance themselves from failure. Some believe that if they forbid failure or erase it from the books, it will disappear. With enough slogans, chants, and pep talks, perhaps, just perhaps, they can drive it away.

Geoffrey Canada, president and CEO of the Harlem Children's Zone, wrote in an op-ed in 2010: "Visitors to my public charter school often ask how the students feel about the signs on the walls that say: 'Failure is not an option.' They are surprised to hear that the signs are really for the staff." But if failure were not an option, why would one bother saying so? What's hiding here is the acknowledgment that failure is an ever-present option, one that Canada and his staff fight every day. The Harlem Children's Zone aims at breaking the cycle of poverty for Harlem children through a combination of education and social services. Using a "conveyor belt" model, which takes children from infancy up to college, it strives to provide seamless supports so that no child falls through the cracks. Yet failure happens even in the Harlem Children's Zone. In March 2007, Canada announced that he was phasing out the Promise Academy middle school, which he originally had intended to expand into a high school. All the graduating eight graders would have to find a high school elsewhere, and there would be no incoming sixth grade. Why? The preliminary test scores weren't high enough, and Canada felt he had to change course.[27] It was a wrenching decision for him, and the question remains: if failure is not an option, what does one do with it when it appears?

In many situations, the stakes demand that one try to prevent failure at all costs. This is the case in surgeries and wars, in high-poverty schools at testing time and earthquake rescue missions. Even in safer places such as concert halls, there is tension and expectation when the moment comes. Laxity in those cases will not do. But even there, failure happens, and one must have a way of reckoning with it. One must have a language for it, a kind of dignity around it. If all one hears about is success, then those who fail are left stumbling and bewildered, and the audience, equally confused, points fingers and makes noises of blame.

If we try to exclude failure, we deny much of existence: we disregard wars, famines, and other disasters; we wish away low test scores, college rejections, romantic rejections, divorce, poverty, addiction, death, injustice, car accidents, lost jobs, misspelled words, stutters, misunderstandings, and our daily mistakes and slippages. Those who take on the slogan "failure is not an option" wittingly or unwittingly paint over their lives and the lives of others, and the result is not only false but flat. Such a paint job can't render anything close to a human life. Hochschild observes that "the ideology of the American dream includes no provision for failure; a failed dream denies the loser not only success but even a safe harbor within which to hide the loss."[28] Failure happens, yet it isn't supposed to be there. The contradiction is each person's private secret; it has driven some to despair.

In rejecting failure, we reject a resource as well. Failure can be inconsequential, crushing, or anything in between, but we need it as much as we need success, and even when we don't need it, it happens and must be taken into account. Our successes and failures, in combination, teach us about the world and ourselves; they push us beyond ourselves. They help us understand history, literature, science, arts; they show us who we are, what we do well, whom we love, what we desire, what our limits are and aren't, and how our private and public lives meet and part. When they have no explanation, they stand as stubborn reminders that not all of life bends to our will or understanding. Explained or unexplained, they are not always what they seem.

The narrator of Robert Browning's poem "Rabbi Ben Ezra" (1864) suggests that failures may be successes in disguise and vice versa.[29] The poem is solemn, exuberant, witty, soulful, and jagged—a vigorous call to repose. Its overall meaning is that old age is the mirror opposite of youth; where youth strives, old age rests and contemplates; where youth acts, old age trusts in the action of God. The ideas are somewhat cryptic until one grasps the underlying symmetry of youth and old age, and with it, the ambiguity of success and failure. Near the beginning, the narrator tells us,

For thence,—a paradox
Which comforts while it mocks,—
Shall life succeed in that it seems to fail:
What I aspired to be,
And was not, comforts me:
A brute I might have been, but would not sink i' the scale.

Toward the end, he repeats the idea, but in stronger, more resolved language, as he speaks no more of comfort, but of isolation and God:

Thoughts hardly to be packed
Into a narrow act,
Fancies that broke through language and escaped;
All I could never be,
All, men ignored in me,
This, I was worth to God, whose wheel the pitcher shaped.

"All I could never be"—what does that mean? There is a sense that his failures are, in God's eyes, part of his beauty, part of the shape of his life. Yes, the failures themselves—unrecognized, unmitigated, unrepaired.

Our failures may count among our greatest assets; they may show us the outlines of who we are. In her note to the second edition of *Wise Blood*, Flannery O'Connor writes, "Does one's integrity ever lie in what he is not able to do? I think that usually it does, for free will does not mean one will, but many wills conflicting in one man. Freedom cannot be conceived simply. It is a mystery and one which a novel, even a comic novel, can only be asked to deepen."[30] By this she means that our impossibilities and incapacities end up defining what we *can and must* do. A person may try to be someone or something else but will eventually hit upon an obstacle. That obstacle—which seems to make us fail—ultimately brings us back to ourselves.

This does not mean that failure is always illuminating or redemptive, or that we are always capable of seeing it that way. The shame of failure drives people to suicide; the fear of failure can overpower the mind. The writer who feels she has passed her peak may not be able to put that thought away; each new work, even each sentence, seems to limp along while the earlier writings surged and sang and sparkled. The scientist who has spent decades trying to solve a problem may feel that all the effort went to nothing. The immigrant worker who spent long hours, day after day, year after year, cleaning homes, only to see her children drop out of school, may wonder what all that labor was for. The retired stockbroker who made himself a decent living but had longed to do something different all along may ask whether the money was worth it. In these cases there may be nothing rewarding about the situation except for the questioning itself, which may or may not open the way to more understanding.

Insofar as we believe that we were "meant" to do something in life, we dread to find out that we failed to do that very thing. It is all very well if I fail as a gymnast; I was not meant to be a gymnast. But if I fail as a teacher, then I am left with the question, what has my life been worth? Was I deluded to think it had any purpose at all? It is not surprising that those with the strongest sense of vocation may also be tormented by failure; they are called not only to action but to excellence and certainty. If these are flawed or absent, what, then, was the calling? Was there one at all? Did they mistake it somehow? Or did they fail in fulfilling it? While the idea of a calling may seem a little antiquated, each of us, in some way, tries to find out what our life is about, where it is headed, and how to make the most of it. Answers do not come easily, but when they do come, it seems shameful not to live them out.

Even those who know their calling do not necessarily have an answer. Mother Teresa lived with doubts, bleakness, and loneliness; in a letter to Father Neuner, a Jesuit priest, she wrote, "I have nothing—since I have not got Him—whom my heart & soul long to possess. Aloneness is so great.— From within and from without I find no one to turn to. He has taken not only spiritual—but even the human help. . . . How terrible it is to be without God—no prayer—no faith—no love."[31] For one who has devoted her life to God, what failure (other than cynicism or apathy) could be worse than the failure to find God? Yet she showed the possibility of persevering even without the sense of God's presence. There are few like Mother Teresa, but many of us find ourselves at times without assurance or comfort, without any sign of success. Such absence of hope may be an opportunity to grow stronger, to see our lives more deeply, or even to rely less on our own conception of our lives. Or else it is just there, unexplained.

Ernest Hemingway's *The Old Man and the Sea* can be regarded as a parable of the ambivalence of success and failure. The old man catches the marlin but loses the flesh; he comes home with the skeleton, proof of both his defeat and his victory. But the skeleton cannot tell the private part of the story: the conversations with a bird, with the fish, with himself. A tourist spots the skeleton tied to his skiff and asks a waiter what it is. He replies, "Tiburon, Eshark," meaning that the sharks ate it. The tourist misunderstands him and replies that she didn't know sharks had "such handsome, beautifully formed tails."[32] Already the history has been lost, through broken telling and misunderstanding. The old man is alone with his experience; be it success or failure, it is unknown to anyone but himself, and perhaps not even to himself. His explanation to himself is that he went out too far; perhaps this means that he has no explanation or that he went out to a place where there were no answers. Perhaps this is the nature of a serious endeavor: if we go very far, we reach a point of private conversation, where nothing is clear and where success and failure are no longer opposites.

What, then, might success be, if our current understanding is too narrow? It is not simply personal fulfillment; fulfillment in itself can be empty. One can take Prozac and feel fulfilled for a while, or at least less unfulfilled; does that make one successful? One can join a group of like-minded people and shut out conflicts; is that success? One can be electronically matched to the things one likes, and only those things, but what happens, then, to ruggedness and adventure? Why not take a rougher route? Success may have to do with wending our way through swamps and clambering over logs. It may have something to do with living ourselves out, as Friedrich Wilhelm Nietzsche suggested—becoming strongly and purely ourselves. But there is more. Success has to do with a certain empty-handedness, a willingness to do something out of love or dedication or curiosity, without predictable reward. That includes spending time with a partner, child, or close friend; it includes playing an instrument and hearing the tones grow fuller and clearer. Maybe there is grace in it too. Ferry writes, "What is the use of growing old? . . . To enlarge one's view: to love the singular and once in a while to experience the abolition of time that the presence of the singular permits us."[33] We are not used to thinking in these terms, but perhaps true success is something we may achieve when false success falls away.

The preoccupation with outward success (money, image, power, and success itself) deceives us out of a hardier success. Failure, our twin, becomes the exiled leper, so we come to loathe ourselves even as we buff and propagate our image. Whatever seems awkward, unformed, or tentative gets pushed aside. Confidence trumps competence; we hesitate to do things that we do not already do well. But in ridding ourselves of all unsuccessful things, we make a bleak utopia, an empty dome. Our internal misfits may be things in motion: ideas in formation, projects in progress, difficult challenges. They may be private thoughts or things for which we do not yet have words. They may be concerns and hopes for another person. They may be part of the human rumble: suffering, confusion, unexpected joy. They may not always shape themselves for job applications, promotions, or million-dollar prizes, but we do not live by such shapes alone.

8

~

Mass Personalization and the "Underground Man"

In 1851, the World Exhibition at the Crystal Palace in London caused international commotion. Unprecedented in grandeur and sweep, it brought together 13,937 exhibitors from around the world to display their sculptures, railroad engines, metal works, cloths, jewels, machines, model ships, recent inventions, and other prized examples of culture and industry.[1] Over the years, other countries held international exhibitions of their own, and the Crystal Palace declined in importance as a building but not as a symbol. From the beginning, it seemed to herald the progress, prowess, and goodwill of the human race; over time, it swelled into a concept and a dream.

Fyodor Dostoevsky, who visited the Crystal Palace in 1862, saw an ominous side to it: "You sense the frightening force that has here united all these countless people, who have come from all over the world, into a single herd; you recognize a gigantic idea; you feel that something here has been attained, that victory, exultation are here. You even begin to feel afraid of something." What was there to fear? For Dostoevsky, it was the sense of having reached a destination: "Must one not recognize this as the full truth and go completely numb?"[2] The question remains perplexing today: can one strive for a richer, better life while preserving human freedom? Is there progress that allows us our full liveliness, or do the very formulas for social improvement end up constraining us? By examining Dostoevsky's critique of the Crystal Palace, we may see our own crystal palaces more clearly—particularly the crystal palace of technology.

The Crystal Palace seemed to mark the end of one era and the beginning of another. Prince Albert announced in 1849 that the exhibition would "give us a true test and a living picture of the point of development at which the whole of mankind has arrived in this great task, and a new starting-point from which all nations will be able to direct their further exertions." He believed that it would inspire people to realize God's blessings through "peace, love, and ready assistance, not only between individuals, but between the nations of the earth." With the assistance of the structural engineer Charles Fox, Joseph Paxton undertook the design. Made of cast-iron frame and glass and completed in less than a year, the glittering structure measured about 1,848 feet long by 454 feet wide, with 18,392 panes of glass in the roof. According to a popular journal, hours before the exhibition opened on May 1, 1851, "every possible point of access to the building was thronged with well-dressed persons—a great proportion of them ladies—eagerly waiting for admission." Public admission took place between nine and eleven in the morning. At exactly ten minutes to twelve, Queen Victoria arrived, dressed in pink satin, with crowds cheering throughout the building.[3]

From the opening day to October 15, six million people came to view the displays. Charlotte Brontë wrote, "It is a wonderful place—vast, strange, new and impossible to describe. Its grandeur does not consist in *one* thing but in the unique assemblage of *all* things." She continued, "It seems as if magic only could have gathered this mass of wealth from all the ends of the earth—as if none but supernatural hands could have arranged it thus—with such a blaze and contrast of colours and marvellous power of effect."[4]

Glorifying both God and science at once, bringing people together from all around the world, the Crystal Palace suggested that some of the most dogged human problems were on their way to resolution. The exhibition showed vast possibilities assembled in one scintillating structure. The displays were often spectacular and the crowds peaceable and courteous. Horace Greeley called it "magnificent in conception, and most triumphant in execution" and saw in it an indication of the "practicability and ultimate certainty of Universal Peace."[5] But there were cracks in the utopian dome, troubles fermenting below the glitter.

Praise of the Crystal Palace was neither unanimous nor unequivocal. John Ruskin was to quip later that it was "neither a palace, nor of crystal." John Tallis, author of a laudatory three-volume description of the exhibition, at which he was present, devotes some space to reservations and doubts. At one point he quotes a pseudonymous "Christopher North" who imagines Voltaire coming back from the dead to visit the exhibition. This imaginary and solitary Voltaire is less than enraptured: "What a din this age makes about its progress! It travels fast enough, if that were all. Rapid progress of that kind. For the rest—let us see whether the world is revolving in any other than its old accustomed circle." He inspects a locomotive, which a professor of mechanics proudly introduces as "one of our iron slaves." Voltaire points out that it has not put an end to dreary human labor: "Putting my head out of the window of my railroad carriage, whilst we were yet at the station, I saw an industrious mortal going from wheel to wheel with a huge grease-pot, greasing the wheels. He greases wheels from morning to night; eternally he greases."[6]

This fictional Voltaire has no patience for the exhibition's "ornamental nonsense": "If I pour water from a ewer into a basin, must I seize a river-god by the waist?" Continuing on his tour, he sees the printing press with its "wonderful celerity," capable of bringing parliamentary debates to the reader on the very same morning that they occurred. "I hope," he reflects, "that the orations are equally wonderful. They should be. From what I remember of such matters, I think I could wait a few more hours for them without great impatience; and perhaps the well-written comments would not suffer by the delay."[7] Finally Voltaire returns to the realm of the shadows, and Tallis continues with his own description of the exhibition.

Tallis was not alone in glimpsing the underside of the exhibition. Even the hyperbolically enthusiastic Samuel Warren describes, in his eulogy *The Lily and the Bee*, a "grey-haired harmless idiot" who is not permitted to enter the Crystal Palace, causing the narrator to enter "with a spirit saddened." Others bitterly criticized the overwhelming emphasis on England's contributions. In a letter to the *New York Times*, the Honorable W. C. Rives, minister to France, complained that the exhibition was "so contrived as to leave upon the mind of the beholder a strong impression of the material superiority, if not supremacy, of one of these nations over all the rest. England has the vast advantage in the Exhibition of being *at home*."[8]

After the 1851 exhibition, the Crystal Palace was relocated to Penge Place on Sydenham Hill and reopened in 1854. In 1889, the Exposition Universelle in Paris eclipsed the English show, and other exhibitions followed. By the early twentieth century, the Crystal Palace was starting to fall into disrepair, and in 1936 it was destroyed in a fire. The ideas, in the meantime, had taken off on their own. The Crystal Palace had come to represent the future—a godly future and a scientific future at once.

In 1863, the Russian author Nikolai Chernyshevsky published his utopian novel *What Is to Be Done?* which he had written in prison. The novel's heroine, Vera Pavlovna, sees the Crystal Palace in a dream: "But this building— what could it be, what kind of architecture is this? There's nothing like it now. No, there's one hint at it—the palace that stands on Sydenham Hill."[9]

Here the Crystal Palace represents a place where life is beautiful, where there is no more inequality, where people enjoy their work and can be heard singing in the fields, where thousands dine together in elegant and diverse attire, and where moral wisdom, physical energy, talent, and joy combine.

Chernyshevsky's novel was to inspire Vladimir Ilyich Lenin and other revolutionaries, but early on it found a fierce critic in Dostoevsky. His short novel *Notes from Underground* (1864) snarls and fumes at Chernyshevsky's Crystal Palace (and even some aspects of the original exhibition). *Notes from Underground* influenced many anti-utopian writings that followed it—in particular Yevgeny Zamyatin's *We* (1925), which describes a city made entirely of glass buildings, where everyone is subject to surveillance. Dostoevsky's critique of the Crystal Palace (through his narrator and protagonist, commonly known as the "Underground Man") remains one of the most powerful and yet cryptic takedowns of utopias. Playful, mischievous, and contradictory, it is a literary work, not a statement. Nonetheless, it gives utopian schemes a good shaking, and whoever is attentive and shoeless can feel the tremor today.

Dostoevsky wrote *Notes from Underground* in 1864, after serving a five-year prison term for his participation in the liberal intellectual Petrashevsky Circle and an additional five years in the Siberian Regiment. During his time in prison he underwent a religious conversion and reexamined many of his earlier views. Dostoevsky wrote *Notes from Underground* during an unhappy time in his life, when his wife was dying; he turns his disillusionment into a bristling character, a creation who does not go away once we know him. The Underground Man is impossible yet omnipresent, self-contradicting and elusive, opposed to any conclusion, even his own utterances. He writes from his filthy apartment on the edge of Petersburg, having lost desire to participate in reality. He writes and writes, knowing his writing is futile. He addresses his readers ironically as "gentlemen" (*gospoda*), argues with them, contradicts himself, mocks himself, and continues writing, aware that he accomplishes nothing.

The very opening of *Notes from Underground* has confounded translators: *Ia chelovek bol'noi . . . Ia zloi chelovek* ("I am a sick man . . . I am a spiteful man").[10] *Zloi* has been translated as "spiteful," "wicked," "mean," "nasty," "angry," "evil," and more; it is all those things, but no matter what the translation, it is difficult to replicate the sound of these opening lines. In Russian, *zloi* rhymes with *bol'noi*, and the word order (*chelovek bol'noi zloi chelovek*) suggests mirror symmetry. The opening sentences ring like biting, toothaching poetry; ideas as well as words rhyme and collide.

The Underground Man has no faith in the perfectibility of humankind; he sees rational systems as worse than human problems. "Two times two makes four is no longer life, gentlemen," he declares, "but the beginning of death." For the Underground Man, the Crystal Palace is essentially "two times two makes four"; it is "an insufferable thing." He would rather bang his head against the wall and protest "two times two makes four" than give into it just because it is reasonable. He would rather be miserable than succumb to a formula that does away with questions and actions. There is something we hold dearer than happiness, he argues; it "destroys all our classifications and constantly demolishes all systems devised by lovers of humanity for the happiness of mankind." This thing flies in the face of the most reasonable laws: it is "one's very own free, unfettered desire, one's own whim, no matter how wild, one's own fantasy, even though sometimes roused to the point of madness." Man wants one thing: "his own *independent* desire," even though it does him no good.[11]

The Underground Man explains his preference for independent desire. First, desire is more encompassing than reason; second, history shows over and over that humans will defend their right to choose something stupid, just for the sake of having that right; and third, in preserving that right, man preserves his own individuality, without which there would be no humanity. History, he says, can be described in many ways, but one cannot possibly call it rational; "you'll choke on the word." Man will do anything, he will cause destruction and pain, just to "have his own way" and to prove that he is "a man and not a piano key."[12] The Crystal Palace, he argues, is untenable as a way of life, because there is no room for the human mind in it:

For instance, suffering is not permitted in vaudevilles, that I know. It's also inconceivable in the crystal palace; suffering is doubt and negation. What sort of crystal palace would it be if any doubt were allowed? Yet, I'm convinced that man will never renounce real suffering, that is, destruction and chaos. After all, suffering is the sole cause of consciousness.[13]

To the Underground Man, the Crystal Palace (as an idea) is frightening not because it has flaws, but because it is perfect and unassailable. If we have no choice but to revere this palace, if we may not mock it, then there is no possibility of full life in it; one must be polite and reverent within it. This fills him with dread:

You believe in the crystal palace, eternally indestructible, that is, one at which you can never stick out your tongue furtively nor make a rude gesture, even with your fist hidden away. Well, perhaps I'm so afraid of this building precisely because it's made of crystal and it's eternally indestructible, and because it won't be possible to stick one's tongue out even furtively.[14]

Then comes the crown of his argument, where he points out that a thing's usefulness does not make it grand or splendid.

> Don't you see: if it were a chicken coop instead of a palace, and if it should rain, then perhaps I could crawl into it so as not to get drenched; but I would still not mistake a chicken coop for a palace out of gratitude, just because it sheltered me from the rain. You're laughing, you're even saying that in this case there's no difference between a chicken coop and a mansion. Yes, I reply, if the only reason for living is to keep from getting drenched.[15]

It is not immediately obvious how the Crystal Palace might be a chicken coop. The logic is this: any scheme for a perfect world is a short-term shelter, no matter how glorious it may seem. To draw crowds of believers, panacea promoters dress up ordinary things in grand verbiage. The Underground Man declares this a sham. If a chicken coop keeps him dry, it is still a chicken coop. Those who claim it is no different from a mansion (in terms of keeping one dry) are implying that staying dry is a high enough aspiration in life. The Underground Man wants more—or perhaps he does not.

The Underground Man has put himself in a bind, and he knows this. Robert Louis Jackson observes that he is "an embodiment of the very rationalism he rejects."[16] He has made himself a negative Crystal Palace of sorts: a perfected attitude of self-defeat, sneering, and caprice. He even recognizes this; he imagines his critics telling him, "You long for life, but you try to solve life's problems by means of a logical tangle."[17] Indeed, a tangle he has made. In his rambling, several arguments are intertwined: man is irrational and does not always act in his own best interest; man needs his suffering; perfection would be awful because we could not suffer or make fun of the perfect thing; and we need not exalt something just because it serves a limited purpose. His arguments are perversely enchanting, yet they suffer from narrowness. He lives, survives, seethes, but participates in nothing, believes in nothing but his own will. "The reader is without a Virgil in this hell," writes Jackson, "and his journey is a difficult one."[18] The Underground Man's actual behavior ranges from hapless to cruel (as the second part of Notes from Underground shows). He is trapped in his resistance to a trap.

Throughout the work, Dostoevsky poses an implicit spiritual puzzle. Is there a way through the Underground Man's conundrum? How does one resist a panacea or grand movement while still participating in the world? Is it possible to improve one's life and the life of society without succumbing to slogans and formulas? Is it possible to see keenly without slipping into a snarl? Part of the brilliance of the work is its irresolution. The underground rumbles on, and the reader is left to puzzle out the questions. They are urgent today as ever; we are surrounded by spin and sales pitches, in education and elsewhere. To counter the spin, one must come close to the matter at hand—but in doing so, one runs the risk of acquiescing to it. One must be willing to inform oneself, to see past platitudes, to take part in solutions—but one must also be willing to roar.

TECHNOLOGY MAY BE our new Crystal Palace; it not only makes certain tasks easier in the present, but holds great promises for the future. Technology is enveloped in future-talk; this is part of its appeal. David Gelernter has suggested that we have lost our sense of future; that if we want to recapture some of the energy and optimism of the late 1930s, we need "to see something where today we see nothing; to imagine the future, period."[19] Technology offers precisely that: a sense of future. We read of inventions around the corner, miraculous things like invisibility cloaks. We read that technology—especially mass personalization—is transforming our very conception of school. Mass personalization is under rapid development and has the potential to influence culture, education, and individual life. It is dangerous because it is not personalization at all; it is streamlining and standardization in disguise. At the same time, disturbing as it may be, it will not go away; we have to learn about it in order to use and criticize it well.

Mass personalization is the automated tailoring of products to individuals. For example, Amazon recommends books and other products to customers on the basis of data it collects about them. The more data it collects, the more accurate its predictions supposedly become. Ultimately a customer will buy one of the recommended products and then go on to buy more. The engine and the human will come closer to each other; the recommendations will seem more fitting, and the customer will start to trust them. Of course, this only applies to people who are looking for recommendations in the first place. Some people have no lack of books to read and no interest in a program that offers them more. But for those who do want the recommendations, the "personalized" appearance is deceptive.

Amazon relies on trends, after all, not on knowledge of individuals. The recommendations are based on what others with similar purchase patterns have bought. Rather than personalize their offerings, Amazon and similar programs may bring about an insipid sameness of tastes. Facebook targets its advertisements on the basis of users' "likes": it encourages users to indicate what they "like" and then uses this data to sell things to users that supposedly suit their tastes or the tastes of their peers. Beyond the Internet, there are now robots that not only perform tasks but empathize with people, have sex with people, and assume whatever personality the owner chooses (within a set of options). "Robotic companionship may seem a sweet deal," Sherry Turkle writes, "but it consigns us to a closed world—the loveable as safe and made to measure."[20]

Some companies use a combination of data gathering and behavioral targeting—advertising based on a customer's perceived personality type. According to the *Wall Street Journal*, Capital One's website uses the calculations of the online-marketing company [x + 1] Inc. to determine which advertisements to show the visitor. These calculations are based not only on his web-browsing and purchase history but also on his demographic group. Similarly, Google uses a form of advertising known as "behavioral targeting": it assigns users to categories based on the web pages they visit, and selects ads accordingly. Developers are also working on "relevance engines"—engines that deliver precisely the information likely to appeal to an individual in a given situation. In these cases, the engines target the product or information to the individual's supposed category or circumstances. In September 2010, Google rolled out Google Instant, which gives results in real time as one types. This is part of an effort to predict and even influence users' searches; Google cofounder Sergey Brin called it an attempt to make Google "the third half of your brain."[21]

In education, personalization is a sweeping concept and, to many, the holy grail. At face value, nothing could be more important than tailoring school to each student's needs. Especially in schools where students work at widely disparate levels, the challenge is to find ways to instruct them all, leaving no one behind. Most acknowledge that this can be an overwhelming task, but few question its ultimate value. For this reason, reformers see great hope in technology, which can automate the customization of lessons and exercises. Computers could tailor instruction to students automatically on the basis of their test performance. Teachers, relieved of some of the more difficult planning work, could then assist students individually and deliver targeted lessons. Every child would have a unique and changeable instructional plan. Every child's achievement would rise, because no one would have to fail at all; each would be working at his or her level and pace.

Salman Khan, creator of the Khan Academy, a carefully planned library of instructional videos, sees video instruction as the future, a way to free up teachers to assist individuals in the classroom instead of teaching the whole class.[22] On first consideration, his argument makes sense. As he points out, students watching a video can pause and repeat as many times as they like. Then, in class, they may work with peers on problems. Khan states that this model flips instruction on its head; students watch videos at home and solve problems in class, instead of the other way around. But is this a desirable scenario? One is stuck with that video, willy-nilly—and one must solve problems in the presence of peers, in the buzz of the classroom. As resources, these videos may be a great boon; as a global solution and model, they may constrict rather than liberate education. Such tailoring may leave students with little more than videos and peer groups; it may take away the challenge of a teacher posing questions, or an assignment that requires full mind and concentration. Students may need things that don't always match them; they may need to be confronted with things they don't understand or like.

In a November 2010 lecture at the Dallas Institute of Humanities and Culture, the scholar Louise Cowan spoke about education in Faulkner's story "The Bear." She observed that "the boy has had two sorts of education: a classical one, no doubt given him by his Uncle Cass, in which he has read the *Iliad*," and a spiritual and practical education given him by Sam Fathers. The rest of his education comes from "the wilderness and the bear itself." The first two kinds of education prepare him for his encounter with the bear. But when the moment comes for him to meet the bear, he has to set aside the aids on which he has relied: his gun, his watch, and his compass. When the time comes, the bear "shows himself, as in a theophany, like a god, to the boy." The boy's life, according to Cowan, "will be shaped by this experience, which would not have been possible for him without Sam's tale-telling and his coaching and drilling." Isaac's encounter with the bear is solitary; he must follow the bear into "strange and dangerous territory." This territory is the subject matter, according to Cowan, and it does not bend itself to the student. It requires that the student encounter something beyond the comfortable and familiar. It is "not tailored to his preferences . . . or his abilities; rather, he has to take in the material and have an openness to it. He has to accommodate himself to it, measure up to it."[23]

We may not serve students well by trying to match instruction to them exactly. The problems are compounded when computers do the matching. According to Lauren Resnick and Larry Berger, the assessments accompanying the Common Core State Standards will be frequent and customized, based on each student's needs. Aided by this "mass personalization process," teachers will not have to determine which tests to give their students; this will be decided automatically, and the results will guide their instruction.[24] If this means that each student has an individualized skill-building plan, this may affect the presentation of the subjects themselves. Teachers may be under pressure to teach to students' individual levels instead of presenting topics that encompass many levels.

Let us consider three examples of mass personalization in education: virtual learning, in which students may study from home at least part of the time and take courses online; the School of One, piloted in New York City, in which lesson plans are generated by software in response to classroom data; and mood-detecting learning software, which gives students hints and emotional encouragement as they try to complete a task. In all cases, the technology is supposed to bridge a gulf between the subject and the student—by giving students more options, tailoring the instruction to their levels and needs, giving teachers more data on student progress, and mitigating student frustration and boredom. This bridge is both the strength and weakness of such technology.

VIRTUAL LEARNING—THAT is, online and computer-based learning—has enthralled education reformers with its possibilities. In 2001, the National Association of State Boards of Education released a report titled *Any Time, Any Place, Any Path, Any Pace* (borrowing a slogan from the Florida Virtual School). It declared that virtual learning "will improve American education in valuable ways and should be universally implemented as soon as possible." Virtual learning can take a number of forms. In some cases, it replaces regular classroom schooling; in other cases, it supplements it or is combined with it in a "blended learning environment."[25] Some virtual schools and courses are public, some private; some include meetings in person, and some do not.

Because of virtual schools' variegated nature and their accessibility, proponents see endless potential in them. If students can attend classes virtually, from home, then school districts do not have to hunt for new buildings to relieve overcrowding. Advanced and struggling students alike would find their needs met; students interested in advanced chemistry could study it, while students needing remedial math could receive just the help they needed. School communities would not be confined to a geographical location; students could study with peers across the United States and even around the world. Students could receive online tutoring; teachers relieved of the physical classroom duties would have more time and energy for instruction. Supposedly everyone would have a place in such a system. But would it be a satisfactory place?

Journalists and proponents of virtual learning have cited the U.S. Department of Education's 2009 meta-study of online learning studies as evidence in favor of blended and online learning. The meta-study concludes that "students in online conditions performed modestly better, on average, than those learning the same material through traditional face-to-face instruction." It notes, furthermore, that "instruction combining online and face-to-face elements had a larger advantage relative to purely face-to-face instruction than did purely online instruction." However, the authors point out that such blended learning often included additional instructional time and that "the positive effects associated with blended learning should not be attributed to the media, per se." Moreover, this meta-study focuses largely on higher and specialized education, as there were few rigorous studies of K–12 online learning at the time of its writing. The researchers warn that while the findings may have implications for K–12 education, "caution is required in generalizing to the K–12 population because the results are derived for the most part from studies in other settings (e.g., medical training, higher education)."[26]

Despite these disclaimers, education secretary Arne Duncan cited the report as evidence that "effective teachers need to incorporate digital content into everyday classes and consider open-source learning management systems, which have proven cost effective in school districts and colleges nationwide." The Heritage Foundation cited the study in an article titled "How Online Learning Is Revolutionizing K–12 Education and Benefiting Students." The *New York Times* article about the study shows a picture of a nine-year-old searching the Web and boasts the headline "Study Finds That Online Education Beats the Classroom."[27] In their enthusiasm, these articles apply the study's conclusions to situations that lie outside its parameters. The press exaggerates and always will, but here the press has ignored, distorted, or skirted the study's disclaimers and caveats.

The euphoric headlines not only misrepresent the study but ignore some of the losses of online learning. Its drawbacks are especially pronounced for K–12 education, where students rely on adults for daily guidance. It would be hard to compensate, even in blended instruction systems, for the loss of face-to-face contact. It would be hard to protect students (and even districts) against scams or mediocre online programs. Some homes might not be good environments for learning; they might be loud, violent, or lacking in equipment and resources. The study environment could become lax and distracted; students might "attend" online class with the TV on, the cell phone flashing text messages, and the iPod playing. School districts would have to take extra measures to ensure that students were receiving appropriate instruction and taking responsibility for their studies. They might even engage in some form of surveillance (for instance, with webcams) to track down problems.

Virtual schools may well have something to offer to students with special needs and abilities; they may well supplement and strengthen the regular curriculum. But they must be handled with care; to this end, skepticism is not only helpful but essential. Yet proponents of virtual schools and virtual learning promote their cause with swaggering optimism, impugning the integrity of those who question them. In a 2002 paper published by the Center for Education Reform, Neal McCluskey writes that cyber charter schools "offer greater opportunities for the dissemination of knowledge than have ever existed before." He claims that critics of cyber charters are mainly concerned with control and money, not with serious educational matters.[28] Proponents' unwillingness to take critics' concerns seriously can only heighten the concerns.

In *Saving Schools: From Horace Mann to Virtual Learning*, Paul E. Peterson makes a curious case for virtual learning. He enumerates problems with the Florida Virtual School yet praises it as a harbinger of "disruptive innovation." The Florida Virtual School allows middle and high school students to complete their entire education online. The school's CEO, Julie Young, has stated her belief in "teaching *kids*, not teaching content"; not surprisingly, the two most popular courses in the Florida Virtual School are Life Management Skills and Health/Physical Education. There is little emphasis on books, according to Peterson; rather, the curriculum designers rewrite the material in a way that will appeal to the students. Florida Virtual does not receive funding when students fail a course, and only the Advanced Placement courses have externally proctored examinations. Thus there is plenty of incentive to pass students whether or not they have learned much.[29]

Yet, while admitting that "the Florida story gives no assurance that technology will transform American education," Peterson argues that "the *opportunity* to learn will be equalized." In Peterson's view, virtual learning has the potential to be transformative in ways that would have pleased Horace Mann, John Dewey, Martin Luther King Jr., Albert Shanker, James Coleman, and William Bennett. The strange part of his argument is his willingness to rely on the future, even in the face of shaky evidence. There are no guarantees that the benefits of online learning will outweigh the losses, or that it will be anything more than a temporary cost-cutter. In 2011, in Miami, many students walked into their classroom to discover that it was an "e-learning lab"—that there would be no teacher, only a lab facilitator.[30] These labs came as a response to a new law limiting class sizes; since the class size limit does not apply to labs, students could be placed in an enormous lab—hardly a palace, hardly a glorious future.

Those who are closest to the action may be less than euphoric about virtual schools. In February 2011, *GothamSchools* reported that principals in New York City were ambivalent about the pilot program iLearn, which is funding experiments with online learning in eighty New York City schools. According to some, this online learning program helps advanced but not struggling students, who need intensive instruction and support. But even those who praise the program bring up problems unwittingly. One principal said in the program's defense that "the children we have seem to be more facile at thumbing through an online text to go back and get notes than they are a book."[31] This very admission is unsettling. If students become unused to books, then literature will be lost to them, no matter how much is available online. Students may end up nimble at best—grabbing main ideas, bullet points, and conclusions, but missing the trickier aspects of language and arguments.

VIRTUAL SCHOOLS VARY widely; other forms of mass personalization take specific forms. The New York City Department of Education piloted the School of One in seven middle schools in the summer of 2009. This program, which currently focuses on mathematics, gives each child a daily schedule that changes according to his or her performance of the tasks and demonstrated mastery of skills. The mathematical skills are arranged in sequence; students move along at their own pace, working on computers in small groups, with virtual tutors, and with the teacher. A student's individual assignments may be tailored to his or her interests: a student who likes baseball may be given a problem with baseball statistics, or two students might compete in a video game that requires the use of arithmetic. The classrooms are redesigned to support various groupings; they are large, carpeted, open spaces with various work areas. At the start of the year, students take a "learning preferences" quiz and receive a "profile" of their learning styles. There are daily multiple-choice assessments as well as assessments at the end of each unit.

The system has three main components: student profiles, a "learning algorithm," and a bank of lesson plans. Every day, the computer gathers performance data, analyzes which skills each student has learned, generates a "playlist" and schedule for each student (based on his or her performance and learning profile), and selects lesson plans for the teachers. The teachers receive their lesson plans for the next day by eight in the evening.[32] Teachers may revise them, but since they receive new lesson plans each day, it might be difficult for them to plan a series of lessons or to alter the grouping dramatically. Since the algorithm takes the school's resources into account, one teacher's change to the lesson might throw off other teachers' planning. Thus it is likely that most teachers use the computer-generated lesson plans, with only minor edits.

The School of One has turned into a symbol of hope. *Time* magazine heralded the School of One as one of the top fifty inventions of 2009. Arthur E.

Levine, president of the Woodrow Wilson National Fellowship Foundation, praises the program for the promises it holds. "Today's schools are an anachronism," writes Levine. "They resemble the assembly lines of the industrial era, when they were conceived. . . . The School of One turns the current model of education on its head, flipping the relationship between teaching and learning. . . . It is the future." He points to the software's capacity to create individualized plans that allow students to "advance by mastery" in different modes of instruction—"small- and large-group instruction, peer tutoring, individual tutoring, asynchronous instruction, and independent study."[33] Levine fails to consider how this affects the very study of mathematics. What happens to the student's ability to see beyond the skill at hand? What happens to problems that come clear only over time, or that take on new meaning as students understand more? Do students get to struggle with problems "above level"? Do they return to problems they have encountered before? Do teachers have the opportunity to teach difficult concepts gradually? Levine does not raise these questions; he simply praises this harbinger of the future.

The School of One presumes that mathematics consists of a linear progression of skills. Certainly there is a progression in mathematics instruction, though it may vary from one curriculum to another. Certainly it is possible to identify what students should know about each concept, at least to a degree. But a great part of mathematics is synthesis: the conjoining of disparate concepts and parts. Euclid's *Elements* is presented in a linear fashion, but it could not be taught adequately through the School of One program. To understand Euclid's progressions, one must move back and forth often between the definitions, postulates, common notions, and propositions. One must not only comprehend each proposition but see how it follows from what came before as well as what it may imply. In other words, mathematics, like other subjects, involves frequent movement backward and forward to concepts learned before and not yet learned. It also involves turning concepts every which way in order to grasp them thoroughly.

There is yet another problem with the School of One. As students reach more advanced topics, it may become harder for them to progress on their own, and multiple-choice tests may become less and less appropriate for the topics. Students may need more extensive instruction and complex homework (instead of work in class). If students have grown used to computerized instruction, games, and playlists, they may struggle in courses where they are expected to pay attention to the teacher for extended intervals and do difficult work on their own.

Promising or not, the School of One is poised for expansion and media attention. In November 2010, News Corporation announced that it had signed an agreement to purchase 90 percent of Wireless Generation, the leading partner in the development of the School of One. Only two weeks earlier, New York City schools chancellor Joel Klein had announced that he would be leaving the Department of Education in order to accept a position of executive vice president at News Corporation, where he would lead the pursuit of business opportunities in the education marketplace.[34] With these developments, it appears likely that the School of One will remain a heavily promoted, proprietary program and that critics will have very little information about it. Without open-source code and a publicly available curriculum, there can be no public deliberation over the program's merits and drawbacks. In such circumstances, skeptics must continue to raise questions, even in vain, even from underground, even alone. The point is not to deny the merits of the program but to make room for questions and doubts, even when no room exists. The mind has room, after all, when the media do not.

FOR SOME, THE ultimate dream is to meet students' needs through software—not only their intellectual needs, but their emotional needs as well. Researchers around the world have been developing software with "affect-aware tutors," that is, animated characters that respond to the users' mood. In one ongoing project, teams of researchers at Massachusetts Institute of Technology (MIT), Arizona State University, and the University of Massachusetts, Amherst, have been investigating how technology can use emotion-sensing devices to help students stay focused and motivated.

The researchers have conducted experiments that integrate emotion-sensing hardware with Wayang Outpost, a multimedia tutoring system for high school geometry and algebra. When the hardware detects a negative emotion, an "intelligent tutor" (i.e., a cartoon character) may intervene with empathetic comments and suggestions. The ultimate goal is to help students out of negative learning experiences and thus boost their performance. The researchers—Beverly Woolf, Winslow Burleson, Ivon Arroyo, Toby Dragon, David Cooper, and Rosalind Picard—acknowledge that "no comprehensive, validated, theory of emotion exists that addresses learning, explains which emotions are most important in learning, or identifies how emotion influences learning." Yet they state that "research shows that efforts to build models of a less understood phenomenon will aid in improving the understanding of that very phenomenon."[35] In other words, they are conducting psychological experiments as they develop the software.

The researchers used three approaches: human observation, hardware sensors, and machine learning techniques (self-improving algorithms). They began with the premise, based on the work of Mihaly Csikszentmihalyi, that there are two basic categories of learning experience: "flow," the optimal experience, where the student is focused and in control, and "stuck," the non-optimal experience, where the student is frustrated, out of control, fatigued, or bored. They broke down these categories into combinations of positive or negative emotion (valence), high or low arousal (physical excitement), and "on-task" or "off-task" activity. They then drew connections between these behaviors and students' emotional states. Realizing that emotional states in themselves might not correlate strongly with student performance, the researchers also considered whether or not the student was focusing on the task. Thus, the "highly desirable" states involved (a) positive valence, high arousal, and on-task activity, or (b) positive valence, low arousal, and on-task activity.[36]

The observers entered classes and labeled students' behaviors according to the prearranged categories. From there, the researchers looked for connections between behavior and performance. They found many correlations: for instance, between positive valence and pretest mathematics score (suggesting that those who were already good at mathematics were likelier to experience positive emotions while using the software).[37] The goal from here was to detect students' behavior through sensors and use animated characters to direct them to a more positive state.

The sensors are intended to detect students' emotions or "affect." Developed at MIT and Arizona State University, they consist of a camera, posture analysis seat sensor, pressure mouse sensor, and skin conductance sensor. The "mental state camera" picks up on "head nod and shake behaviors, blinking, pupil dilation, mouth fidgets and smiles." The "pressure sensitive chair" detects the student's posture; the "pressure sensitive mouse" detects the student's hand pressure (and, supposedly, level of frustration). The "skin conductance bracelet" measures the skin's electrical conductance.[38] The hardware reads the student's behavior and transmits the data to a database.

The researchers developed animated characters that would "mirror" the student's emotion when appropriate and respond with encouragement or suggestions. For instance, if the student showed signs of frustration, the animated character might assume a facial expression of concern and say, "That was frustrating. Let's move to something easier." Then it would ask, "Would you like to choose the next problem? What kind of problem would you like?" The researchers have begun experimenting with animated characters whose cultural and ethnic "background" matches that of the user. They continue to refine the program so that the character's words will have the desired effect. They claim that the students who use the software not only perform better on tests but have a more positive attitude about mathematics than they did before.[39]

There is some nuance in the researchers' arguments. They acknowledge, for instance, that "labelling emotional states as desirable or undesirable is problematic as often an undesirable state of confusion precedes learning gains, thus making it a desirable state pedagogically."[40] Yet they seem to ignore some of their own wisdom. They express hope that the cartoons will go beyond responding to students' moods and actually influence students' behavior: "We propose that the tutor will identify desirable (e.g. flow) and non-desirable (e.g. boredom) student states. Different interventions will be tested in an attempt to keep students in desirable states as much as possible (e.g. a confused student might be invited to slow down, reread the problem and ask for a hint)."[41] Why is it desirable to steer a student's behavior at every moment?

This "intelligent tutor" technology leaves many more questions unaddressed. Does one learn mathematics best by staring at a computer screen in the first place? The researchers state that the act of looking away from the screen correlates with negative feelings. "It is possible," they write, "that students avoid the computer screen when they do not feel good about the software or the learning situation."[42] Yet it is also possible that the students turn away in order to think. A student's negative emotion could reflect on the difficulty of the problem, not his or her desire to learn the material. Also, an "empathetic" tutor may not even be enjoyable, let alone helpful. Some students might find themselves annoyed with the empathy; some might want an instructor who focuses on the subject, not on their feelings. Some might get nervous about a cartoon's impending appearance and thereby bring it on.

The greatest promise of the software is also its greatest danger. The researchers hope to prevent students from getting "stuck" in their work. Ultimately, with such software, all students should be in a state of "flow," all or most of the time. But the researchers themselves have acknowledged the role of confusion and frustration in learning. Is it good for students to have a cartoon or anything else respond to their fluctuations in mood? Is there not some value in leaving them alone to struggle with the material? The more complex the math problems become, the higher the likelihood of frustration along the way. Moreover, there is value in living with frustration, working on something without finding an answer, and persevering. The researchers' desired scenario, where students would experience more positive emotion and less frustration, may have severe consequences. Perhaps one day we will all have personal coaches in our pockets, telling us when our behavior is going off track and proffering empathetic cartoons when we show signs of sadness. Soon no one will have an excuse to be in an "undesirable state." Like antidepressants, these devices will leave no room for a bad mood, since a device will be there to fix it on the spot.

This is where the Underground Man would rear up and say, I do not care what your software does for my achievement or my attitude. I refuse to be part of your perfect world where everyone is flow-minded. If I am bored, let me be bored. If I am frustrated, then frustrated. If I fail, it is my right to fail. It is my right to be ugly, awkward, angry. I want no part in this solution, even if you insist it would be good for me, even if you are right. Why? Because I have the right to say no.

IT WOULD BE FOOLISH to take the Underground Man too seriously; he does not take himself seriously. Just when we think we understand him, he slips away from us, contradicting himself, defeating his arguments, and cackling through it all. There is something relieving and disturbing in his growl; having read *Notes from Underground*, one starts to hear him everywhere. He is not policy or platform; he is anything but a talking point. But somewhere in the midst of this grim play, Dostoevsky raises unsettling questions. How does one stand up to those who are sure of their solutions? How does one point out the flaws in those solutions without condemning oneself to isolation or ridicule? How can one strive for a better life while steering clear of facile formulas? How does one confront the uncomfortable world, instead of groaning underground? How does one uphold and pursue good things while retaining some humility (which the Underground Man lacks)? The Underground Man seethes on, and it is good that he seethes; still we must go out and face difficulty. *Notes from Underground* may guide us, indirectly, if we do not take it as a guide—if we allow it its life and ourselves our own.

Taken down a notch, personalized technology has many uses. It can give students practice with specific skills. It can gather information, limited as it may be, on what students have and haven't learned. But we must have access to it—the underlying code as well as the resources. If we have no idea what reasoning and ideas went into the software, then we fall prey to marketing pitches, shibboleths, and bromides. Schools will buy software with hopes that it will bring them into the future, whatever that might be. Precisely because so few understand new technology, it arouses utopian excitement and paranoid fear, but not intelligent criticism. We must take the path of intelligent criticism. We must deepen our knowledge of mathematics and computer programming, in conjunction with humanities, so that we are not simply end users. We must demand that education products be made available for public scrutiny and discussion. We must consider their benefits and dangers, their implications, and their future developments. Such discerning judgment navigates between the cynicism of the Underground and the hyperbole of the Crystal Palace.

If we were to have an international exhibition today, it might be in a large space with many booths. Each company would have its own demo; visitors might sit down, don the headphones, seize the mouse, and enter a personalized virtual world. Perhaps their facial expressions would be read and interpreted; perhaps the computer would give them back their very selves, as it perceived them. Perhaps they would see animated characters in their own likeness crossing their favorite landscape or helping them solve a problem. They might be able to direct the character's actions with their thoughts alone. In a certain sense this is a lonely scenario: each person in his or her customized world, which can be perfected over time. Yet no one in such a world is left alone: the program nestles up close to us and responds to our gestures and thoughts. There is no room to be puzzled or baffled; to dislike something; to spend a day in a strange mood, between cheer and melancholy; or to keep much to oneself. Our screens become a world where nothing is at odds with us and nothing is very hard.

That is not the kind of world I want. I want to walk among people who know nothing about me, so that I may come to know someone slowly or catch someone's eye in passing. I want a maple tree that changes according to the time of year but not according to my whims and moods; a sea that laps its own irregular rhythms, not for me in particular; a language I cannot understand; an unassisted Internet search, perhaps without results; an instrument I practice without the cajoling of cartoons; the crash of thunder and downpour when I am out on a walk; and a dear friend I miss but cannot bring to my side at will.

9

~

The Need for Loneliness

Solitude has a ferocious aspect at times. It rips up its clothes; it drenches pillows with brine. It takes out its paintbrushes and daubs the stars with red, then tosses the brushes aside. It stumbles on the floor's cracks and nails; it argues with the shadows, fist against fist. It shivers and shudders; it spits on its own diary, crosses out words, and rewrites the same ones in smudged hand. It sleeps and sleeps to get rid of the hours, then wails over hours gone by. It runs from its shadow and into its own image, in a mirrorless room. It tears screaming out the door; the neighbors lock their doors and pull their shades. Who wants this ugly thing—solitude? Why sing the virtues of a thing that has no virtue at all, no strength, no will, only bruised elbows and a burning throat? A great part of solitude is lonely, and in loneliness something is missing or amiss.

Loneliness is not the only trouble with solitude, of course—there are obsessions, uncontrolled thoughts, despondencies, and many other extremes of mind and passion—but loneliness affects us all, sometimes more than we wish to admit. Who has not, on any given day, wished for a good talk with a friend, or a game of Ping-Pong or whatever it might be? Even those whose lives pass in company are waiting for the real connection, the credible gleam. The psychiatrist hopes for the breakthrough, not only for the patient's good, but for her own. The cabdriver gives his number to a friendly passenger, knowing she probably won't call, but thinking just maybe she will. The worker at a coffee stand looks forward to the slight lull when he can talk with the customers. Once in a while, when he feels comfortable, he starts to tell someone about his life in Afghanistan and his reasons for coming to America. But then the customer stammers that she has to be going, she's late for work, and he sets himself to arranging the donuts and pastries again.

Some assert that solitude and loneliness are two different things: that solitude is full and contented; loneliness, lacking and needy. Examining solitude in schools, psychology professor Evangelia Galanaki distinguishes between solitude, "beneficial aloneness," and loneliness, "painful aloneness." Sherry Turkle goes so far as to call loneliness "failed solitude."[1] But solitude and loneliness overlap; each can be found in the other. Even the most contented solitude contains an ache, and even the most painful loneliness has room for insight and shaping. This is how it must be; we must struggle a bit in order to know ourselves and the world. We tend to regard loneliness as a disease or aberration, simply because it is painful—but the pain of a thing does not mean it should be taken away. Without loneliness, there would be no need to wait for anything kindred or recognize it when it came along.

To say loneliness has a place is not to say it belongs on the throne. In his essay "No Door" (1935), Thomas Wolfe writes, "For you are what you are, you know what you know, and there are no words for loneliness, black, bitter, aching loneliness, that gnaws the roots of silence in the night."[2] Our lonelinesses today have less of that silence and outdoor sound, as more and more people rely on digital communication. Wolfe heard loneliness in the conversations between neighbors; we hear it, muted, in the patter of keys on the keyboard, in the click of the mouse. On the one hand, we have more resources at our disposal than people did eighty years ago; on the other, many of these resources are unreliable and disposable. Invisible strangers often do not give us what we need, yet we depend on them, often to our embarrassment. There is an unspoken message, even as we rely on digital communication, that those who *really* depend on it (emotionally and otherwise) have a problem. We are all supposed to "have a life," even when tethered to our screens and jobs.

Yet this gnawing, troubling, pervasive loneliness shapes our actions. There is something wrong about loneliness, but the wrongness is not a blip on a screen; it is everywhere, part of everyone. It fills our understanding of ourselves and others. In his sermon "You Are Accepted," published in 1948, Paul Tillich states boldly that "sin is separation." Not only that, but this separation is our very existence, beginning before our birth and continuing beyond our death. He calls on the listener to think of sin—and its inherent separation—not as a moral wrong, or as the opposite of righteousness, but as our "fate *and* guilt." We cannot escape it or rectify it, but we can know grace, which comes to us precisely because of our sin.[3]

His statement seems to topple the very premise of this book. If sin is separation, how could one possibly argue for solitude? But Tillich does not say that separation is sin; he says that sin is separation. That is, he does not say that we do something wrong when we separate ourselves. Rather, he says that our lives are made of rupture. There is no way to escape or mitigate it; it is there whether we wish it c∴ not, from our birth until our death. But it is this very rupture that provides the occasion for a crossing. There could be no grace, Tillich writes, without this fundamental separation: "For sin and grace are bound to each other. We do not even have a knowledge of sin unless we have already experienced the unity of life, which is grace. And conversely, we could not grasp the meaning of grace without having experienced the separation of life, which is sin."[4]

In secular terms, this means that if our separateness is a flaw, it is inherent in human existence and a precondition for connection with others. How bland! Though not religious in any formal sense, I would rather say "sin is separation," as Tillich did. Tillich found all substitutions for these words unsatisfying; he said that "there is a mysterious fact about the great words of our religious tradition: they cannot be replaced."[5] Tillich was right: there are no replacements for "sin" and "grace," but to discuss Tillich in secular terms, one must rely on some translation. Secular language is the cross that a secular culture must bear.

What is grace, in secular language? Again, any translation is crude—but it might be something like an unexpected crossing, something apprehended from far away. It is an understanding that comes to us by surprise, a knowledge of being heard and answered, or even none of this, but a quiet that suddenly becomes not only bearable, but sweet. Such grace would not be possible unless we were indeed separate and suffering from the separation.

It is strange to defend loneliness. It is painful; it seems a hindrance. No one wants it—or, at least, so we believe fervently. Loneliness has been one of the most difficult and persistent aspects of my life; I could fill this book with stories of loneliness. But the most interesting ones would not be directly autobiographical; to get at loneliness, one cannot be literal, as loneliness itself is not literal. To say that this or that event made me lonely or that I had some quality that isolated me from others—this may be true, but it is rather humdrum. Loneliness need not be invoked by its own name; it is found in things that do not call themselves lonely. The genius of Wordsworth's "I wandered lonely as a Cloud" is that the loneliness of the cloud is not known until it appears in those words.

Rid ourselves of loneliness, and it is unclear what would be left, if anything. Wolfe writes that loneliness, "far from being a rare and curious phenomenon, peculiar to myself and to a few other solitary men, is the central and inevitable fact of human existence."[6] Loneliness is as basic as the cat wandering in the woods in search of his lost sibling, or the dog waiting anxiously outside the store. Growing up is filled with loneliness: there comes a day when we can walk without holding someone's hand, or read a story on our own. It is strange that we seek to push loneliness away, cure it, hide it, turn it into jargon, or otherwise rid ourselves of it. It can bring agony and shame; it can seem too much to bear. But once we build the strength to hold it and know it, it becomes many things, like the pariah who turns out to have beautiful eyes and who knows a thing or two about ships.

Loneliness is somewhat like the three-dimensional manifold mentioned in the seventh chapter. Donal O'Shea explains this manifold by comparing it to the space inside a transparent shoe box, where the region around any point is a space, not a surface.[7] Loneliness, likewise, has space in all directions. It is like the ice in Gabriel García Márquez's One Hundred Years of Solitude: "an enormous, transparent block with infinite internal needles in which the light of the sunset was broken up into colored stars."[8] Loneliness is so many things at once that we often don't know where to go with it, yet we feel that we must go somewhere. It carries a sense of wrongness, but this wrongness can take many forms.

Without loneliness, there would be no motion of the spirit. Sometimes loneliness contains a paradox: the thing we long for is actually present but concealed. In those cases, loneliness may call us into closer listening and observation. We find, through the loneliness, the very thing we thought we lacked, and sometimes much more. Sometimes there is no culprit; the loneliness is simply there, without answers or escapes. Sometimes this comes from a fixed condition, sometimes from a loss. It may take the form of grief. The most common kind of loneliness seems temporary; it seems to be caused by a minor defect in ourselves, in another person, or in the world. It seems fixable: all we need to do, supposedly, is repair, work around, or ignore the defect. But the fixing makes its own royal mess.

LET US LOOK first at loneliness as desire. The suffix -ly in lonely suggests a semblance; it derives from the Old English lic, meaning "a body, dead or living," and ge-lic, meaning "having the same body or form."[9] A lonely person is "like someone who is alone"—that is, somewhere in between aloneness and non-aloneness. In that intermediary state, there is room for movement; such movement requires either an external force or longing. What is this longing? It pulls us from one place to another; it helps us see something that we want to know or become. The longing, therefore, contains both a lack and a presence. We are aware of our own lack and need, but we also perceive that needed person or thing, even dimly. We may retreat, move closer, move around in orbit, or even stay still, but in any case we are responding to the pull. This longing is everywhere: in our appetites, games, greetings, and gestures. It is often the unspoken part of things: to say "I want" may seem too direct, so we show it in other ways.

Julio Cortázar's story "Final del juego" (End of the Game) shows such longing hidden in a children's ritual. Three girls—two sisters and a cousin—meet in secret by the train tracks, their "kingdom," every day, while the mother and aunt are resting. Once they have escaped to the tracks, they draw lots; the winner then assumes the pose of a statue or an attitude. If it is a statue, the other two dress her up in ornaments from a special ornament box; if it is an attitude, no ornaments are required, but expressiveness is needed in great quantity. Leticia, the cousin, is partially paralyzed, and capable of "gestures of enormous nobility"; she does particularly well as both statue and attitude.[10]

The ending (not to be disclosed here) makes the reader wonder just where the game began to end, or whether the ending was there from the very start. It seems that the game depends on a secret that is broken and that would have been broken, in some way, no matter what. We do not learn what the secret is. Maybe it is desire, maybe loneliness, maybe Leticia's illness, maybe some other human state or limitation. It is possible that this breaking is contained in the game all along and gives it its meaning. The sparkling granite, the regal poses, the clandestine jewels allow for a shimmering episode in the girls' lives, precisely because they are part of a ritual that cannot last. One could think of it not only as the end of a game, but as the game of the end, the game that is the end. Somehow ending and game are bound together.

Imagination may require a degree of loneliness. In *Solitude: A Return to the Self*, Anthony Storr writes that "man's extraordinary success as a species springs from his discontent, which compels him to employ his imagination." He argues that creativity is the bridge between inner imagination and outer reality—and that it relies on a gap between the two. Some may do a better job of bridging the gap than others, for a variety of reasons, but both the gap and the desire to bridge it are part of artistic and scientific work and part of children's play.[11] One could define loneliness (at least partially) as the awareness of the gap and the desire to bridge it. But the imagination does more than bridge gaps; it also creates illusions, deceptions, and masks. Loneliness contains the desire to withhold as well as the desire to reveal—for the revelation must not be cheap. Emily Dickinson writes, "Tell all the Truth but tell it slant"; this very "slant" contains loneliness, as it requires that the message not be conveyed directly.[12] That is, to be understood, one must be willing to risk misunderstanding.

Through its very pull, loneliness involves the outside world; even in its bleakest forms, it contains hidden answers to itself. One finds such paradoxical loneliness in E. B. White's *Charlotte's Web*, a wise and beautiful tale of loneliness and friendship. At one point in the story, Wilbur finds himself lonely. He goes from animal to animal, asking each one, "Will you come over and play with me?" or "Will you please play with me?" or "Will you play with me?" Each one refuses, and Wilbur eventually succumbs to sobbing. It seems an unbearable situation; nothing makes it better, not even his breakfast, which he leaves untouched all day.

But this sobbing eventually leads into quiet, and in this quiet there are specific sounds, ordinary but calming. The sobs no longer drown out everything else; in fact, the darker it gets, the finer are the sounds he hears, right up to the voice of his friend-to-be, the spider Charlotte.

> Darkness settled over everything. Soon there were only shadows and the noises of the sheep chewing their cuds, and occasionally the rattle of a cow-chain up overhead. You can imagine Wilbur's surprise when, out of the darkness, came a small voice he had never heard before. It sounded rather thin, but pleasant. "Do you want a friend, Wilbur?" it said. "I'll be a friend to you. I've watched you all day and I like you."[13]

Charlotte was there all along, but Wilbur probably would not have heard her voice if he had ended up frolicking with one of the other animals. Moreover, Charlotte addresses him here because she knows he wants a friend. Had he not wished so badly for one, she might have kept to herself. Charlotte has her own loneliness, which stays hidden until the end of her life; after she has saved Wilbur's life and brought him to glory, after Wilbur has carefully taken her eggs away from the fair so that her children may hatch at home in the barn, after the fair is over and the grounds deserted, she dies alone. What she contains in her last moments, no one knows.

Loneliness, then, may hold a hidden companionship, but such companionship does not stop the loneliness. There is a part of loneliness that refuses to be pat. Many people spend their lives feeling awkward, out of place, unloved, without having done anything to deserve such isolation. Many are given more than a fair share of loneliness; they may be born with a disability, lose their family in a catastrophe, or suffer humiliation and oppression. Many live as outcasts and endure ostracism, rumors, and attacks. Some live their lives unknown except to a few. Charlotte is not unhappy, it seems; she does her good work for Wilbur and catches flies, and that is enough. She may have her secret unhappiness, but she does not let it show. But few are as lucid and resourceful as Charlotte. If told to endure the loneliness, someone might legitimately respond, "But just how long am I expected to endure this? How long can anyone endure this?"

In his sermon "Waiting," Tillich writes that waiting "means *not* having and having at the same time." We are waiting for something we do not have, but our very waiting for it signals that we know it is there and therefore have it. The first part, the *not* having, is essential, he says, for if we focus only on the having, we are creating an image of God in our minds. "I am convinced," Tillich writes, "that much of the rebellion against Christianity is due to the overt or veiled claim of the Christians to possess God, and therefore, also, to the loss of this element of waiting, so decisive for the prophets and the apostles." He reminds the listener that "waiting is a tremendous tension. It precludes all complacency about having nothing, indifference or cynical contempt towards those who have something, and indulgence in doubt and despair."[14] Loneliness, too, is a "tremendous tension." It requires both stillness and willingness to act. It is both of our own making and made for us, both awful and hopeful, both singular and communal.

Much loneliness is vague: a sense of something missing, but little knowledge of what or who it might be. There are also sharper, more specific kinds, such as when we miss someone whom we can't bring back, or wish to repair a mistake and cannot. We often call such loneliness grief. Such loneliness can rise up and rattle all our assembled meanings and purposes; the one whom we counted here is gone, and nothing makes this right. It rages and calms in its own time, and sometimes rises up again after the calming. No one but the sufferer knows what it is like. And yet, at some point, this grief joins a larger grief, the grief that everyone knows at some time or another. It is this joining that allows Priam and Achilles to weep together at the end of the *Iliad*; it is this joining that allows Tommy Wilhelm in Saul Bellow's *Seize the Day* to attend a stranger's funeral and sob his heart out. In that sense, grief carries its own paradox. It forces each of us into complete aloneness, yet eventually we see a similar aloneness in others. We come to see our loss as intensely singular and yet not singular at all. Sometimes we even see how mild our losses have been compared to others' losses—though, when it comes to loss, nothing is mild, not even the loss of leaves on trees.

In Gerard Manley Hopkins's poem "Spring and Fall: To a Young Child," loneliness is both slow and brief—wrapped up brilliantly in a very short poem, but long and lingering.[15] The poem creates a young girl Margaret grieving "over Goldengrove unleaving." All we know, or think we know, is that she is watching this "unleaving" and grieving over it in some way, maybe crying. An older and wiser speaker addresses her, telling her that her grief is common to all, "the blight man was born for," and that it is herself that Margaret mourns. This is the poem in full:

> Márgarét, áre you grieving
> Over Goldengrove unleaving?
> Leáves, líke the things of man, you
> With your fresh thoughts care for, can you?
> Áh! ás the heart grows older
> It will come to such sights colder
> By and by, nor spare a sigh
> Though worlds of wanwood leafmeal lie;
> And yet you wíll weep and know why.
> Now no matter, child, the name:
> Sórrow's spríngs áre the same.
> Nor mouth had, no nor mind, expressed
> What heart heard of, ghost guessed:
> It ís the blight man was born for,
> It is Margaret you mourn for.

This speaker comes to Margaret's "fresh thoughts" with wonder and weariness: he asks her, "Leáves, like the things of man, you / With your fresh heart care for, can you?" In those lines one can hear the leaves falling and the branches creaking. Here is a girl in sorrow over the "unleaving" of "Goldengrove"—which already is more than falling leaves alone. In it we sense the end of a beloved world, the end of childhood, the end of a grove as Margaret has known it. The speaker, though hardened to such losses, sees their dignity and seriousness; he recognizes that this has no name, that "Sórrow's spríngs áre the same."

Throughout the poem, one senses that Margaret is not alone—that there is another presence, besides her and the speaker. This comes across through the insistent pairs (and sometimes triplets) of alliterating words or phrases: "grieving/Goldengrove," "care for/can you," "such sights," "By and by," "spare a sigh," "worlds of wanwood," "leafmeal lie," "wíll weep and know why," "Now no/name," "Sórrow's spríngs are the same," "Nor mouth/no nor mind," "heart heard of," "ghost guessed," "Margaret/mourn." Similarly, over the course of the poem, one grief is paired with another: leaves are paired with the "things of man," and grieving Margaret with Margaret who will one day die.

If one reads the poem slowly, one hears in it a world of innocence and experience, of strangeness and familiarity, of coldness and tenderness, of immediacy and eternity, all under the trees in fall. Here is a girl, weeping alone over the falling things and, without knowing it, for herself; here is the absence of the girl, as we don't really know what she is doing; here is an adult telling her that her grieving is "what heart heard of, ghost guessed." Thus in this grieving there is company—the company of the Margaret being grieved, the company of the speaker, the company of our imagination, and the company of all sorrow, ghostly and alive. Yet the company makes the loss even more profound; the presences are a reminder of what will be taken away.

These are big lonelinesses: the paradoxical loneliness that contains company, and the grief that is private but part of all grief. They contrast with everyday loneliness, which is weak and overpowering at once. This is the loneliness of not quite fitting in, of feeling rejected, of having no good friends nearby or of not feeling satisfied around friends. It is the loneliness of being without a partner or of being unhappy with one's partner. It is the loneliness of separation from family, even (or especially) during family gatherings. It seems in these situations that something can and should be *done* about it, and often that is the case. But there is a trap in the doing: one can come to believe that loneliness should never be, that it should be fixed instantly. This is not so; no matter what we do, the loneliness resurges in some form, and sometimes there is good in it. In fact, we are sometimes crippled by the notion that we mustn't be lonely—for when it does come, it seems shameful, and the shame is worse than the loneliness itself.

Loneliness can spring from the very feeling that we should not be lonely. In *The Lonely American*, Jacqueline Olds and Richard S. Schwartz argue that Americans retreat into themselves not only because they are overwhelmed by the demands of modern life, but because they believe in the American ideal of self-reliance and nonconformity. They think they *should* be able to live without needing others—and so, when they feel lonely, they retreat still more. The authors write that the ideal of the independent outsider "exerts a powerful pull, shaping the stories we want to tell about ourselves and directing the choices we make in order to live out those stories." Often these "outsider-hero-myths" surround us without our knowing it; they "operate in the background, just out of view, making people feel uneasy when they fall short." We are plagued not only by our busy lives, but by our sense that we should not need community, except for an imaginary community of heroes.[16]

The problem here is not loneliness, but the very rejection of loneliness. Loneliness becomes all the more overwhelming because it has no place. The person who denies his need for others is not so different from the one who seeks to gratify his need for others instantly. Loneliness is the range in between, the rough expanse where things are not quite right, cannot be quite right, and indeed would lose something if they were quite right. This expanse is a necessary space; with a little roaming (not too much), we may start to find our way around.

This is not to say that we should be complacent about current forms of loneliness. It is hard to measure its rise and fall, but certain kinds of loneliness have grown more acute over the past fifty years. More adults live alone today than ever before in U.S. history; at the same time, institutions that support friendliness, charity, and a sense of community (such as religious institutions) have grown weaker. Still, loneliness is hard to track down; according to Olds and Schwartz, people are often ashamed to admit they are lonely, even to their therapists. Therapists themselves have difficulty admitting to loneliness; their profession demands that they conceal it to some degree. In *Welcome to My Country*, Lauren Slater writes of the contradictory messages that psychologists in training receive. On the one hand, they are supposed to bare their emotional secrets so that they can better understand those of their patients; on the other, they are supposed to keep such emotion within limits, maintaining a distinction between "us" and "them" and using jargon to mark their privilege.[17]

We may exacerbate loneliness by trying to get rid of it. John T. Cacioppo, a research psychologist at the University of Chicago, argues that loneliness serves an evolutionary purpose: it has helped our survival as a species by alerting us to the need for connection with others. It becomes a serious problem "only when it settles in long enough to create a persistent, self-reinforcing loop of negative thoughts, sensations, and behaviors."[18] But that "persistent, self-reinforcing loop" can result from unwillingness to face it. What does it mean to do something about loneliness? It need not mean rushing to act; it need not mean quelling the loneliness at all costs. Such impulsive action can lead us right back into the loneliness, the way a scared child runs down one path and another at the county fair, only to end up once again at the haunted tent with the glowing eyeballs and rumbling laugh.

Loneliness has given rise to numerous online dating and networking services, which seem to take away the need ever to be lonely again. Yet we remain doggedly lonely. The sheer multitude of antidotes can make it more upsetting still. One quick fix is "speed dating," in which each participant goes through a series of "dates" that may last no more than five minutes. At the end of a speed-dating event (usually held in a particular place), each person submits a list of people with whom he or she would like further contact. A similar practice is "Chatroulette," a game where players encounter randomly selected strangers online, with audio and video feeds. If they don't want to interact with someone anymore, they just hit "next" (a practice known as "nexting").[19] These activities are extreme variants of much more common antidotes, such as online dating and overscheduling. Frequent metaphorical references to speed dating suggest that there is more to it than the specific practice. We have learned to escape disappointment by moving on from it very fast, yet the rapid motion and changing stimuli almost guarantee disappointment from the start.

A recent study suggests, not surprisingly, that speed daters often find the variety of options confusing and are unable to make good choices in the limited time frame. The disappointments of automatic and guaranteed company are not just human letdowns; there is something subhuman about such activity, a trivialization of contact. There is humiliation in this incessant availability that contains no warmth, no true connection. Up for grabs, speed daters reduce themselves to grabbing, as though they were little more than dresses and jackets at a flea market. Even in milder forms of online dating, people come to see themselves as marketable products. The dating columnist April Masini advises readers to repost their profiles if they aren't getting responses. "Like real estate," she writes, "if a property is on the market too long, people assume there's something wrong with it."[20] Dating has always had attributes of a market, but its online forms take the market to extremes, as people present themselves in any way they wish, sometimes as multiple personae, and must be ever responsive to the reactions of invisible strangers.

But real-life human contact is not always the cure; it can be alienating as well, especially when it goes against what we are hoping and longing for. Tillich asks, "Who has not, at some time, been lonely in the midst of a social event? The feeling of our separation from the rest of life is most acute when we are surrounded by it in noise and talk. We realize then much more than in moments of solitude how strange we are to each other, how estranged life is from life."[21] One can surround oneself with people, but even the closest of them can seem like strangers at times. Yet we are seduced by the idea of company; we think that maybe this time it will click, that there is a secret to it all, within our grasp.

In Flannery O'Connor's novel *Wise Blood*, Enoch Emery joins a long line of children waiting to shake hands with a gorilla, who finally arrives in a black truck and is led out on a chain. At first frightened, the children advance one by one to shake hands with him. When Enoch's turn comes, the gorilla takes his hand with "an automatic motion"; it is the first hand that has reached out to Enoch since he moved to the city. He starts to stammer and mumble things about himself; then he sees two human eyes behind the gorilla eyes and hears a voice telling him to go to hell. Later he returns to the truck, slips inside the van, and manages to wrest the gorilla costume away from its wearer. He changes into the costume in a pine grove, and starts to beat his chest and let out "low and poisonous" growls. He practices extending his hand and shaking a nonexistent hand (in O'Connor's words, he "clutched nothing, and shook"). Happy as can be, he heads back for the highway, ready, one presumes, for a long series of handshakes. But when a man and a woman catch sight of him, the man disappears into the woods, and the woman runs away screaming. There is a stark and comic epiphany here. The formula for human contact did not work; it ended up scaring people away, because it was fundamentally scary.[22]

When trying to cure loneliness, one may flit from cure to cure, not dedicating oneself to any of them. "I have tried everything, and I'm still lonely!" the exasperated patient tells the psychiatrist. But part of the problem may lie in the restlessness of "trying everything." The one who tried joining a church, tried going to the gym, tried online dating, tried volunteer work, tried spending time alone, tried spending time with family, tried to go to parties, tried getting a haircut and buying new shoes, tried meeting people through Facebook, tried quitting Facebook, has not tried much at all. To say one "tried" something is often the same as saying that one gave up on it. One may even develop a habit of giving up.

WHAT, THEN, DOES a person do with loneliness? What can adults do to help children understand it better? How can adults grapple with it better themselves?

There is no good answer to this, as loneliness takes so many directions and forms. Just as one can become too pat about waiting, one can also latch onto some comforting maxim about loneliness—about how it passes, or how there's good in it, or how it makes one stronger, or something along those lines. Comforting maxims are not the point. To a degree they are dishonest, and they ignore loneliness's rough ground. If the answer to loneliness were somewhere out there, most of us would don our adventure gear (whatever that might be) and go out to find it. But you can experience loneliness when sitting with your spouse by the fire. You can find it in a kitchen amid boisterous chefs, on stage in a play you have rehearsed for months, or at a graduation where everyone is cheering and taking pictures. You may experience it in moments of honor. One of my most severe attacks of loneliness came during the performance, in college, of a short semi-autobiographical scene I had written. The person playing "me" performed beautifully, as did the one playing my cello teacher. I had watched the rehearsals with admiration; the performance should have been an occasion for pride. But instead I was bewildered by the applause for something that seemed unlike me, that seemed not to come from me. Over time, I learned that this was to be expected, that a performance takes on its own life. I did not fully understand this at the time.

It takes time to sort out loneliness, to come to know it like a xylophone: its different tones, its mallets, its pounding and rippling. For young people, loneliness seems a crack of thunder, an alarm. But over time, some tones may seem softer than others, and some lonelinesses more bearable, some even enjoyable. Sometimes loneliness may bring up a thought of a friend. Sometimes it brings to mind a favorite piece of music or a passage from a story. It may pull a person out the door and into the street. It may fade and then return. Sometimes lonely times seem peculiarly happy in retrospect, because there was so much desire in them, so many vivid sounds and faces. Sometimes they have forced us to confront ourselves. Sometimes what we take for loneliness is not loneliness at all; it is a restlessness of conscience, which calls for time alone, not company.

It takes many years to learn these distinctions. In childhood, loneliness may seem a curse. Children look wistfully across the playground at their peers, who are laughing with friends and not letting others join them. Some find, over and over, that they are the last to be picked for teams. Many suffer from bullying; some become bullies so as not to be bullied. Unlike adults who know that loneliness is everywhere, children may believe that they alone are lonely and unhappy. Not having lived long enough to see loneliness change form, they think the form they know is the only form and that it will never go away. Or they may think the opposite: that it will go away immediately if they can just get through to someone. Turkle describes a high school student who sends text messages to her friends whenever she has an "emergency"— that is, whenever she is experiencing a strong emotion that she cannot share right away.[23]

Not all children avoid being alone, however; not all feel compelled to send text messages every few minutes. A study by Galanaki suggests that children are able to distinguish between aloneness and loneliness, and the percentage of children able to make this distinction increases with age. Many of the children in the study recognized that one is not necessarily lonely when alone; one may have things to think about, things to do, or imaginary companions. A substantial percentage—again, increasing with age—answered, when asked, that loneliness itself was not always a bad thing. As for solitude ("beneficial aloneness," in Galanaki's definition), seven-year-olds had difficulty understanding the concept, but nearly two-thirds of the twelve-year-olds recognized its existence.[24] If young children are able to distinguish among different kinds of aloneness, it is possible, especially as they grow older, that they will come to perceive different kinds of loneliness as well.

Nonetheless, teachers and parents should treat children's loneliness with care. Children work out their own relationships, but only up to a point. It is not reasonable to expect children to grapple with ostracism, bullying, and isolation on their own; most lack the experience and perspective for this. So when a child is being mistreated, in school or elsewhere, the adults should intervene, making clear that the ones doing the bullying or taunting are in the wrong. At the same time, schools can help children understand what it means to be alone. Most serious study involves solitude and even loneliness; through such study, students come to learn that their loneliness is neither theirs alone nor a cause for despair. They may find that loneliness allows them to come closer to things they would not otherwise have noticed. The very ache pulls them in. For some, loneliness can turn into an intellectual or artistic pursuit—of a solution, a sound, an idea, a line of poetry, a drawing of a face in shadows.

This does not mean that children should be confined to their loneliness or to their studies. They should learn ways of forming bonds: participating in activities together, starting conversations, helping others, and showing interest in others. Adults can remind children and teenagers to focus on the simple steps and to be forgiving of mistakes, both their own and those of others. Schools can provide occasions for students to come together over common interests. When things do not go quite right during the school day, when an activity goes awry, teachers can help them overcome the distress, whether by repairing the errors or by letting them go. In order to know themselves, young people need to see a little beyond themselves; schools can help them do this.

And adults—what about us, bumbling beings that we are? We excel at making things complicated; we are even better at oversimplifying our jumble. Something of the reverse is needed: simple gestures and the ability to see into them. We will always be a garageful of things, but when we go on a bicycle ride, we may leave the rake behind. It's an awkward thing to carry on a bike. Company is not difficult to find, when we come to it somewhat bare. The complexities, the jangling implements, will still be there when we need them.

Tillich's statement that "sin is separation" gives little comfort, yet it helps us see our discomfort in perspective. Religions and civilizations are filled with ruptures: Lucifer cast out of heaven; Adam and Eve cast out of Eden; wars between countries, within countries, or within the self; an unhappy family or a broken family; toppled towns and ghost towns; disappointment or confusion in love. People are laid off from their jobs after years of service with no advanced notice; a friendship of many years ends in a petty squabble. At the end of the story of Ivan Ivanovich and Ivan Nikiforovich, Nikolai Gogol's narrator lets out the surprising cry, "It's dreary in this world, gentlemen!"[25] What seemed a play of words, a bending of logic, a story for its own sake, turns into intense sadness. In Gogol's story, there is no end to the loneliness, except in the storytelling itself, and maybe not even there.

Yes, loneliness calls for fixing, but it is slow work, and it often takes subtle forms. Ernest Klein wrote the *Comprehensive Etymological Dictionary of the English Language* in response to the deaths of his father, wife, only son, and two of three sisters at Auschwitz. In his introduction, he reveals the hope that fueled the work: "May this dictionary, which plastically shows the affinity and interrelationship of the nations of the world in the way in which their languages developed, contribute to bringing them nearer to one another in the sincere pursuit of peace on earth—which was one of my cardinal aims in writing this dictionary."[26] Perhaps words themselves come out of sorrow and hope; perhaps language itself breaks and mends.

In Tillich's words, our lives consist of a "struggle between separation and reunion." This struggle occurs in all aspects of our lives; both sides of the struggle are in each of us. "Are we not almost always ready to abuse everybody and everything," Tillich asks, "although often in a very refined way, for the pleasure of self-elevation, for an occasion for boasting, for a moment of lust? To know that we are ready is to know the meaning of the separation of life from life, and of 'sin abounding.'" In other words, to admit to our capacity for abuse is to recognize who we are. This recognition is the first step toward something greater. For Tillich, this greater thing is grace, in which "something is overcome," in which the self is reconciled with the self.[27] In nonreligious terms, it might be a sense of responsibility and resonance, our place in a larger story. In a moment of loneliness, a person may experience rage, calm, jealousy, generosity, hurt, confusion, tenderness, and much more, all mingled; it is in these moments that barriers fall, because this loneliness contains everything, or at least a good part of it. One hears the wind in it.

To understand loneliness, we must consider how it can be shaped—imperfectly and unevenly, sometimes messily, but with conscience, discipline, and good craving. Our loneliness, like our solitude, is too often unwieldy; it gets pushed to and fro, sucked into society and flung out again. The task is to discern one kind from another and to hear the patterns. But such understanding comes from the specifics. It is not enough to say that loneliness is universal; one starts to sense the sweep of it when tracing one of its lines. Still, the lines may turn unlinelike, as loneliness mixes with solitude and other things.

Waiting out loneliness does not mean waiting passively or waiting forever. Sometimes it means just waiting past the nervous impulse to blot the loneliness out. It is like the waiting required of a violin student, whom the teacher is trying to show how to move from one position to another. The student interrupts with attempts to get it right, nervous about having played badly. The teacher keeps telling the student to stop and pay attention for a moment. Unless the student does this, he will not know how to practice when he gets home and will stay caught up in the same mistakes. Letting those mistakes exist is the first step toward overcoming them; so it is with loneliness. The person who does not want a second of loneliness becomes a pest; the person who can hold it for just a few minutes may come to understand it or at least see past the panicked scramble for a fix.

One more point about Tillich's sermon: the title is "You Are Accepted." He does not say "You will be accepted one day" or "You will be accepted if you do the right thing." The acceptance is already here, but we may see it only in flashes, if at all. We find it in our very grasp of language: "We understand not merely the literal meaning of the words, but also that which lies behind them, even when they are harsh or angry. For even then there is a longing to break through the walls of separation."[28] Right there, in that longing, there is the possibility of acceptance; as soon as we recognize the longing in ourselves and others, it is partially overcome. But how fleetingly this is grasped, and with how much difficulty! It is much easier to cling to a wounded ego and wail away into the dawn. It is possible that in loneliness we resemble the Underground Man; despite our protestations, we don't want to get rid of it entirely. If we can't have our heart's desire, at least we can have the loneliness, or so we believe.

We are taught to measure ourselves by the things we can clinch, be they dates, grades, jobs, homes, burial sites, understandings, love, or loneliness itself. But loneliness and love are both empty-handed; both require the ability not to possess. This concept of nonpossession is all too easy to get wrong; hackneyed notions of "letting go" are not the point. The answer to loneliness is not the surrender of need. To find one's way between need and autonomy, one must make way for both. Loneliness is room, sometimes too roomy for comfort, but room nonetheless.

It is the very discomfort that makes for marvels. In the first ode of *Antigone*, the Chorus describes man, who rides the tops and bottoms of the waves, turning up furrows in the tireless land, the eldest of the gods. Even today, stationed behind our screens, we know the ups and downs of endless toil, the leaps of hope, the plunges of fault, and then the inverse: hope diving, fault soaring, a key turning in the wild sky, and somewhere, maybe in this very chair, a place to sit awhile and find a thought.

1 0

~

The Practice of Solitude

There is only one practice of solitude: to make a choice and carry it out well. The particulars assemble around this simple principle. One may later regret the choice; one may end up reversing or abandoning it. The choice may consist of doing nothing or refraining from a decision until the time is right. But no matter what it entails, one must entrust oneself to it in order to see it clearly. In our hectic lives, we have difficulty making choices; we have even more trouble living them out, as the alternatives flash and jingle around us. Solitude allows for a gathering of the intentions.

Practice involves much more than routines, but routines of some kind are essential. It is by making certain things automatic, relaxing into certain good habits, that one can reach other choices. Not every moment should be filled with an agonizing "What should I do?" Much of the time, the answer should be obvious. Habits lay certain things to rest. Taken in their other senses, habits are also clothing and home. They provide for us; they take care of the necessities so that we can do the other things we want and need to do.

The practice of solitude requires education and experience. None of the choices of solitude can be made without insight, if they are to be made well. Martin Luther King Jr.'s "Letter from Birmingham Jail" is filled with philosophical, religious, and historical references. These are not ornaments; they give dimension and urgency to his argument. They help explain why, in his view, nonviolent protest is the one viable response to the injustice of segregation. This simplicity of view is anything but simplistic; it draws on study and experience, wisdom and anger. One senses the years of thought in it.

We receive mixed messages about choices every day. On the one hand, we are supposed to choose from a great variety of just about everything, from toothpaste to friends. (In reality, the choices are not as many as they appear, but the dazzling array makes us rub our eyes nonetheless.) On the other hand, we are supposed to go about our lives with an untrammeled sense of purpose, not lingering on uncertainties, not thinking the questions through, but moving on and up toward one goal and then another. We have no chance to get to know the options well, nor is that the point. The point is to scan quickly for the winner, the one that will supposedly pay off. If it doesn't, we need only toss it aside and choose something else. The meaning is subordinated to the scramble. To step out of the scramble, one needs a bit of agility, stillness, and gumption.

This chapter will look at the practice of solitude in three ways: first, in terms of the commitment it requires; second, in terms of the choices it involves; and third, in terms of the education required for it. This is not a how-to guide; instead of prescribing a specific practice, it examines some of the underlying principles. Essentially, the practice of solitude consists of decisions, whether large or minuscule. Sometimes the decision is nothing other than the last remaining option, the thing we do because nothing else is acceptable or possible. In such cases it may not be a rational decision at all; it may seem as basic as a glass of water, or it may stay murky in our minds for a long time. But whether simple or complex, manifest or hidden, the decision requires some aloneness.

It requires sincerity as well—a concept that tends to raise hackles. Lionel Trilling writes about the word, "When we hear it, we are conscious of the anachronism which touches it with quaintness. If we speak it, we are likely to do so with either discomfort or irony."[1] We know that "saying what you mean" is not as straightforward as it seems, as part of the meaning may be unknown even to the speaker. We know, also, that "speaking from the heart" does not necessarily mean speaking truth, as the heart has deceptions and is a metaphor to begin with. Yet all good work requires some sort of sincerity in motion—that is, the shedding of falsehoods and errors. Robert Frost wrote in one of his notebooks, "There is such a thing as sincerity. It is hard to define but is probably nothing but your highest liveliness escaping from a succession of dead selves. Miraculously. It is the same with illusions. Any belief you sink into when you should be leaving it behind is an illusion. Reality is the cold feeling on the end of the trouts nose from the stream that runs away."[2]

One feels the swift cold water as one reads Frost's words: the excitement and chill of leaving an illusion behind. If one looks at sincerity as a sloughing off of falsehoods or mirages, then it becomes more believable. One cannot possess truth permanently, but one can experience flashes of it now and then. When working on a poem, one decides which parts belong and which don't, which words jar the ear and why. When working out a mathematical proof, one keeps an eye out for hidden flaws and pitfalls, things that might render the proof invalid or possibly strengthen it. When learning a language, one becomes increasingly aware of idiom and syntax. All of these sharpenings are forms of sincerity. To work on anything sincerely, or with hopes of sincerity, one must sink into it enough to hear and see it. One must give oneself over to it for a time, over time, with full mind.

There is something miraculous, indeed, about sincerity. But there would be no room for the miracle if one did not make way for it and stay on the alert for it. A person must be willing to practice whatever it may be. The practice, while it goes on, must be all that exists, or almost all—and within that practice, the mind must be listening, doubting, correcting. Some argue that they practice best on the fly—that they play the instrument here and there throughout the day, or carry a notebook wherever they go. But such people still work with dedication, with full ear. The work may be scattered across the day, but the intent is not. The final work requires more than scattered efforts; those who write or practice in bits and pieces must still take time to put them together and sort out what is good from the rest.

In the fourth of his *Letters to a Young Poet*, Rainer Maria Rilke writes that "if you have this love of inconsiderable things and seek quite simply, as one who serves, to win the confidence of what seems poor: then everything will become easier, more coherent, and somehow more conciliatory for you, not in your intellect, perhaps, which lags marveling behind, but in your inmost consciousness, waking and cognizance."[3] Winning "the confidence of what seems poor" means tending to the details of one's work, listening for those things that usually escape notice. It runs counter to the pressure to get one's work "out there" or win praise from high quarters. The poverty is not only the visible kind but the poverty of things unseen: the book one reads alone; the sentence one struggles to get right; the piano scales, which may sound clumsy at first; or the quiet act of generosity. One relaxes into being unremarked.

Of course, we need some kind of response from the outside. Much of our work depends on outside responses and collaboration. But even so, we must give ourselves over to the work. Actors, who depend on immediate response much more than poets do, must enter into their roles without reservation. They sense the audience as they go along but also shut it out. Teachers, similarly, must enter into their lesson plans, even as they adjust to the students and the events of the day. They must do what they have set out to do, even as they make minute adjustments. A musician must be vigilant to every sound that comes out of the instrument, every movement of the fingers, but must also surrender to the piece and play out its life.

It is all very well to say that one must sink into something in order to do it well. But what is that thing into which one sinks? It is hard to do anything without having already chosen to do it. The ten-year-old who doesn't know whether to do homework, go out and play, practice trombone, send text messages, or make a birthday card is not too different from any of us in times of indecision. We must decide what to do with our time alone—but even when we have little or no time alone, we decide between play and work, action and contemplation, speech and silence, agreement and dissent, and more. Having made a choice, we must then take it into ourselves and carry it out, watching it as we go.

But we do not make these choices by sitting down and asking, "Shall I do A or B?" Sometimes the choice that makes the most sense is A and B with a hint of C; or sometimes we think we choose A, and it turns out to be W. There is more to the practice of solitude than becoming resolute or simply making good use of time. It has also to do with recognizing and honoring our mixtures. It has to do with detecting the vitality of what is right, what is true for us, or what we know. Sometimes to find this vitality is simply to stop escaping it. Sometimes it comes only through recognition: doing it and sensing the pulse.

ONE OF THE fundamental choices we make is between purposeful activity and play. The word "play" has many definitions; for now, let us take it to mean whimsical activity that is not primarily aimed at a goal or finished product. One can understand it by considering the way children and adults walk on the sidewalk. Often a five- or six-year-old makes an adventure of every step, hopping this way and that, leaping over the cracks, zigzagging, or circling around. Adults, by contrast, tend to walk at an even pace, in a straight line. Walking, for them, is not an experiment or a game; it has a specific function. Now and then they may find themselves whirling in the streets, frisking and laughing in the rain or snow, but most adults do this less and less as they get older (unless they are playing with children). Still, adults play like five-year-olds in other areas of their lives. Within the work they do, they may find themselves leaping over cracks and rushing this way and that, or moving straight toward a goal. Often there will be a mixture of both.

Finding the right mixture of play and purpose is a tricky matter; they switch roles with each other or combine. Both have their dangers: too much play can resemble doodling, and too much purpose can become plodding. A good mixture requires self-knowledge, knowledge of the work at hand, and the skill of calibrating one's actions. Richard Hofstadter writes that the intellectual lives in tension between playfulness and piety and that "the tensile strength of the thinker may be gauged by his ability to keep an equipoise between these two sides of his mind."[4] This is true not only for intellectuals, but for others who need a mixture of the two. Some will tend more toward one side than to the other, but they still rely on the other side to keep them in check.

Some have profoundly mistaken themselves, expecting themselves to be serious and purposeful when their nature was playful, or vice versa. Or else they have wavered between seriousness and play, not always finding the right place. Nikolai Gogol, known for his supremely playful stories and his novel *Dead Souls*, longed for a more solemn role in culture, or at least a role different from his own. At the outset of his career, he was crushed when his long poem, *Hanz Kuechelgarten* (1829), met with one piece of sharp criticism and nothing more. He bought up the remaining copies of the poem, burned them, and left for a brief stint in Germany. Later, back in Saint Petersburg, he entertained hopes of becoming an actor, especially a tragic actor; his audition (in both comedy and tragedy) failed miserably, as he had nothing prepared and read in a monotone from the text he was given.[5]

For a while, beginning in 1831, Gogol taught history to girls at the Patriotic Institute in Saint Petersburg; he told them Ukrainian folktales and made them roar with laughter. Soon he began to tire of it; he would feign illness and skip class frequently. In 1834 he was appointed to an assistant professorship in medieval history at the university. He wrote to his mother, "I have thrown off all trivial encumbrances and given up my other occupations. At the moment, I am contenting myself with a position as professor at the University of Saint Petersburg and nothing more. I have neither time nor desire to do anything else." He dazzled his students with his first lecture, which included no names or dates but was, according to biographer Henri Troyat, "a sheaf of general ideas, a sort of mirage, in some places glittering and in others very misty." After this auspicious beginning, his lectures declined, as he was uncomfortable and unprepared. He would miss lectures, end them early, or come in complaining of a toothache, with his head wrapped in a white handkerchief.[6]

Gogol's last failed vocation was that of self-appointed spiritual guide, when he wrote *Selected Passages from Correspondence with Friends* (1847), a series of essays in the form of letters. Some of these essays take the form of literary criticism, some of religious discourse; some offer advice on matters ranging from household management to politics. While a few of his friends defended him, most readers reacted with outrage and dismay. They found some of his claims and his tone of authority preposterous.[7]

All the while, Gogol had become known for his stories, which frolicked, taunted, and conjured. Russian writers and writers around the world have been not only influenced, but even defined by Gogol; it has been said that "we all emerged from under Gogol's 'Overcoat.'"[8] But he was restless with his gifts. Something troubled him about his work; perhaps he could not reconcile himself with his religious ambivalence, his fascination with things diabolical. Toward the end of his life, Gogol succumbed to illness and religious fanaticism; he burned most of the second part of *Dead Souls* and died nine days later. His spiritual struggle destroyed him, but it also charged his work; his playfulness was shaped and tinged by his preoccupations.

Gogol's story "The Overcoat" (1842) shows him at play and in glee—masterful, exuberant, and haunted. The protagonist, Akaky Akakievich, whose very name is filled with play, comes to life through Gogol's language. Akaky Akakievich copies letters for a living; his life is filled with writing, though it is not the content that matters, but the process of copying, which he loves. Although the narrator mocks him and makes him seem somewhat ludicrous, there is a deep affinity between them. In telling the tale of Akaky Akakievich, Gogol's narrator loses himself in language, just as Akaky Akakievich loses himself in the copying. The very explanation of Akaky's name bears witness to this:

> The civil servant's surname was Bashmachkin. From the very name it is clear that it came at some point from *bashmak* [shoe]. But exactly when and at what time and in what manner it came from a shoe, no one knows. Both his father and his grandfather, and even his brother-in-law and all the other Bashmachkins went around in boots, changing the soles only three times a year or so. His name was Akaky Akakievich. Perhaps the reader will find this name a little strange and far-fetched, but he can be assured that no one went looking for it; rather, circumstances were such that there was no way to give him any other name, and it came about as follows.[9]

The narration itself is an exuberant and dark excursion, into words themselves, into meaning and absurdity. The fact that the Bashmachkins "went around in boots" and changed the soles "only three times a year or so" seems hardly relevant, except that the irrelevance is the very point. The words take us into a place where things are not quite sensible and yet make vivid sense. Vladimir Nabokov writes that "the diver, the seeker for black pearls, the man who prefers the monsters of the deep to the sunshades on the beach, will find in *The Overcoat* shadows linking our state of existence to those other states and modes that we dimly apprehend in our rare moments of irrational perception. The prose of Pushkin is three-dimensional; that of Gogol is four-dimensional, at least."[10] Gogol's "play" opens up a perspective on the world; one starts to see the world in Gogolian terms (or, as one would say in Russian, *po-gogolevski*). In Gogol's peripatetic prose, there is a sense of fate; the language does not amble aimlessly, but finds its way to an inevitable place, in this case the very name Akaky Akakievich. Like his name, Akaky Akakievich cannot be anything other than what he is, nor can the narrator.

In poetry, seriousness and play are often one and the same. We cannot sort it into piles, saying "this is serious," and "this is playful," but we see how verse can romp through matters of life and death. Gerard Manley Hopkins's "The Caged Skylark" abounds with play and solemnity at once. The first stanza gives a sense of this:

As a dare-gale skylark scanted in a dull cage
Man's mounting spirit in his bone-house, mean house, dwells—
That bird beyond the remembering his free fells;
This in drudgery, day-labouring-out life's age.[11]

The expression "dare-gale" is unprecedented, but we know instantly what it means: a bird that dares to brave the gale. "Scanted"? Held back, made less than he is. And now we have the whole sense: a brave bird, diminished by his cage, is like man's spirit trapped in his body, his "bone-house, mean house." But the meaning is only part of it. The other side is the sound—strange, insistent, brooding, yet subtly ecstatic. The meaning of "bone-house, mean house" comes out of the sounds themselves—one hears a slight jeer in them, as though this house, about to be surpassed, could use a little mockery. One also hears a cage in the first line, as "skylark" and "scanted," alliterating, are held within the almost-alliterating "dare-gale" and "dull cage." The play of the poem contributes to its dignity.

Outside of poetry, we fall prey to the notion that seriousness is only serious and play only playful. Teenagers who sneer at their studious classmate may not recognize how much enjoyment can be found in those studies. To them, the studiousness is nothing but an attempt to win the teachers' favor or to attain a goal. Schools reinforce this belief by emphasizing goal-setting to the extreme; in many schools, every student must have an individual learning goal in every subject. Goals are necessary, of course, but they can be overdone. Likewise, the school that focuses on test preparation elevates the tested subjects above the rest; arts become frills, side endeavors, in comparison with the "serious" subjects. This does an injustice to tested and untested subjects alike. All subjects have their discipline and delight. Anyone involved with music and theater knows how strenuously demanding they are; anyone who falls in love with English or mathematics knows that the tests do not approximate what the subjects contain.

One should not have to point to the seriousness of play in order to justify it. There is a place for dreaming and exploring, taking a bike ride just to look around, browsing through this and that book, speaking in a made-up language, writing an experimental poem without worrying about whether it will be good, learning a magic trick, pulling off a good-natured prank, acting out a scene for fun, or looking out the window and thinking. By the same token, one should not have to apologize for taking something seriously—taking a hobby beyond the point of hobby, staying up late with a book, or staying with a job despite pressure to move on and up. If one wants to shape the expanse of seriousness and play, one must allow for the expanse to begin with.

The choice between action and contemplation is as complex as the choice between serious pursuit and play. Again, there are mixtures and combinations: active contemplation, contemplative action, and different kinds of each. In *Summa Theologica* (completed in 1274), Thomas Aquinas asks whether life is "fittingly" divided into the active and the contemplative. He raises the possibility that it might not be, as "the soul is the principle of life by its essence" and "the soul is the principle of action and contemplation by its powers." But he counters that there is indeed a difference: that "the life of every man would seem to be that wherein he delights most, and on which he is most intent," and that "certain men are especially intent on the contemplation of truth, while others are especially intent on external actions." In other words, the distinction holds but should be understood properly.[12]

Let us define action as the translation of thought into something that affects the outside world. A speaker at a public forum acts through speaking; a writer, through writing (arguably, even when the writing is unpublished). Activity, by contrast, may not affect the outside world at all (except in minute ways—for instance, through the consumption of supplies). Clearly there is a gray area between action and activity, but the two are distinct.

Likewise, contemplation is not simply "thinking"; in religious terms, it is thought that abstains, at least temporarily, from action, concentrating instead on the divine. In secular terms, it may range from a prolonged gaze to quiet reflection or some kind of meditation. Perfect contemplation may be known only to a few; for the most part, it is defined through its contrast with other states. We often use the word "contemplation" in a broad sense, to encompass musing, observation, consideration, and focus.

On the whole, with variation and exceptions, everyday American culture tends to favor busyness, not action or contemplation. "Work hard. Be nice," goes the motto of the Knowledge is Power Program (KIPP) charter schools; this is not bad advice, but its value depends on the substance of the work. Similarly, many businesses embrace the slogan "work hard, play hard." Hard work is necessary for many endeavors, but we have turned it into an end. Students in school are supposed to be working constantly—that is, visibly doing something whenever anyone peers in the room. Adults work longer hours and with shorter vacations than many Europeans in similar positions. Our escapes, such as TV or the Internet, may be symptoms of working too much; the tired mind seizes them to relieve the burdens for a little while. This is the inverse of busywork and just as numbing; it prevents contemplation and quiet thought. Susan Jacoby notes that the video and audio media "demand that everyone take his or her place as a member of the audience"; and "the more time people spend before the computer screen or any screen, the less time and desire they have for two human activities critical to a fruitful and demanding intellectual life: reading and conversation."[13] The loss of *desire* for reading and conversation is especially dangerous, for without desire, we do nothing to combat our excesses.

Our vacations become brief periods of recuperation, not time for thorough rest or pursuit of our own interests. We see advertisements for "getaways," deals that take vacationers to a resort for a few days. Everything is planned for the traveler, to the point where there may not be much of a getaway at all. Sometimes we need to get away from the getaway. Many wish for vacation that takes on a life of its own, a life as important as the work life. It takes some determination to find a way of resting that is not an escape from daily life, but an integral part of life, and to find time for one's own interests outside of work.

The idea of the getaway is not new or particularly American. One finds a form of it in Chekhov's "Ward No. 6," a story about an unhappy doctor, Andrei Efimych Ragin, who spends his evenings immersed in reading. In contrast with his profession, which to him seems hypocritical, the reading offers him not only tranquility, but a chance to spend time in a world he enjoys. This is much more than a getaway; it is a separate existence.

With the pleasant thought that he has had no private practice for ages, thank God, and that no one will disturb him, Andrei Efimych, upon coming home, immediately sits down at his desk in the study and begins to read. He reads a great deal and always with great pleasure. Half of his salary goes to the purchase of books, and of the six rooms of his apartment, three are filled to the brim with books and old magazines. . . . The reading always continues for several hours, without interruption, and does not exhaust him. He reads not quickly and fitfully . . . but slowly, with penetration, often stopping at places that he likes or doesn't understand.[14]

One day, the doctor befriends (or hopes he has befriended) a paranoid mental patient, Ivan Dmitrich Gromov; he finds in him a kindred soul, interested in similar philosophical questions, and begins visiting the ward in order to continue the conversation. Once the news breaks about Andrei Efimych's new association, his colleagues begin to suspect him of insanity. Eventually they do to him what they have done to others. Before things reach that point, his acquaintance Mikhail Averianych coaxes him away on a trip to Moscow, Saint Petersburg, and Warsaw, supposedly to help clear his mind and refresh his spirits. As it turns out, Mikhail Averianych makes him miserable the entire time, talking to him constantly and not leaving him alone for a moment: "The doctor's ears started to ring and his heart began to pound, but out of politeness he was unable to ask his friend to go away or stop talking."[15] The hypocrisy of Mikhail Averianych comes clear: he ends up losing all his money gambling; needing a loan, he turns to Andrei Efimych, who gives him almost everything he has, without complaint. By no means is Andrei Efimych a hero—Chekhov portrays him with a mixture of sympathy and contempt—but this failed getaway shows the discrepancy between his society and the kind of life he would like to have.

The more closely one regards any particular endeavor, the more likely one is to find both action and contemplation in it. The memorization of poetry is both contemplative and active: active because it requires learning the words, sounds, rhythms, structures, and meanings; contemplative because of the surrender to the poem as one learns it, the willingness to take it in without fully understanding it. Fixing a car is both active and contemplative: the person is doing something to the car but often spends much of the time peering into the engine. Sailing is not nearly as contemplative a sport as it may seem; one has to be alert to the winds and in control of the ropes at all times. Nonetheless, once one learns how to do it, one can find room for quiet thought.

Busywork is neither action nor contemplation, but for some reason it is very important to look busy; whoever does not may be accused of laziness or accuse herself of the same. This is particularly clear in the teaching profession, where fingers point at the teacher who leaves the school at the end of the school day and takes full weekends to herself. According to some, the great teacher is the one who does "whatever it takes"—who gives her phone number to students for homework assistance, works at the school six days a week, performs cafeteria and hallway duties, attends meetings after school and over the summer, and visits homes if necessary. Taken together, such activities leave little time for planning lessons, working out ideas, immersing oneself in the subject, and leading a reasonably full life. Without this quiet work, teachers have little to bring to their students. To uphold the teaching profession, one must allow for its unseen work and stillness; one must also allow for true action. Many teachers are involved with some of the larger issues of education, from curriculum writing to policy. They must have room to speak their views, participate in projects, and pursue their own interests.

This brings up another choice we have to make through solitude: the choice between speech and silence, or between public and private action. Every day, in one situation or another, we have to decide whether to speak up or not (and when to speak). The student has to decide whether to contribute to a discussion or hold back and listen. Adults and children decide whether to give a compliment, bring up a problem, argue a point, try out a joke, reply to an insult, put forward an incomplete thought, admit to an uncomfortable feeling, or protest a policy. We make these decisions at work, at home, by phone, by email, in various gatherings, and on the Web. To find our own mixture of silence and conversation, we must see beyond the influences on us. We must understand the value of both speaking up and refraining from speech. We must, moreover, choose our speech well, so that we are not simply babbling. We must be capable of silence, so that we have a choice. This silence is not only withholding of words; it may be abstinence from many kinds of public display.

While there is great pressure on us to make our work known and public, we may need to keep certain kinds of work to ourselves until it is ready, even if this takes years. Pablo Casals first encountered the Bach Suites at age thirteen. In his biography (the result of many conversations with Albert E. Kahn), he recalls, "I had never heard of the existence of these suites; nobody—not even my teachers—had ever mentioned them to me. . . . I hurried home, clutching the suites as if they were the crown jewels, and once in my room I pored over them." For twelve years, Casals worked on the Suites daily before daring to play them in public.[16] In the recording, one can hear the effect of those years of private study. His cello sounds like wood and strings that speak and cry and narrate and proclaim. One can imagine, when listening, that the sounds contain those twelve years alone with the music—but whether or not the years can be heard in the sounds, they are present in Casals's performance.

Silence comes in many forms and is part of sound. Good conversation requires a degree of silence, in order to make room for thoughts. If we lose a sense of silence in conversation, we use talk to fill the air; we become afraid of the pauses. The discipline of silence can allow us to have richer conversations and to speak with more precision. Not needing to have an opinion on every subject, not needing to have words for every occasion, not needing always to be right, we are at liberty to use words and listen well. But there are also cruel, careless, or defensive forms of silence—for instance, when a person does not reply to a well-meant letter, when one family member stops speaking to another, or when a gift goes unacknowledged. There is silence that comes from fear: the student in class who does not speak up because he thinks the others will laugh at him, or the politician who does not take a stand out of fear of losing votes. One must sort out the different kinds of silence and recognize where each one may do good or harm.

Just as we choose between speech and silence, we choose between agreement and dissent, many times a day, in ways large and small. The argument between Antigone and Ismene is in some way our daily inner argument. In some ways this may not seem like a choice at all; after all, if we agree in our hearts with something said or done, we should agree out loud, and the same is true for disagreement. But agreements and disagreements are not always so clear-cut. Sometimes we agree with part of an argument but not all, and we must decide which to emphasize. Is the point of disagreement the central point? Or is it peripheral? If we find ourselves in disagreement with a group, should we leave the group? Or is there enough common ground to justify remaining in it? Are we willing to risk our associations, careers, lives by dissenting? Will our dissent do damage? These questions have run through history: the decision whether to break with a church or religion, to revolt, to speak against the abuses of the state, to influence a group from within, to make peace, to withhold judgment, to wait for a better time.

Decisions regarding dissent are as vital as they are difficult. Schools depend on the willingness of teachers and administrators to speak their minds about policy, yet teachers may be disciplined for publicly criticizing their school or even the programs within it. Teachers resort to writing on blogs under pseudonyms, never knowing for sure whether what they say could jeopardize their employment. Even personal expression (not necessarily dissent) is fraught with danger. Frequently we hear in the news about teachers who were disciplined or fired for posting an inappropriate photo on Facebook or saying something about their students. Some of the cases are egregious, but they raise serious questions about the division between workplace and private life, about freedom of speech, and about the monitoring to which we subject ourselves. Most learn to be cautious in their expression, but caution comes at a cost.

Tobias Wolff's story "In the Garden of the North American Martyrs" concerns Mary, a reclusive professor who accepts a former colleague's invitation to apply for a position at her college. Throughout the visit, the colleague (Louise) ignores or pretends to ignore how serious this occasion is for Mary; she maintains a flighty and chatty attitude almost to the end. Mary realizes during the visit that it was all a setup, that they have someone in mind already for the position and are interviewing her only as a formality. The ending (not to be revealed here) suggests that to be pushed over the edge is sometimes to be pushed into being. Having been secretly different from others all her life, Mary finally seizes her difference, leaving the likes of Louise far behind.[17]

In all these choices and mixtures, something must be at stake. We must have the sensation, at times, of being on the peak of a roof, about to slip one way or another. This can only happen when we understand the choices and their importance. Without taking ourselves too seriously, without making a melodrama of every decision, we can give the decisions their dignity and comedy. Why comedy? Because we will always make mistakes, and most of these mistakes are not fatal. There is room to brush ourselves off and try again.

Practice, then, is little more than carrying out these decisions. There is regular practice (such as studying and exercising) and situational practice (such as speaking up in defense of someone). Both kinds require fullness of intent. From there, each has its particular requirements. Practicing a language involves both drill and spontaneous conversation; practicing an instrument requires the playing of technical exercises and musical pieces. Defending someone is also a kind of practice. To defend someone well, a person must have courage, knowledge of the situation, and good judgment. Such practice needs commitment in order to take shape. To commit to anything, a person must be with it as in a stained-glass dome, aware of the exit but stilled by the colors and patterns. Such stillness is built over time.

HOW CAN SCHOOLS help students learn to make such choices—between play and seriousness, contemplation and action, silence and speech, agreement and dissent, and more? Giving students many choices is not the answer; students may end up bewildered, as they do not understand the choices yet. Students need first to learn about the nature of these choices—by studying history and literature, discussing ethical questions, working out mathematics problems, learning languages, practicing instruments, and reading about the lives of others. In high school, students may start to take electives, but these should be in addition to a core set of studies, so that they may continue to build a foundation as they start to branch off. Even in college and graduate school, students need the structure of a syllabus; they need to know the field in order to stake out independently in it. There are exceptions: some students may find their interests early on and do substantial work on their own. Yet even the most precocious students need some guidance.

Some argue that students will not be motivated unless schools give them opportunities to choose what to read, what to learn, and which topics to pursue. But students will not be motivated unless they know something about the subjects in the first place. Students may find excitement and possibility in specific assignments, as they open up new knowledge and associations. I remember the delight of memorizing the declension of the Latin demonstrative pronoun *hic, haec, hoc*. The sounds were enjoyable; they reminded me of "kuplink, kuplank, kuplunk" in Robert McCloskey's *Blueberries for Sal*. Later, when taking poetics and linguistics courses, I became interested in the ablaut (the linguistic term for a vowel gradation that distinguishes closely related words, such as *sing, sang*, and *sung*). Besides awakening new interests, structured study allows students to look more closely at a problem than they might otherwise. Students do need some time for exploration, but much of this will spring from the specifics they learn in class. There is room for a degree of choice (of essay topic, for instance), but choices may be richer when they are fewer and more focused.

Students' lack of motivation comes not from structured study, but from elsewhere. As I mentioned in the third chapter, many students are distracted by mild or severe despair, overt or concealed: a sense that their studies don't really matter and are not as important as personal concerns, and that it will soon be over anyway (school or even life itself). Schools try to give students a sense of urgency, but their methods are often misguided. They may try to make the learning superficially relevant to students' lives, whip up their enthusiasm through chants and pep rallies, or impress upon them that their studies will help them toward their career or college goals. None of these approaches is sufficient. The "relevance" approach confirms for students that their personal preoccupations come first; the pep rally is off-putting to many; the "goal-oriented" approach ignores the questions: what happens when the goal is met? Does all of this lose its meaning? The student gets good grades, passes the courses for the year, goes on to the next grade, graduates, goes on to college or gets a job, and what then? What is the larger point?

Deborah Meier writes that education has long meant more than jobs and money; it has meant something "precious." Yet what that "precious" thing actually is, we do not often explore in the public domain: "We instead encourage children from ages 4 to 18 to think it's mostly about doing better in school *so you'll do better in school* OR, big step forward, you'll get a better-paying job. (Or ANY job.) We actually offer them statistical proof of this, over and over." Indeed, the economist Eric Hanushek has argued that "effective" teachers "produce" higher salaries; according to his calculations, a teacher in the 84th percentile (according to value-added ratings, which are based on test-score gains) with a class of twenty students will increase their collective annual earnings—each year—by four hundred thousand dollars.[18] Such calculations rest on the assumption that education translates directly and lineariy into salary: that is, the better the teacher, the more the students will ultimately make. It discounts the many choices that an education permits.

Beyond giving students a fou.ıdation, schools must teach them what commitment means. Without apology, they should teach students to read, write, and practice without any distractions from the Internet, cell phone, or TV, and to make a daily habit of this. It doesn't matter if they claim to know how to "multitask"; multitasking amounts to compromise, and they need to learn to offer more of themselves. Schools should make use of technology but should also teach students how to do without it. Otherwise they will depend on text messages during class, musical practice, lectures, daydreams, and even rest. Over the long run, the setting aside of distractions will give students permission to take the work seriously. Many young people latch onto a casual attitude about their studies; they need to be helped out of this. Many secretly long to be pushed into greater seriousness.

Schools must assign homework that goes beyond the trivial, that requires persistence and sustained concentration. When asked what he would recommend to readers who had trouble understanding his work after reading it three times, William Faulkner answered, "Read it four times."[19] This advice could apply to many endeavors. Students should learn to read closely and carefully, bearing with things they do not immediately understand. Assignments should be designed to combine routine practice with difficult challenges. Teachers should not hesitate to correct students, as students need to strive for accuracy when working alone. Students should learn how to put their full mind into their work, sometimes heartily, sometimes grudgingly, but with regularity and determination.

The psychologist K. Anders Ericsson refers to this kind of work as "deliberate practice": sustained, analytical, regular, focused practice that makes the difference between an amateur and an expert, or a good expert and a top expert. Students engage in deliberate practice in between lessons; professionals engage in it on their own. According to Ericsson and colleagues, deliberate practice is not inherently enjoyable; individuals practice not because they like doing so, but because they know that such practice improves their performance. Upon conducting several studies of the practice habits of musicians, they found, among other things, that expert performers practice more than others over the years; practice alone, with full attention; practice regularly, for limited periods at a time; and get plenty of rest.[20]

This idea of deliberate practice is promising, if one recognizes a few caveats. First, practice can be inherently enjoyable. For many it is a private, precise dialogue between the self and instrument (or pen and paper, or other material). It is a time for close listening and watching, for tuning and tinkering. It can be dull or painful at times, but there are also times of insight and amazement. It is possible to conceive of a somewhat warmer version of deliberate practice, with all of the focus and structure but with love of the work as well. Second, there are many principles of practice, but it is still idiosyncratic. One might learn from the example of the Scottish virtuoso percussionist Evelyn Glennie, who as a child persuaded a teacher (and later the Royal Academy of Music) to take her on even though she was deaf. She showed them that deafness in the ears did not impede her from hearing; she could hear with her body. What fueled and sustained her practice, it seems, was not just pursuit of a goal, not just the belief that she would get better over time, but love of the sounds right then and there, and her own forays into them.[21]

Technique is essential to playing, but technique is more than mechanics. The cellist Aldo Parisot said in an interview that "students don't concentrate on technique like they should. Instead they are taught how to hold the bow, how to finger, and then all their teachers talk about is the music, as if that's all that matters. Meanwhile their fingers continue to struggle and the years go by." His observation may surprise those who equate technique with holding the bow correctly and fingering properly. In the same interview, Parisot spoke of the importance of relaxed playing: "Sometimes I worry about the kids that play for me. They are so tense that they stop progressing after they reach a certain point. When they reach the age of 25 it's often too late and they may never be able to play fast pieces up to tempo."[22] The principles of relaxation and fluency—two essential components of musicality—should guide students as they practice. They should be listening to the sound, the textures, the transitions from string to string. They should remember to breathe properly, stay flexible, and play with as much ease as possible. This may be called technique, but there is musicality in it as well.

Many practices of solitude can be conveyed only through example. Teachers who practice their subjects—who think about them and work on them in their own time—can show students a way of life. They need not "model" for the students in any canned way; their very conduct is a model. When a teacher reads a poem aloud or presents a mathematical proof, her tone conveys whether she has thought about it at length, played with it, argued about it, and more. Students will likewise learn from teachers' handling of conflicts that arise in class and in school. Problems and dilemmas will arise, and teachers will be put to the test. How does a teacher respond when one student taunts another, when one student seems far more advanced (or less advanced) than the others, or when one of the students objects to the tenor of discussion or the premises of the lesson? How does the teacher respond to events affecting the whole school—a new principal, a change in the rules, or an emergency? A teacher's bearing in these situations is complex and influences students enormously. But teachers must also let themselves be fallible; students will not be harmed by a teacher's minor mistakes. And when a teacher handles a large mistake with grace, students learn that they, too, will survive mistakes.

There is some truth to the existentialist idea that we give things their meaning and importance. Practice allows for this; through honoring something regularly, we come to value it more. Nonetheless, not all of importance is of our own making. Casals did not make the Bach Suites important; he recognized something in them. Gogol's stories are wonderful not because people read them closely, but because of the worlds they contain. If practice makes meaning of things, it makes only part of the meaning. The rest comes from the things themselves. Practice is not solipsism; at its best, it is a relationship with something outside us, a relationship that grows more intimate over time. Sometimes it goes through periods of estrangement, when we realize how little we know and what beginners we are.

One cannot enter such a relationship with a sneer. Solitude allows a person to cast off the pretense of casualness. Even in solitude there are masks, but some of them drop off the face as soon as they are no longer in vogue. In solitude, nothing is in vogue. The elastic band disappears, and the plastic clatters to the floor. What's left has permission, at last, to be brave. Once alone in this manner, many will not settle for less. The compromise, the leveling of the self, the efforts at smoothing the edges all create extra work for nothing. What does a person receive in return for fitting in? Not love, not excellence, not prosperity, not even fitting in, as the fit is false, like the boots that look stylish but crunch the toes.

Students find their way by knocking their heads against a subject, by struggling with ideas, by learning things by heart and then carrying them around. They find themselves on their own, through their wanderings, friendships, and thoughts, but this takes place alongside structured study.

Sometimes, when working on an assigned essay, a student sees an unusual phrase wriggle through, or stumbles on a source that lights up the topic and leads to more sources. That may be the first sign of an individual voice; it grows stronger as the student learns, listens, and writes more. Through such practice, students learn how to be alone; they learn that they will always have something to do in solitude, including nothing at all. For some, solitude becomes the only place where they can do what they truly want. For others, it remains difficult and unpleasant, but they make room for it in some way. The relationships with solitude vary widely, but students learn that it is essential to doing certain things well.

But there is more to the practice of solitude than simply doing something well or working toward good performance. The person who shapes something is also shaped. We think of "character building" as something that takes place outside, in the world, but much of it happens in private. Reading, playing an instrument, memorizing the elements—all of this makes a person just a little different from before. Seeing the world a little differently, he is slightly altered in turn. All he needs to do is honor this new shape, not hide it under paint and plastic, not try to shake it away or sleep it off, not apologize for it, not slur its syllables. It is possible, even with abundant foibles, to live up to the way one sees the world. For some, there is no other way.

All of this is easily misunderstood. What does it mean? What is the relationship between routine habits and the larger choices? And what do we make of those choices that make themselves without our say? Is there such a thing as a practice of solitude, or is it an illusion? Well, it is a bit of all of these things. The routine habits make room for some of the larger choices, but the larger choices are never completely within our grasp, no matter how much solitude we give them. Something always does what it does despite itself; it slips away from us like a minnow. What remains is a robust sort of refusal. We learn, over time, what we will not and cannot do, what we will not and cannot give up. Sometimes the practice of solitude comes down to a simple "no." That "no" protects all sorts of other possibilities. It guards a life.

In February 1949, Flannery O'Connor wrote to editor John Selby at Rinehart in response to his comments on the manuscript of *Wise Blood*:

> I can only hope that in the finished novel the direction will be clearer, but I can tell you that I would not like at all to work with you as do other writers on your list. I feel that whatever virtues the novel may have are very much connected with the limitations you mention. I am not writing a conventional novel, and I think that the quality of the novel I write will derive

precisely from the peculiarity or aloneness, if you will, of the experience I write from. . . . In short, I am amenable to criticism but only within the sphere of what I am trying to do. I will not be persuaded to do otherwise. The finished book, though I hope less angular, will be just as odd if not odder than the nine chapters you have now. The question is: is Rinehart interested in publishing this kind of novel?[23]

The "aloneness" of *Wise Blood* is part of its magnificence. O'Connor had the strength and wisdom not to give it up for the sake of a book contract. She would accept criticism, but only if it meshed with what she was doing. This is the practice of solitude: distinguishing what is essential from what is not, and standing firm on the former. It is difficult, if not impossible, to teach aloneness of this kind, but if students see it, if they read *Wise Blood* and take in the language, they may come to love its jagged clarity and understand why it should not be softened for anything in the world.

11

~

Discernment and
the Public Sphere

A t age ten, in 1974, I traveled with my family to the Netherlands, where we were to spend a year (my parents were on sabbatical). We crossed the Atlantic on the *Mikhail Lermontov*, a Soviet cruise ship that had recently been converted from an ocean liner. It was my first time at sea, and the first moments were thrilling: pulling out of the New York harbor at sunset, with passengers cheering from the deck and others waving from land; watching the Statue of Liberty recede into the distance; feeling the rumble of the motor; and soon seeing nothing but waves upon waves.

I shared a cabin with my sister, Jenna. We had the run of the ship; no one worried about our whereabouts. There was a swimming pool, a lounge and dining area with a stage, an exercise room, a slot machine room, a gift shop with balalaikas and Matryoshka dolls, and a few canteens and bars. At night, the deck was aglow with lights; by day we could sometimes see dolphins leaping. At sunset, we would watch the changing colors over the sea and taste the salty chill; even the sounds grew darker as night fell.

On the second day of our voyage, when we were out on the deck, my parents struck up a conversation with the parents of a British family. There were five children: Anne, seventeen years old, John (fifteen), Ginny (ten), Diana (three), and David (eighteen months). Ginny and I became friends for the duration of the trip. We took lessons in Russian language, song, and dance—the crew kept us quite busy—and spent the rest of the time romping around. But I jump ahead.

While our parents were talking, I saw Anne walk away to the edge of the deck and lean over the railing. No one said anything about it for a few minutes, but then she started to lean farther. Her mother called her, and she ambled back in their direction, with a vague look in her eyes. As the trip progressed, I saw more hints of something unusual and precarious. She would walk away in the middle of conversation or give befuddling answers to questions. During the dance lessons, she would sometimes go in the wrong direction or leave the stage and wander around the hall. But while aloof and of her own world, she was never unkind. There was something captivating about her ways, so different from other people's.

As our Russian song and dance performance approached, we all chose partners for the show. Anne was left without a partner; either she was the odd one out, or someone finagled her way out of dancing with her. Her distress was visible; she would walk around repeating mournfully, "Who will be my partner? Who will be my partner?" Ginny and I were already dance partners and didn't want to change that, but we did want to find a partner for Anne. So we knocked on the cabin door of a woman in our class. The door opened; she stood tall before us, her long hair in a hurried bun with some wisps falling out. We explained the situation to her and asked whether she would be Anne's partner, just for this occasion.

This woman (I'll call her Mrs. Barrow) told us flat out that she wouldn't do it and there was no point in pushing her. We stood in the hallway, pleading, telling her how much it would mean and how hard it was for Anne not to have a partner, but none of this moved her. "This is a free country," she said, "and I have to consider my reputation." In fact, we were on Soviet territory, by maritime law, so it may not have been the country she thought it was. I doubt, moreover, that her reputation would have been harmed if she had agreed to dance with Anne. Dancing with someone of the same sex was not the issue; most of the people in the dance class were female. Nor would anyone have thought badly of her for dancing with Anne in particular. Her response says something about how she perceived her country and her life. Americans often use the expression "free country"; it rolls off the tongue like a chocolate ball. Sometimes it has specific meaning; at other times it is a way of saying no. At other times it is a way of explaining things that would be difficult to explain otherwise.

In the end, it worked out somehow; Anne ended up with several dance partners (including Mrs. Barrow, if I am not mistaken). The performance was a great occasion; I had never imagined, before the trip, that I would one day be performing Russian dances and singing Russian songs out at sea. The crew gave us ample stage time; in addition to the singing and dancing, we had a talent show and costume contest. Anne, Ginny, Diana, Jenna, and I dressed up as Matryoshka dolls, with kerchiefs and rouged cheeks. Ginny's father dressed up as a someone who had gotten seasick; he carried a giant blue pill, provoking a roar of laughter from the adults, who had been seasick for a great deal of the voyage. We sang "Kalinka" and another Russian song; for the talent show, we got to take turns at the microphone. Anne sang some songs and rattled off jokes, charming the audience.

I have often thought back on this experience—not with indignation at the woman who said no (she was within her rights, as she said), but with sorrow, bemusement, gratitude for the experience, and thoughts of the English family and how they are now. I recently made contact with Ginny, through the Internet; both parents have passed away, and Anne is doing well, living in sheltered accommodation and enjoying life. Ginny works in education management, as an advocate for arts education. The *Mikhail Lermontov* no longer crosses the seas; it hit rocks and sank near New Zealand in 1986.[1]

If Mrs. Barrow was at fault, it is because she lacked discernment. For whatever reason, she mistook us and the very ground on which she stood. She responded to us as one might respond to aggressive political canvassers or missionaries, not as one might to two girls trying to help someone. While relying on the concept (or cliché) of a "free country," she did not consider what that meant or where she actually was.

Of course, as the details of this event grow fuzzy over time, its symbolic significance increases—so it is possible that I would see it quite differently if I could replay it exactly. Yet, even with the distortions of memory, there is something monumental about that moment in the hallway of the Soviet ship, far out at sea. It ended happily, but there was a speck of tragedy in it all the same.

DISCERNMENT IS THE practice of distinguishing two similar things or recognizing something for what it is. It is not easily taught, nor does it necessarily transfer from one area to another. Someone with good character judgment may be unable to tell a good poem from a bad one, or a solid historical analysis from a shaky one. Someone with excellent business sense may fall for a medical fad or political ploy. Nonetheless, if one learns to make fine distinctions in one field, one becomes alert to the possibility of such distinctions elsewhere. Through ear training of the mind, one may learn to guard against hasty judgments and false generalizations. In discernment there is also an element of courage: the willingness to look at something or someone, even when the thing or person causes discomfort. To look someone in the eye is to let down one's own guard, to let one's own flaws show.

To the extent that it can be taught, discernment relies on a degree of common ground. For example, students are much more likely to recognize the allegory in George Orwell's *Animal Farm* if they have studied something of Russian and Soviet history; they are in a better position to distinguish Johann Sebastian Bach from Carl Philipp Emanuel Bach if they have studied the works of both. Common knowledge provides a common language; when people are reasonably confident that they are talking about the same thing, they understand or can at least ask for clarification of each other's terms. At the same time, an individual's particular knowledge can light up the discussion; one student may have read Orwell's "Politics and the English Language"; another might have advanced knowledge of harmony and counterpoint.

Thus, to teach discernment, schools should foster both common knowledge and individual interests. Finding the right proportion is a tricky matter. Many Americans are wary of a common curriculum, which they equate with homogeneous, "cookie-cutter" instruction and the imposition of a set of views. But diverse views and interests can thrive only when people have something to differ over.

In his 1902 essay "How the School Strengthens the Individuality of the Pupils," educator William Torrey Harris wrote that recitations foster and develop individual thought. "All of the pupils," he wrote, "concentrate their attention on the statements of the pupil who is reciting and on the cross-questioning of the teacher. It is a dialectic which calls for alertness and versatility of mind in the pupils who take part in it." In an earlier essay, he wrote that "the pupil can, through the properly conducted recitation, seize the subject of his lesson through many minds. He learns to add to his power of insight the various insights of his fellow pupils."[2] The very idea of a recitation would be derided today as a form of "rote learning," but his description makes it seem anything but rote. Harris assumed optimistically—perhaps too optimistically—that the students would all be concentrating intensely and trying to refine their understanding. Without such focus and desire, a recitation could easily turn dreary. But that is the case no matter what the approach. In a recitation, class discussion, or other format, the principle remains the same: through coming together over a subject, through straining to understand it better, students may find their individuality, even eccentricity.

It is not that American public schools lack any sort of common study; we have textbooks and the usually vague specifications of state standards. These half measures have grown out of a longstanding resistance to common curriculum, yet they have come to define curriculum. Except where such textbooks and standards are of high quality, this bears little resemblance to a curriculum as it should be. A curriculum is an outline and sequence of the works, concepts, and skills that students should learn, along with a rationale. It should be flexible enough to allow the mind to play, yet specific enough to provide rich working material. Whether it exists at the school, district, or state level, it should do justice to the word. From there, one can determine the proper balance of common and individual learning.

TO FIND ONE'S way in the world, intellectually and otherwise, one needs a place to put one's ideas to the test. Or, rather, one needs two places: the public sphere and the private sphere. These spheres have been defined in many ways, by Jürgen Habermas and others; let us define them simply here.[3] In the public sphere, one speaks one's mind and allows oneself to be challenged by others (theoretically). In the private sphere, one works out ideas alone and with friends, testing them against one's best knowledge and conscience. The private sphere also holds the things that one keeps separate from the public; it is a place for rumination, intimacy, and rest. Neither the private nor the public sphere is sufficient in itself; the two complement each other. But if either the public or private sphere is missing or compromised, the ideas themselves suffer, as does public discussion.

In *The Human Condition* (1958), Hannah Arendt argues that the *social* sphere has eroded both public and private spheres and changed the meaning of both. Modern society, she writes, "has not only blurred the old borderline between private and political, it has also changed almost beyond recognition the meaning of the two terms and their significance for the life of the individual and the citizen." According to Arendt, this phenomenon is peculiar to the modern era. The ancient Greek political life, the *bios politikos*, was "reserved for individuality; it was the only place where men could show who they really and inexchangeably were." The private realm, which complemented the public realm, was a physical place; private property gave the individual a retreat, a place to guard the things that were unknown or unknowable to others. "Privacy," writes Arendt, "was like the other, the dark and hidden side of the public realm, and while to be political meant to attain the highest possibility of human existence, to have no private place of one's own (like a slave) meant to be no longer human."[4]

Society, according to Arendt, corrupts both the public and the private; it tends "to 'normalize' its members, to make them behave, to exclude spontaneous action or outstanding achievement." It places high value on statistics, which elevate norms above "rare deeds" and substitute behavior for action. It turns labor into a public matter, defining people by their very struggle to survive. In a society of laborers, she writes, "all members consider whatever they do primarily as a way to sustain their own lives and those of their families." With family life made public, and public life made practical and material, the distinguishing characteristics of both realms are softened, normalized, and compromised; in Arendt's words, "greatness has given way to charm everywhere."[5]

This ubiquitous charm comes at the expense of meaning. With people talking in their own ways about their private and economic selves, people are neither gathered together nor distinguished from one another. Arendt's description of this phenomenon seems to anticipate the Internet era: "The weirdness of this situation resembles a spiritualistic séance where a number of people gathered around a table might suddenly, through some magic trick, see the table vanish from their midst, so that two persons sitting opposite each other were no longer separated but also would be entirely unrelated to each other by anything tangible."[6]

Arendt observes that when people are talking about different things, they can no longer discern what others are saying. "Men have become entirely private," she writes, "that is, they have been deprived of seeing and hearing others, of being seen and being heard by them." The diversity of public life, according to Arendt, depends on "the sameness of the object"—that is, a true common cause, in relation to which "everybody sees and hears from a different position." Without this common cause, all perspectives are ultimately reduced to one or none, as there is no way to compare them in the first place. We have lost the distinctiveness of the public and private realms—so while in one sense the private realm has disappeared, in another sense it has spread everywhere.[7]

As historical commentary, Arendt's analysis has flaws; she simplifies both the ancient and modern eras, glorifying one and deploring the other. As philosophical and political theory, her analysis seems somewhat exaggerated; we have not lost all vestiges of public and private spheres, nor do we lack regard for exceptional acts and deeds. Yet the idea itself—that our social emphasis endangers public and private life—sheds light on many of our problems. One can see how American schools' social emphasis has coincided with a social conception of democracy, in which various groups vie for power and prominence, and where relationships and networks determine the ideas themselves. If one perceives democracy as social, then group work is excellent preparation for participation in it. But if democracy is also to involve a meeting of independent minds, then schools must provide a foundation for such meeting.

To put it plainly: as long as schools emphasize working in groups, getting along with group members, completing tasks together, and networking online, students will not learn to put forth ideas *as ideas*; they will not learn to stand apart from the group, either in public or in private. Relationships and products will take priority over clear and independent thought. But if schools emphasize the subjects themselves, and structure class in a way that best serves the topic at hand, then the ideas will take priority over the relationships, and students will learn to challenge each other and refine their thoughts. Of course, schools can and should do both; they need not confine themselves to one or the other. But the social emphasis deserves critical scrutiny; it did not always dominate our educational vision, nor should it always do so.

As E. D. Hirsch Jr. illustrates in *The Making of Americans*, the Founding Fathers saw the urgency of educating for the public sphere. Benjamin Rush wrote in 1798 of the necessity of "laying the foundations for nurseries of wise and good men"; he argued that the schools, "by producing one general, and uniform system of education, will render the mass of the people more homogeneous, and thereby fit them more easily for uniform and peaceable government." This homogeneity was to be the *basis* for independent thought: "if our youth are disposed after they are of age to think for themselves, a knowledge of one system, will be the best means of conducting them in a free enquiry into other systems of religion, just as an acquaintance with one system of philosophy is the best introduction to the study of all other systems in the world."[8]

The founders were concerned about the dangers of factions; to prevent disintegration, they sought to promote a spirit of deliberation. Deliberation would allow for individual differences yet preserve a common spirit and cause. To this end, they called for public education in the liberal arts and sciences. Their hopes and plans were not identical; they themselves had been educated in very different ways, and their ideas gave rise to a variety of educational institutions. Hirsch notes, "Our early educational thinkers conceived of the United States as *both* a salad bowl and a melting pot—a federated union." William Deresiewicz observes, "Without solitude—the solitude of Adams and Jefferson and Hamilton and Madison and Thomas Paine—there would be no America."[9]

American schools of the eighteenth and nineteenth centuries varied widely in quality, and many young people were excluded from them or discouraged from pursuing education past the early years. Yet the idea of education for the public sphere persisted, thanks in large part to the efforts of Horace Mann. As secretary of the board of education in Massachusetts (established in 1837), Mann established teacher preparation schools; founded the *Common School Journal*, in which he laid out the principles of a common education; visited schools in Europe and brought back ideas for lively and practical instruction; met frequently with teachers and community members throughout Massachusetts; and argued fiercely for an equalizing public education, accessible to all children. According to the historian Lawrence Cremin, Mann sought to build "a *public philosophy*, a sense of community which might be shared by Americans of every variety and persuasion."[10]

As a result of Mann's work, a common school system grew in Massachusetts, and many states emulated it. In the second half of the nineteenth century, free high schools proliferated. While there was no single curriculum, these schools had a general understanding of what students should learn. Opportunities for self-education also multiplied, through printed material ranging from advice columns to textbooks, and through cultural institutions. Lyceums, which offered courses and lectures to adults for affordable fees, featured speakers such as Thoreau, Emerson, Daniel Webster, Nathaniel Hawthorne, and Emma Willard.[11]

In the early decades of the twentieth century, the goals of education shifted. Where high school used to be for students headed for college or the seminary, now it was charged with meeting the needs of all students. One by one, states enacted compulsory attendance laws; the last state to do so was Mississippi in 1918. Schools now faced a dilemma: how should they address the needs of their new school population? Progressive education reformers tried to make schools more responsive to the needs of students and communities; they emphasized not only connection with the outside world but continuous revision of curricula in order to keep the schools in step with the times. Twentieth-century school reforms took place under many banners, including efficiency, creativity, practicality, activity, "real life," the "whole child," social efficiency, and social action.

According to Hirsch, reformers in the 1930s and onward, believing that "the public cohesion of the country was firm," turned toward educating for the private sphere and away from a common curriculum. "Instead of placing at the center of emphasis and concern the knowledge and skill that *all* citizens should possess," writes Hirsch, "the new center was to be the individual child and his or her interests, talents, and needs." The idea of preparing citizens for participation in public discourse had receded; it was "as if the public school had decided to train students more for private than public life."[12]

One might add, in the spirit of Arendt's argument, that some reformers sought to prepare students for the social sphere or social life. Reformers repeatedly referred to the social group in school as a microcosm of society; the new curriculum was to be born of social activity or at least shaped by it. In *Democracy and Education* (1916), John Dewey maintained that school should reflect life: "For when the schools depart from the educational conditions effective in the out-of-school environment, they necessarily substitute a bookish, a pseudo-intellectual spirit for a social spirit." He saw the "social spirit" as the essence of education; in his view, even individual work was subordinate to it. "Individuals are certainly interested, at times, in having their own way," he wrote, "and their own way may go contrary to the ways of others. But they are also interested, and chiefly interested upon the whole, in entering into the activities of others and taking part in conjoint and coöperative doings."[13] While Dewey did not deny the importance of individuality, his words appear to equate independent thought and action with "having one's own way."

The child-centered movement had a contradictory attitude about "having one's own way." It celebrated the individual child on the one hand and the conditioning of the social group on the other; the latter became more important over time. In his 1918 essay "The Project Method," William Heard Kilpatrick described a project as "a wholehearted purposeful act carried out amid social surroundings." This work, he argued, should be conditioned by peer approval: "Now there are few satisfactions so gratifying and few annoyances so distressing as the approval and the disapproval of our comrades. Anticipated approval will care for most cases; but the positive social disapproval of one's fellows has peculiar potency." The peer group (guided by the teacher) would regulate the interests and impulses of the individual child: "The pupils working under his guidance must through the social experiences encountered build the ideals necessary for approved social life." The children would thus become "an embryonic society," making "increasingly fine distinctions as to what is right and proper." The teacher's interventions should diminish over time, according to Kilpatrick: "The teacher's success—if we believe in democracy—will consist in gradually eliminating himself or herself from the success of the picture."[14] To Kilpatrick, democracy and the social group were not far apart; once adequately educated, the social group at school would resemble the kind of society that a democracy needed.

Some schools gave students vigorous practice in group operations. Harold Rugg and his colleague Ann Shumaker praised the Francis W. Parker school in Chicago, where elementary school students took part in numerous committees: "housekeeping committees, assembly committees, library committees, playground committees, lost and found departments, attendance committees, the school court, the jury, further handling of individual and group behavior in the corridor, lunch room library, rest room, or on the school grounds."[15] For the person who dreads committee meetings, this sort of education seems like an early induction into hell. Beyond that, one can imagine the amount of time devoted to the very management of the school's social activities. Parker was (and is) a remarkable school that combined progressive approaches with an inspiring curriculum; by no means did com- mittee work dominate school life. The point is that the school, like other progressive schools at the time, strove to build social units and to integrate social activity into the lessons and school life.

An emphasis on groups can also be found in the "integration" movement, led by L. Thomas Hopkins, professor of education at Teachers College from 1929 to 1954 and curriculum director of its Lincoln School. "Integration" was a nebulous concept; it referred to the integration of the personality, the integration of the individual in society, and the integration of subjects, among other things. Jesse L. Newlon, director of the Lincoln School from 1927 to 1934, saw integration as practical education and personality devel- opment. Hopkins took this idea further, saying that the "experiences" of the curriculum "cannot be set out and organized in advance of the life of the individuals who will participate in it." What kind of individuals should these be? Not individuals with strong opinions and eccentricities, not individuals who preferred to work alone, but individuals who worked well in groups.[16]

The "integrated" individual, according to Hopkins, makes "wide contact with the environment" and successfully "resolves the ensuing disturbances." By contrast, a "disintegrated" individual "moves within a narrow, increas- ingly circumcised environment," acts with "undue caution and restraint," and may withdraw in response to disturbances. Those who fail to integrate will likely be rejected by "certain persons" or "certain groups"; will "not concur with the goals, ends, or values set by the group"; will "not agree with the methods or means utilized by his fellows in pursuing their ends"; and will "resist attempts to enforce conformity upon him through dominance." To promote integration, argued Hopkins, schools must revise or eliminate all things that stand in its way: "grades, schedules, credits, records, reports, promotions, examinations, departmental organizations, minimum essentials, required subjects, and the like." The most important thing a school can do, he argued, is promote an *environment* for growth. A decade later, he described this as a "cooperative process": "This means a curriculum based upon the experiences of children, for it is only when working on their own needs that children learn genuine cooperative action. And so the whole basic subject structure of schools must be remade."[17]

By the late 1930s, according to Hopkins, four out of five schools in the United States were affected in some way by integration. In 1934, the *Jour- nal of the National Education Association* called this a "momentous shift of emphasis"; it stated that "the isolated subjectmatter [sic] compartment type of curriculum is rapidly losing ground" and that "the primary objective [of integration] is the substitution of 'pupil goals' for 'subjectmatter goals.'" Not everyone was swept up in the enthusiasm. Teachers College professor W. D. Reeve cautioned that "before teachers can properly correlate mathematics with other fields, they ought to learn how to correlate the various parts of mathematics." Many teachers found the integrated courses lacking in substance. One teacher in California wrote that "the vitamin content was far too low" and "the necessary nourishment was lacking." Her senior students, who had gone through the school's core program, complained that they had not read a single book together; she could "scarcely pry them loose from *Hamlet* because it was the first time that they had had a chance to argue about characters that they all knew." William C. Bagley, a brilliant educator and a colleague of Hopkins and Reeve at Teachers College, criticized the vague goals of the integration movement, noting that "integrative learnings are most effective when there is something to integrate."[18]

Like students, teachers in this era were expected to form and work within social units. In *Left Back*, Diane Ravitch gives a striking description and analysis of the curriculum revision movement of the 1930s and 1940s. Similar in many ways to the integration movement (with some of the same advocates), it emphasized the socialization of students and teachers alike. Influenced by psychologists and sociologists, schools used social engineering techniques to convince teachers of the necessity of change and to drive curriculum revision. An administrator might announce to the staff that an overhaul of the curriculum was needed. Consultants would then visit the school to direct the teachers in this process. Working in study groups, teachers would read works of Dewey, Kilpatrick, Rugg, and other theorists; conduct surveys in the community to find out whether the schools were meeting students' and parents' needs; and revise curricula accordingly. The new curricula would reflect and shape students' life experience.

From district to district, the groups concluded that the old academic curriculum was outdated and that the new curriculum should be based on children's own experiences. Many districts dropped their academic curricula, including courses on mythology, history, classic literature, and geography, and started offering courses on "basic living" and vocational skills. Teachers who resisted such changes would encounter pressure from the group. Indeed, that was part of the purpose of such group activity. In her study *Changing the Curriculum: A Social Process* (1946), Teachers College professor Alice Miel recommended that administrators assess teachers' readiness for change and use group processes to stir up dissatisfaction among the complacent. She also recommended hiring a heterogeneous staff—with the exception of people who might appear as "freaks" to the school community or those "whose social and educational philosophy is known to be reactionary. . . . In other words, differences to be *sought after* should be productive ones." In a 1945 article, the psychologist Kurt Lewin and his associate Paul Grabbe wrote that everyone desired to be part of an in-group—so the establishment of an in-group was an important step in bringing about change.[19]

Over the decades, the social emphasis has risen and fallen, but it has gone largely unchallenged as an idea. Some have objected to its particular manifestations; some have pointed to the weakened curriculum and called for a renewed emphasis on academic knowledge. Yet the social idea has great tenacity; we see this in classrooms where processes and strategies, not knowledge, serve as the common ground, and where students work in groups more often than not. We lose a sense of school as a place where *things* are taught—and where individuals grapple with these things in different ways, under the guidance of the teacher. The Common Core State Standards, which point in the direction of a strong common curriculum, still call for a variety of group interactions, thereby suggesting that the variety itself has value. The English language arts standards state, for instance, that third-grade students will "engage effectively in a range of collaborative discussions (one-on-one, in groups, and teacher-led) with diverse partners on grade 3 topics and texts, building on others' ideas and expressing their own clearly."[20] This is a laudable attempt to combine clear expression with various forms of group discussion—but it could turn into a distraction if teachers felt compelled to vary the "collaborative discussion" format for the sake of varying it.

In current standards for teachers, one likewise finds a social emphasis. Teachers are supposed to show awareness of the school community and students' personal backgrounds in relation to the subject matter. The proposed Model Core Teaching Standards, prepared by the Council of Chief State School Officers, state that "the teacher brings multiple perspectives to the discussion of content, including attention to students' personal, family, and community experiences and cultural norms." In addition, the teacher "reflects on his/her personal biases and seeks out resources to deepen his/her own understanding of cultural, ethnic, gender, and learning differences to build stronger relationships and create more relevant and responsive learning experiences."[21] In other words, teachers are expected to pay close attention to the social aspects of the subject matter. This can be a trap for both students and teachers; there are students of every ethnicity who do not think the way a culturally sensitive teacher thinks they might. Cultural sensitivity can easily turn into stereotyping. Moreover, a subject does transcend culture to some degree; instruction that ignores this may shortchange both subject and students.

A school is inevitably a social entity of some kind; at its best, such an entity provides a warm, nurturing environment for learning. But when the social emphasis goes unquestioned, it has serious pitfalls. First, when students spend a great deal of time in groups, the teacher must focus on their behaviors. The substance of the lesson takes a backseat to the processes. The teacher may sit down for a few minutes with this or that group, but she does not have time to challenge the students rigorously; she usually checks to see whether they are working well together, employing the appropriate "strategies," and getting things done. Another danger is that the groups, in order to stay cohesive and "on task," may disregard ideas that seem too complicated or challenging. Group work, even when conducted well, tends to bring the members toward the middle; it takes an extraordinary group to do otherwise. Yet another danger is that personal and social experiences may obscure the subject matter. Students may cloak themselves with their feelings and personal opinions, and teachers may hesitate to point out errors.

The social aspect of school needs counterbalances. To bring students together, schools must give them a basis for such a gathering. To encourage students to express their thoughts, schools must challenge students to refine them, both alone and in class. Without such challenge, students may not learn to push beyond their own limits. Those who lack the knowledge and skills to do the work may give up; those who are getting by may persist in getting by; and those who excel may develop a habit of ranting without realizing it.

RANTING IS THE spewing forth of an unconsidered, unchecked opinion; the ranter is both ignorant and sure. Ranting makes so much noise and takes so much space that it is hard for any other view to enter in. Sometimes it may come from a feeling of isolation, of being unheard, but it exacerbates the problem. As it goes unchallenged, it continues. It is often promoted unwittingly by schools and districts; those who *seem* convincing are applauded, whether or not their argument has merit. The appearances of the argument take precedence over the substance.

An example can be found in a sample comprehensive high school ("Regents") English examination on the New York State Education Department's website. For the main essay, students are supposed to agree or disagree with a quotation from Antoine de Saint-Exupéry, "It is only with the heart that one can see rightly." They are asked to offer a valid interpretation of this quotation, agree or disagree with it, and support their view with an analysis of any two literary works.[22]

Taken out of context, as it is in this sample examination, the quotation seems a bit maudlin and vague. Only by reading The Little Prince can one glean what Saint-Exupéry meant. The words are spoken by the fox, who has asked the prince to tame him. This taming involves a ritual: they meet every day, at the same time and place. Through that routine, the fox comes to trust the prince, and the prince learns the meaning of friendship. But as the sample examination does not require the students to have read The Little Prince or to know anything about the context, it leaves them at liberty to take the quotation in any way they please.

The sample examination comes with sample student essays at varying levels of proficiency; the top-scoring essay flagrantly misinterprets the quotation. The student writes, "Sentimentalists and overly romantic persons are the ones who believe that through love, 'one can see rightly.' However, what they see is a false veneer; they see a facade that provides a semblance of truth, but neglect to notice the myriad flaws of thinking with one's heart." The student supports this argument with examples from Romeo and Juliet and The Great Gatsby.[23] Because the essay fulfills all the requirements of the rubric, it is given the highest possible score. Yet it is based on a reaction as impulsive as the passions it criticizes. Part of the problem lies in the lack of common curriculum; if students were required to read any work in common, then the examination could use a quotation from that work, and students would be expected to interpret it carefully. If students are rewarded for uninformed arguments, if the substance of the argument doesn't matter, then they may rise to the role of national pundit before anyone calls them out.

Ranting is easily confused with dissent. Students who speak their uninformed minds are all too often praised for speaking up and out, being different (although they may not be), and questioning the status quo, which may not be what they think it is. Thoughtful dissent may not even be noticed, as it may take a quiet form. Ranting is self-satisfied and limited; it precludes discernment, as it goes unchecked and wants no checks. This runs counter to what Learned Hand called "the spirit of liberty," that is, "the spirit which is not too sure that it is right."[24] To develop this spirit, one must be willing to learn from others; to do this, one must establish what one is talking about in the first place.

Interpreting a quotation such as the one from The Little Prince is no trivial matter. To understand it correctly is to understand possibilities in the world. While life and literature exist in skewed relation, it is through literature that we become aware of some of our capabilities. To know what it means to "see rightly" and to see "with the heart" is almost to imagine oneself doing so. Having taken in the friendship of the prince and the fox, one starts to recognize it in other friendships and rituals: meetings over coffee, walks in the park, and letters that take on a special meaning over time. Without this recognition, we may perceive the heart as inherently impulsive, or reason as cold and calculating. It is an excellent book or poem that allows us to see combinations of truths, such as the reason of love and the poetry of reason.

Ranting seems solipsistic, but in some ways it is intensely social. When people cluster with others who think as they do, they feel at liberty to put forth opinions without carefully scrutinizing them. Those who disagree with them can be written off; they, too, must belong to a group and must have an agenda lurking. The mutual suspicion leads to trivialization of the points on both sides. A group member is relieved of the obligation to look both inward and outward, to question the self and to challenge the opponent. Ranting is checked only in solitude or in a forum where all sides lay down their weapons except for those of fact, intuition, argument, and respect. The lone thinker is more at home in such a forum than in a clique where everyone is in agreement. One of the most important aspects of the public forum is that, ideally, all members may walk off on their own afterward; they are not beholden to the association. The public space is vast, precisely because it has a boundary but confines no one.

FOR A SCHOOL to enjoy the benefits of a common curriculum, it cannot be all-encompassing; it must not be a Crystal Palace. Yes, students need a common basis; they need to learn together and challenge each other, and they need inspiring, lasting, well-organized subject matter. But they need to take their own directions as well. Probably everyone with a serious interest has pursued it in spite of what others were doing. Some have studied an instrument or language outside of school. Some have taken special courses at their schools. Some discover an interest through tinkering or chance. Many have spent evenings wrapped up in projects that people around them couldn't understand—constructing a computer program, drawing a house, deciphering a code, or writing a villanelle.

Discernment relies on respect for each person's separateness of mind. It is thus dependent on difference. Difference is not the same as loudness, nor does it always take the form of protest. It occupies a wide range, from a subtle qualification of a point to rejection of an entire system of thought. It may be right or wrong, wise or foolish; it may be gentle or abrasive in style or anything in between. But without it we would be at a loss. There would be no urgency, no passion, if no one knew how to take off from the group.

We often hear about how our schools and workplaces cannot afford to be individualistic as they were in the past, how we must view ourselves as members of a team and citizens of the world. But individualism and individuals are not the same. One need not be out for oneself in order to think for oneself. Teams, groups, and societies need individuals in order to maintain integrity and vitality. Paul Woodruff points out that "democracy has many doubles, but the most seductive is majority rule, and this is not democracy."[25] We need those who are distinctly unlike the others—those who speak in different terms and do not always get along with the rest. Common ground allows people to define their differences, but there is no point in defining differences unless one can actually have them.

Few works argue as passionately for difference as John Stuart Mill's *On Liberty*, published in 1859. Alexander Bain, Mill's friend and colleague, pointed out some of its logical flaws yet found in it "a combination of reasoning and eloquence that has never been surpassed, if indeed ever equalled, in the cause of intellectual freedom."[26] In this treatise, Mill strives to reconcile the principles of individualism and common good. He warns that when groups become assured of themselves, they lose both their access to truth and their vitality. He argues that a society cannot thrive without dissent—that the "tyranny of the majority" is deadly.

The dissenting individual, according to Mill, contributes to the pursuit of truth even when he is wrong: "Truth gains more even by the errors of one who, with due study and preparation, thinks for himself, than by the true opinions of those who only hold them because they do not suffer themselves to think." That is, we need those who differ thoughtfully—note the phrase "with due study and preparation." What kind of preparation is this? Mill acknowledges that children need formal instruction and guidance: "Nobody denies that people should be so taught and trained in youth, as to know and benefit by the ascertained results of human experience. But it is the privilege and proper condition of a human being, arrived at the maturity of his faculties, to use and interpret experience in his own way."[27]

Mill regards too much common knowledge as a threat; he associates it with uniformity of thought:

> Formerly, different ranks, different neighbourhoods, different trades and professions, lived in what might be called different worlds; at present, to a great degree in the same. Comparatively speaking, they now read the same things, listen to the same things, see the same things, go to the same places, have their

hopes and fears directed to the same objects, have the same rights and liberties, and the same means of asserting them.[28]

Mill claims that "every extension of education" promotes this sameness, because "education brings people under common influences, and gives them access to the general stock of facts and sentiments." These and other forces combine to form "so great a mass of influences hostile to Individuality, that it is not easy to see how it can stand its ground." All the recent political changes, he argues, "tend to raise the low and to lower the high." Economic and social changes likewise contribute to the problem; with the increase in commerce and communication, and the swell of public opinion, there is no longer any power "interested in taking under its protection opinions and tendencies at variance with those of the public."[29]

Mill may have taken for granted the kind of education necessary for understanding his very arguments. Today, in America, many high school and even college students would struggle with Mill's writing and the ideas in it. They might not know what to make of the following sentence: "Instead of being, as at first, constantly on the alert either to defend themselves against the world, or to bring the world over to them, they have subsided into acquiescence, and neither listen, when they can help it, to arguments against their creed, nor trouble dissentients (if there be such) with arguments in its favour." To understand a sentence like this, students would need a firm grasp of grammar and a great deal of practice reading such works, slowly, under the guidance of a knowledgeable teacher. All of this requires a good curriculum and a strong, flexible tradition of instruction. The educator Carol Jago makes a similar point about the opening sentence in Dickens's *Tale of Two Cities*: "How many of our twittering students can parse this sentence? How many teachers have lost the will to ask their charges do so?"[30]

Nonetheless, Mill's argument poses a healthy challenge to the idea of a common curriculum—one that the idea of curriculum can withstand. Students do need to pursue their interests and passions, or they will have little to contribute to society. The question then becomes, how can schools give students a common foundation while also allowing them to take their own directions? One logical approach would be to have a common plan of study through the seventh or eighth grade, so that students could be exposed to many subjects, including languages and the arts, and learn the fundamentals of each. Outside of school, they should have time and opportunity to pursue their own interests—sports, music lessons, independent reading, theater productions, and more. High schools might have different emphases and electives along with a core curriculum. But it is not through electives alone that one finds difference. There must be room for things that stand out in the classroom—the sudden insight, the puzzling question, the supreme effort. We must not overcrowd the schedule or clutter the lesson; there must be time and sufficient tranquility for thinking about the subjects and discussing interesting problems. Difference requires some silence, including the pauses between comments in the classroom.

Writing a century apart, Mill and Arendt were both concerned about the effects of social streamlining on the overall quality of thought. For Arendt, society itself meant streamlining, as it subsumed both the public and the private realms; for Mill, society had integrity only when it made room for difference. For Arendt, common knowledge was essential for difference; for Mill, too much common knowledge threatened to obliterate it. These seemingly opposite arguments are actually compatible; for both, common knowledge is a starting point, not an end. The goal for both Mill and Arendt is to come closer to the truth. While such pursuit of truth may take place in social settings, it requires public and private spirit in order to make headway. The public spirit allows for discussion of a common topic, without the interference of personal relationships (or as little interference as possible). The private spirit allows for the testing of things against the ear and conscience.

Education must show students the way from the surface of a subject to its core; this means, among other things, going beyond opinion to a deeper level of understanding. In the fifth book of the *Republic*, Plato describes opinion as something in between ignorance and knowledge. Those who opine are able to call something beautiful but unable to see beauty itself. They are caught in a conundrum, as things that are called beautiful can also be called ugly, and things that are called just can also be called unjust. The things about which one opines are "rolling around as intermediates between what is not and what purely is."[31] As we are always short of pure knowledge and understanding, we need opinions, but we also need to discern their limitations and perceive something beyond them. To do so, we break from the social realm, for social life is governed by opinion—what friends say, what people on Facebook like, what is proclaimed "in" or "out." Yet in striving for better understanding, in stepping apart from popular opinion, we are able to see others as they are. It is in this manner that we enter the sort of relation that Martin Buber describes in *I and Thou*—a relation that involves one's whole being, a relation in which one is alone.

Consider *King Lear*—a play about many things, but certainly about discernment. We do not know for sure what throws Lear into turmoil and eventually brings him to clarity. When he calls for his Fool, he is in some way acknowledging his foolishness, or at least intimating that something is wrong in his reasoning and in the world. But what pulls him into the storm and out again? It seems to be a movement of the spirit, an inability to rest with error. It could be called conscience or longing for truth, but it seems less rational than that. It is motion of language, of body, of nature; it seems to be caused by an unseen force. At his height of delirium he recognizes the deceit around him: "What! Art mad? A man may see how this world goes with no eyes. Look with thine ears: see how yond justice rails upon yond simple thief. Hark in thine ear: change places and, handy-dandy, which is the justice, which is the thief?" The discerning spirit has a way of returning to itself, even without knowing why.[32]

The resolution of *Lear* is awful, not happy; Lear seems reduced to madness again upon seeing Cordelia dead. "Howl, howl, howl!" he cries. "O, you are men of stones! / Had I your tongues and eyes, I'd use them so / That heaven's vault should crack! She's gone for ever."[33] Yet these very cries, full of the senselessness of the world, show his return to sense and dignity, futile as it seems. We are left to wonder whether there was any justice for him, any reward for his suffering—but there must be some of both, as the false and the true have been sorted out at last. Such sorting requires passion, a relentless desire for truth. To find one's way through error is to restore the public dignity, broken as it may seem.

A bleak equality it would be if we had nothing to do with each other and nothing of which to convince each other. Yet we must also be at liberty to take our own course, to risk disapproval, even censure, even error. Returning to the incident on the Soviet ship, I recognize that there may have been some good that I didn't see at the time. The woman may have been right or wrong in what she did, but if wrong, she was entitled to be wrong. She may indirectly have done us a favor by holding her ground, wobbly as it may have been. Or maybe she heard us, and we didn't realize it. Only she could really know her own motives and actions, and maybe even she did not know them. As equals, we are all tasked with holding our own. We must learn, in our own ways, to lift ourselves, to find our way to nobility. The word "noble," curiously, derives from the Latin *gnobilis*, "knowable," but it also carries the sense of holding something in reserve, of respecting that which cannot be public or fully known.

Such talk of nobility may sound false or pretentious to some. John Hollander writes, "When we hear public discourse invoking nobility, we hold the speaker guilty of being a liar, a knave, a fool, a con man, or a politician until proved innocent." It is common to scoff at the word as though it had lost its use, as though it had nothing to do with equality. But while human equality is our given and our dream, it is a sinking equality unless we try to live up to something greater than ourselves, or at least acknowledge its presence. We need those who help us understand more than we already do, who show us hints of grace in our mess. Hollander sees the nobility of poetry as a complement to democracy; it is a nobility that asks something of us, that calls on us to listen well. "Poetry," he writes, "can exemplify a nobility of expression all the more important in a democracy that sees socially preserved, postfeudal nobility of lineage as a horrible travesty of what an evolved idea of what is outstandingly human might mean."[34]

Wishing no longer to put one human above another, we still need something to look up to, something worthy of admiration. Shoddy, dismissive language wears us down; jargon muddles our thoughts. We need language that does not compromise or condescend, does not throw up its hands, does not pretend beauty is over. When we turn our thoughts fully to it, it is as though the mind straightened its posture. And while buzzwords and glib phrases seem to rule the day, there is still fine language to come, words and rhythms that stride through the noise and chatter.

12

~

Conclusion:
Setting Up Shop

Just how important is solitude? Some might say that it belongs only to the few who want it; others might call it our universal misery. Some might say that it will never go away, so we need not worry about it; others might counter that it is already gone. Each claim is partly true but depends on a slightly different definition of solitude. Let us look at the question in another way: which things deserve the dedication of solitude? Now answers start rolling in. Solitude for the sake of something makes sense.

Solitude gives us room, at least in the mind, to take a break from the churn. Without such room, we entangle ourselves in quarrels, hearsay, and fads. In order to do anything of substance, we need a place that is relatively still, not giddy with updates, not caught up in what others think. This place varies from person to person and from situation to situation, but it needs tending, as do the things in it.

It is at once very lonely and not lonely at all. In that sense it pushes words to their opposites. A person in solitude sees that loneliness contains company and vice versa. Words contradict themselves; sometimes the only way to catch truth is through tousling with language or falling silent and waiting until words rise up again. Sometimes it is a combination of words, or a word used in an unusual way, that catches the mind off guard and shakes the phrases into life. Whether one works with words, music, or wood, solitude has a way of turning the material inside out and upside down until its shape comes clear.

It is difficult to understand today's education discussions—or any con-temporary discussions—without some distance from them. But the distance seems harder to afford than a country villa. Caught up in catching up, many see no respite until they are done, which they will never be. Teachers, who need time to sort through the questions that arise over the course of the day and the longer term, find themselves racing to keep the piles of paper down—reports, conference notes, individualized student goals, portfolio pieces, analyses of test scores, and more. Doctors rushing from patient to patient, or editors from manuscript to manuscript, run as fast as they can just to stay in place, like Alice in Looking-Glass Land.

Stepping out of the mayhem is frightening; we miss the comforting rumble of our assumptions, the unreasoned reasons that keep pushing us onward. To take time for thought is to invite a crisis: What have I been doing all this time? Is it possible—to echo Ivan Ilyich in Leo Tolstoy's story—that my whole life has been wrong? Let us consider the possibility. Which, in that case, would be worse: to keep riding the error, or to take stock of it and change course? If the error is less severe than a lifelong delusion, or if there is no error at all, is it not good to find this out?

But introspection and time alone can mislead, some may say. We need the opinions and advice of others; if we spend too much time alone, distorted thoughts may take over, thoughts that oppress us even more than the out-side world, because we can't get them out of our heads. This concern is well founded; the mind can indeed overwhelm, and outside views can bring clar-ity. But no matter how much good advice we receive, no matter how many sources we consult, all of this is preparation and no more. At the point of decision, we are alone.

In the first chapter, I brought up W. H. Auden's essay, quoting his words, "I shall not attempt, therefore, in this paper, to answer such questions as, 'How good a poet is Yeats? Which are his best poems and why?'—that is the job of better critics than I and of posterity."[1] It is time to return to that essay for a moment.

Auden notes that Yeats was in some ways caught in the arguments of his time, as are those who read his work. The winning side sets the terms of the argument, thus limiting the opposition and the dialogue itself:

Further, Reason, Science, the general, seemed to be winning and Imagination, Art, and the individual on the defensive. Now in all conflicts it is the side which takes the offensive that defines the issues which their opponents have to defend, so that when scientists said, "Science is knowledge of reality, Art is a fairyland," the artists were driven to reply, "Very well, but fairies are fun, science is dull." When the former said, "Art has no relation to life," the latter retorted, "Thank God." To the assertion that "every mind can recognize the absolute truths of science, but the values of art are purely relative, an arbitrary affair of individual taste," came back the counterclaim, "Only the exceptional individual matters."[2]

Education discussions often fall into similar traps. Some reformers assert that teachers must be held accountable; others reply, "How can one be held accountable for passion and dedication?" Some say that schools must show results; others answer, "The best things in education cannot be measured." Some say that educators are resistant to change; the retort comes back, "And rightly so; the proposed changes are wrongheaded." These debates reach a stalemate; the combinations of words lead back to the same place again and again.

But why should accountability be defined so narrowly? What if accountability meant, at least in part, subjecting our actions and decisions to our best thinking and conscience? What if it meant having the courage to stand up for what we do? That would change the argument profoundly. Educators would be responsible for recognizing and honoring what mattered in their work. This would include the substance of education—literature, science, history, and other subjects—as well as the learning demonstrated by students. Such responsibility would require hours of thinking in the evenings; it would require that schools turn their attention toward the subjects and relax any mandates that distract from them.

Someone might object, "You assume that schools have the wherewithal to engage in this kind of thought; in fact, many continue to struggle with practicalities. We need teachers who can teach students to read, period. Forget about thinking about literature and philosophy for now; let's take care of the fundamentals first." Very well; let's take care of fundamentals. But those fundamentals should include suggestions of what is to come. As students learn to read, they should also be listening to poems, myths, and historical tales. A music teacher should give students a glimpse of what they may be able to play or sing later. The teacher of arithmetic should be able to throw a simple algebra problem into the mix, once in a while, so that students start to grasp the abstract forms of their calculations. With these hints, not only are students enticed to the next level but they gain insight into what they are doing at present.

Someone else might complain, "You are giving too much importance to teachers' intellectual lives. Teachers need to learn to get out of the way and let the students do the thinking and talking." Is that really so? If we take the instruction out of teaching, if we turn teachers into assistants and coaches, then students will not see past their own level of understanding. If we stop expecting students to listen to the teacher, then they won't learn how to listen to each other or to themselves, either. A teacher can set the tone of thoughtfulness for the class. He can put students' points in perspective, questioning and affirming them in ways that their peers cannot. In addition, he shows the possibility of spending years with the subject and enjoying it.

Yet another person might say, "Fine. Give teachers time to think about their subjects and their lessons. How many will actually do it? They'll be doing whatever they want. Some of them will watch TV every night or meet up with their friends at the bar." That can be said for any profession. There is no guarantee—nor should there be—that people will use their time the way others wish. Such a risk comes with freedom in any line of work. The undesirable alternative is to require teachers to document everything they do, including their thinking. That creates more busywork and accomplishes nothing. Instead, schools can set examples; they can hold faculty seminars on the subjects themselves and topics within them. Let us say, for instance, that a principal holds a seminar on Matthew Arnold's poem "Dover Beach." By doing so, she not only encourages teachers to think about the poem and discuss it, but makes room for the poem itself in the school day. Although it may not seem so, this is a gesture toward solitude.

Of course, there is the danger that solitude might become a fad: that schools might embrace some sort of solitude movement and mention solitude at every turn. This could be worse than a neglect of solitude. Schools would start having "solitude time," but it would be prescribed solitude: students would have to write in journals and perhaps even "share their solitudes" with the class afterward. There would be a forced sanctity to it: "Shh! the children are in solitude!" There would be solitude charts on the wall. Professional development sessions on "strategies" for "managing solitude" would be conducted. Administrators would go on "solitude appreciation retreats," where they would discuss solitude in small groups and give each other a "Woot!" at the end. Some solitaries might find themselves wishing that solitude had stayed a semi-secret, an outlaw. But there are ways for schools to encourage solitary work without ruining it.

Schools can honor solitude in two ways. First, they should stop pushing group work and technology at all times and places. They are not suited to all subjects, topics, and situations. If they are used wisely, with discretion, they will gain meaning. Second, schools should give students things worth thinking about and show them how to do so. If students are learning things that they can carry through their lives, discuss with each other and the teacher, and practice on their own, there will be room for solitude.

Aristotle writes in the *Nicomachean Ethics* that contemplation is the high-est of the activities because one can practice it alone and love it for its own sake.[3] One can say the same for the study of literature, history, mathematics, music, and other subjects. Though not as pure (in a certain sense) as con-templation, they can all be practiced alone and loved for their own sakes, at least up to a point. Loving a subject is not the same as liking it, enjoying it at every moment, or always being eager to pursue it. It means staying with it even in times of reluctance, and coming back to it after breaks. It means setting aside other things for it, keeping certain rituals for it, and recognizing when to honor or break the rules.

IT SEEMS HARDLY right to leave without a tip of the hat to eccentricity. In a sense, this book has been about eccentrics all along.

Think of the eccentric, and you might recall Nikola Tesla, who enter-tained Mark Twain and his other friends with strange machines and dazzling inventions; Claiborne Pell, who was known to jog in his tweed jacket; or Diogenes, who lit a lamp by daylight and walked around, explaining, "I am looking for a man" (in some versions, "an honest man").[4] Or you might think of someone you knew in high school who would stand up and yodel in the cafeteria. But these are scattered examples of people with outlandish traits. Eccentricity need not manifest itself in outward quirks. It is not just oddity, though it may involve many oddities. It consists of being out of the center—that is, straying from circular orbit.

If you have laughed to yourself when walking down the street, you have known eccentricity. If, at a meeting, you have voiced your disagreement with the general tenor of discussion, not knowing whether anyone would take your side, you have lived eccentricity. If, once in a while, you have sensed the existence of places beyond our knowledge, of ideas not yet formed, of words beyond those spoken, of meanings and ruptures of mean-ing, of inklings sparking forth and melding, you have sensed an eccentricity outside you but involving you. If you have fumbled in another language, trying to sculpt the sounds and syllables while others giggled, you have found the eccentricity that comes from being a beginner. If you have met with a friend, talked for a while, said goodbye, and then walked off on your own way with a surge of sadness, or maybe joy or pensiveness or puzzlement, then you know the eccentricity that is part of every goodbye, every parting of ways. If you have had moments of shivering, tingling, jangling out of the skin, as though the body could not hold it all, then the eccentric is no stranger to you. Such moments may be uncomfortable, but this discomfort is our personal and common wealth; it pushes us beyond our limits, or what we think our limits are.

Sometimes eccentricity is error—inevitable, irrevocable error. In Hermann Hesse's novel *Demian*, the narrating character finds himself criticizing his beloved mentor to his face, only to discover that he has wounded him badly. There is no repairing the harm or retracting the words. Later, when alone, he realizes what has happened:

> For a long time we stayed in front of the dying fire, in which each glowing shape, each writhing twig reminded me of our rich hours and increased the guilty awareness of my indebtedness to Pistorius. Finally I could bear it no longer. I got up and left. I stood a long time in front of the door to his room, a long time on the dark stairway, and even longer outside his house waiting to hear if he would follow me. Then I turned to go and walked for hours through the town, its suburbs, parks, and woods, until evening. During that walk I felt for the first time the mark of Cain on my forehead.[5]

In Hesse's novel, the "mark of Cain" is internal; it is the sense of profound difference from others, a sense of private laws, a sense of the mark that one's actions make on the self. Action, right or wrong, is eccentricity. It is easy to forget action, to rush from activity into activity, without pausing to look at what one has actually done. To look at one's actions is to know one's difference; a day of atonement is in some sense a day of eccentricity. We take to heart the things we have done that stick out like sharp elbows—lovely elbows, some of the time.

Eccentricity may be careless. We let out harsh words to parents, children, friends, teachers, siblings, lovers, colleagues, strangers. We take our own way, sometimes rudely, then wish we hadn't been so harsh. But wish or no, it happens—and to pretend otherwise, to put forth selves that rarely risk a nerve, is to be left with little more than a lump of likenesses and likabilities, a pile of traits that are neither this nor that, moldable into any fashion, moldable out of it again, neither offensive nor memorable, pleasant enough but lacking in the stuff of love, jealousy, loyalty, anger, and awe.

It may be that there are fewer visible eccentrics around than there were forty or fifty years ago. Children are not brought up to think and act on their own; parents and schools plan and monitor their activities throughout the day. Even children's toys leave little room for the imagination: dolls come packaged with life stories, costumes are usually based on TV and movie characters, and video games provide illustration, movement, and sound, leaving little for the mind beyond quick decisions. Textbook and test publishers carefully remove material that might offend, upset, or provoke; thus many students go through school without realizing how interesting and startling the subjects can be.[6] On top of this, children spend hours sending text messages to their peers, instead of writing letters, stories, or diary entries. They can find out instantly what their friends like—and can buy those things instantly if they have the money. In short, they are learning to be like each other and to purchase many things.

In "Solitude of Self," Elizabeth Cady Stanton describes a servant girl who decorated the Christmas tree of the family she served, only to find that there was no present for her. The girl "slipped away in the darkness and spent the night in an open field sitting on a stone, and when found in the morning was weeping as if her heart would break." Stanton comments, "No mortal will ever know the thoughts that passed through the mind of that friendless child in the long hours of that cold night, with only the silent stars to keep her company."[7] Such times of disappointment and raw loneliness come to us all, but we may be losing the ability to endure them on our own. One could argue that the girl *should* have received a present, but that is beside the point. Even in a just world, there is heartbreak and letdown and wrong. Do we go online and try to get sympathy from strangers, or do we call on our own strength? Sympathy from strangers can be genuine and comforting, but it can also wear thin and keep us from ourselves.

Epictetus, a Greek Stoic philosopher of the first and second centuries, argued that one needed to know one's own character in order to make sound decisions. In the first book of his *Discourses*, Epictetus recounts a conversation between Florus, who is trying to decide whether or not to enter Nero's festival, and Agrippinus, who is advising him. Agrippinus says that Florus should go, because he aims to resemble the other men, perceiving himself as "but a single thread of all that go to make up the garment." For his own part, Agrippinus does "not even raise the question," for "when a man once stoops to the consideration of such questions, I mean to estimating the value of externals, and calculates them one by one, he comes very close to those who have forgotten their own proper character." In contrast with Florus, Agrippinus has no need to enter Nero's festival at all, or even to consider going, because he has no desire to be like the majority of the people. He explains, "But I want to be the red, that small and brilliant portion which causes the rest to appear comely and beautiful. Why, then, do you say to me, 'Be like the majority of people?' And if I do that, how shall I any longer be the red?"[8]

If we do not allow ourselves those red threads, we may forget what they are. John Stuart Mill warned in 1859 that "mankind speedily become unable to conceive diversity, when they have been for some time unaccustomed to see it."[9] Today there is much discussion of diversity, but little consideration of its meaning. In its common usage, it seems to have little to do with unusual thoughts and personalities, even less with aloneness of thought. It has more to do with group identity. Workplaces strive to have employees of various racial and ethnic backgrounds, but may reject someone with unconventional ideas, habits, or histories. There may be room for a certain kind of eccentric, such as the software engineer with the unusual project proposal, but not for other kinds, such as the teacher who reads Sanskrit late into the night. It is not that a school would deliberately reject a teacher who read Sanskrit, but it would not value such practice (unless Sanskrit were among its courses). We hear much about the importance of "lifelong learning"—why so little regard for the things one does alone?

WHEN I HAVE told people about this book, no one has responded casually or flippantly. Instead, some have told me that they found themselves thinking about the idea long after our conversation—or had already been thinking about it long before. One colleague wrote me a long letter about solitude in her life; the very mention of the subject brought up many memories. Another teacher told me about her adopted daughter, who needed "thinking time" during the rides to school.

If people are already aware of their solitude and their need for it, where does the problem lie? There are several aspects to it. First, as mentioned earlier, solitude is not immediately lucrative; often it brings few external rewards. Professions that are under pressure to show short-term results tend to sacrifice thoughtfulness in some way. There are certainly exceptions; some companies make time for their employees to explore ideas, with or without results. But the language of results has become dominant in many walks of life. As a consequence, our lives have tilted away from solitude without our full realization or consent. The forces against it are impressive, and it is decidedly out of style. For a combination of reasons I found myself determined to write a book about it.

It is no easy subject. Along the way, I ran into obstacles and paradoxes. For one thing, solitude is meaningless unless it contains something. As I worked on the book, I found myself drawn more and more to the things of solitude, the things I have always done alone, even among others. At times I had the urge to say, to myself and others, "Forget about solitude—just do something that interests you, and do it well! Or walk along the water, or through city streets, and let your mind go scavenging!" But some appreciation of solitude is necessary for all of this. It need not be overt; it can be wrapped up in everyday practice, part of the morning coffee and part of the train ride home.

I had the honor of visiting the Dallas Institute of Humanities and Culture in July 2010. The institute holds year-round events devoted to literature and humanities; at its Sue Rose Summer Institute for Teachers, public school teachers immerse themselves in classic literature. That year, the Summer Institute focused on the epic tradition. I was there for the first three days, which were devoted to the *Iliad*. It was a stirring experience to read this work with teachers and scholars. I had read parts of it in Greek in high school and reread it in English over the years, but I had not read it in full in a long time. Those three days were filled with the *Iliad* and other works from morning to night. Outside of class, I read and reread and talked with my hostess; during the day, I listened to lectures and discussed the *Iliad* with the teachers and Summer Institute faculty.

During the first seminar discussion, Mary Ann Bandiola, a mathematics teacher, began by saying that she had a difficult time understanding literature. Since she came from a mathematical perspective, she was used to making logical sense of things as she went along. She proceeded to ask a question that had come out of careful reading and led to a fascinating discussion. Later in the day, I approached her and told her that I saw such logical thinking as an asset; it involved paying close attention to details and looking for the relation between them. She asked me about my own teaching; I told her that I had left teaching to write a book. When I explained the subject, her face burst into joy. "Math teachers would love this," she said. "We feel the same way. We are always told to use group work, but children need to concentrate in order to learn math. They need to be quiet and think." We had more conversations over the course of my visit; she introduced me to other math teachers there and told them about the book.

At the Dallas Institute, the immersion in the literature brought people together. It seemed, in those discussions, that some kind of virtue was possible, precisely because we were focused on something worthy and beautiful, something we could understand better over time but could not seize or possess. The lectures, seminars, afternoon activities, and solitary reading all gave meaning to each other. There was a seminar room where teachers would read quietly in the mornings before the lecture started; I loved to be in that room with the French windows and the sound of pens and turning pages. The institute was strikingly different from the many professional development sessions I had attended where the subject matter was secondary to pedagogical methods. Here, the processes, though important, hardly made a murmur; yet without being told how to teach, I left the institute with many ideas for the classroom.

In contrast with the Dallas Institute, many institutions of higher education are under pressure to revise their programs with attention to collaboration and concrete outcomes. The Woodrow Wilson National Fellowship

Foundation's Responsive Ph.D. initiative includes a recommendation for "connecting resources to outcomes": Duke University, for instance, allocates budgets on the basis of evidence that departments are bringing in more faculty, attracting students, obtaining outside funding, and increasing student quality. The Council of Graduate Schools' Ph.D. Completion Project recommends increasing the level of socialization in graduate school through groups, workshops, and social meeting spaces. The Yale Graduate School of Arts and Sciences has been instituting regular benchmarks and "collaborative frameworks" to facilitate the timely completion of work. According to a Yale graduate student, an administrator told students that graduate programs in the humanities were costing the university too much; students were taking too long to finish and, unlike students in the sciences, were not usually supported by outside grants. It was time, the administrator said, to step up the process—to get students through the Ph.D. program quickly. To this end, students should work together, not alone; the days of sequestering oneself away in the library were over.[10]

Graduate students should not drag out their studies beyond reason. But if they must limit themselves to what they can do successfully and quickly, they end up sacrificing certain kinds of pursuits and ideas. Worse, they face the hostility of those who distrust uncertainties, who want to raise the numbers. Universities used to have room for a bit of dreaminess, a bit of the tentative, a bit of romping, a few wrong turns. If this disappears, if colleges and universities become career preparation programs, then it is unclear what will happen to studies that do not reap quick profits or result in high-status jobs. Will the pursuit of understanding, outside of strict limits, become too risky? Will subjects no longer be taught for the things that come clear slowly, over many years? There have already been enough limitations, in academia, on intellectual life; departments may be dominated by one view or another, and political relationships may supersede the exchange of ideas. But now, with increased pressure to meet strict deadlines and move on, students may not have time to think apart from others or to conceive of doing so.

It is not that colleges and universities should be protected, isolated realms, detached from the outside world and its practical cares. Many students cannot afford this, nor does such removal necessarily lead to good study. One learns much from the working world—about humans and their ways, about the work itself, and about one's own priorities. Practicality is not opposed to intellectual life. The problem here is not practicality itself but a crude form of it, a form that insists on the tangible and successful and little else. In *University, Inc.*, journalist Jennifer Washburn writes of "a wholesale culture shift" in higher education that is "transforming everything from the way universities educate their students to the language they use to define what they do": for example, administrators "refer to students as 'consumers' and to education and research as 'products.'"[11]

Under pressure to raise their bottom line, many colleges and universities have eliminated less-popular courses and adopted funding policies that rewarded performance and completion. In 2010, the State University of New York at Albany announced that it would no longer be admitting students into programs in French, Italian, Russian, or classics. The Obama administration announced in 2011 that it would offer incentives to colleges and universities to step up their graduation rates and move students through faster.[12] While colleges should encourage students to finish college on time, the very emphasis on rate of completion holds dangers, as it may affect the very content of the courses. If such trends continue, education will lose not only its perspective on the present, but its identity as a giver of perspective. Perspective itself will become a museum piece, an encased specimen of a charmed and outrageous time. Of course that is an extreme scenario; one must keep some perspective on the loss of perspective. Nonetheless, negative utopias keep us on our toes now and then.

SOLITUDE WILL ALWAYS be a bit dislikable, like the one who wears odd clothes, speaks a different language, or harbors plans that no one fully understands. Whoever allows for a bit of solitude, becomes a misfit willy-nilly. The misfit is frightening, not because he poses an external threat, but because each of us might be that very misfit in hiding. Moment by moment we choose whether to differ from the others or from our past habits, and if so, how to do it. To differ is to risk losing friends, making enemies, offending others, losing jobs and opportunities, or being mocked. There is an even greater risk: that solitude set in motion cannot be reversed. A bit of solitude can call old practices into question, and this can be frightening. Solitude shakes the dust from the book that has been with us for years; we thought we knew it, but its words never gleamed so fiercely or shook us so roughly as when we finally sat with it alone.

It is difficult, this solitude, but how much fun it can be. It is in solitude that Tristram Shandy can take his tale wherever he pleases, or the narrator of "The Overcoat" can make tales of his hero's very name. To be solitary is to have language spread out like a peacock's tail (granted, a bit more messily). And despite its difficulty, solitude is remarkably easy to find and strengthen. It takes only an hour with a book, and then another hour, and then another, for the book to take hold and rise up around us. It does not require that we give up our connections with the world. It does require a certain muscle: the ability to concentrate, to leave trivia aside, to put our thoughts into what we are doing, even for a few minutes at a time. That is the beginning of the shaping of solitude. The unshaped kinds are even easier to find, though probably easier to lose as well. Those pleasant mornings with coffee, when there is no immediate need to do anything in particular—those need not always be filled with news updates and email, though news updates and email are enjoyable and important. There are thousands of moments during the day when we may choose where to direct our attention. No movement, no self-help book can teach us how to make such choices.

Poetry might have something to teach us about solitude—not didactically, not directly, but obliquely. Out of the possibilities, a poet finds words that come together in an unusual way. It takes a good deal of honesty to write a poem—not the honesty of "expressing one's feelings" or telling the literal truth, necessarily, but the honesty of fierce, unremitting listening: the willingness to take up rough textures, contradictions, and strange ideas if they are part of the poem that is to be, and the strength to reject what is not right for the poem.

To understand a poem, as readers, we have to be "all ears" in its presence—without distractions inside or outside us. We have to still ourselves enough to take in its sounds; we have to take time with it. Memorizing is a way of coming to terms with a poem, like learning one's way around a house in the dark. We have to be alone with a poem, even if we read it with others or pass it on to others. The poem, in turn, makes us in some ways more alone than before, in some ways less so. It is filled with the minds and voices of those who have read it, even if we don't know who they are. It holds ghosts of poems that came before it and poems still to come.

One of my students, Wen Shi, a seventh-grader from China, delighted in the poems by William Blake and Edgar Allan Poe that I had the class read and memorize. She had been in the country for only two years; she worked hard on English, looking up word after word, writing thoughtful and precise essays, and contributing eagerly to class discussion. I had my students write poems for an assignment; her two poems showed the influence of the poems we had read, as well as a wonderful imagination and ear. One of the poems, "Earth," begins,

Earth was cold:
keep rolling, rolling out loud.
Earth is boil:
people, creatures are fill.

I would be proud if I had written those lines. "Keep rolling, rolling out loud" is ominous and unusual (a little like Poe's "The Bells"); the sounds themselves give the impression of a rolling earth that through its very rotation makes noise. The leap from "cold" to "boil" brings eons into a few lines and has hints of Blake's "A Poison Tree." Her mutation of verbs into nouns (boil, fill) gives the poem starkness and charge. The rest of the poem reads,

And people scold:
because of gold.
Never have any glad:
only left are people's mad.

They make loud voice:
their lives have no choice.
Day is running fast:
but Earthlings are last.

People are killing:
people are falling.
However this is originally:
and happens frequently.

The use of adjectives as nouns, the near anagram of "gold" and "glad," the intriguing word "originally"—all of this contributes to the poem's fierce sense. This is a student who once commented, "I like to be alone so I can have my imagination."[13] I have often returned to her poems; they assure me that poetry is still rolling, rolling out loud.

Poetry is no insipid spread, no placid pool, no nodding head; it does not often mean what we hope it will mean or say what we hope it will say. Tell poetry what to say in advance, and you've got a Hallmark greeting card or a driver's manual. Look into what it says, and you find surprises and openings. It is made of a certain kind of solitude, but it tilts this solitude into something else, a play of singularity and company.

How can solitude be the same for any two people? It cannot. Isn't there a flaw, then, in the very premise of this book, the idea of "our" sense of solitude? Isn't it a subject best left alone for each of us to handle as he or she pleases? I suggest three answers: yes, no, and besides. Yes—the "we" of this book is a loose association, as I have explained earlier. It is not perfect, and the reader may take part or not, as he or she sees fit. No, solitude is not entirely an individual matter, since it is affected by a society's attitudes, structures, and technology. Besides, solitude is filled with contradictions; that is what makes it both terrifying and delightful. The subject of solitude is barely broached, but the broaching opens up the rest.

Yet no matter how rich the solitude, no matter how much we may revel in it, it also holds harm and pain. We separate ourselves because we are already separate, because the communities in our lives do not bring us face to face. Often we walk away from the group because we yearn for something more: a friendship, a relationship, a communion with a book or piece of music, a place where we can be fully ourselves yet forget ourselves, a kind of company that neither allows nor expects nonchalance. We must go into the separation to find our way out of it; most of us do indeed wish for some gleam, some reminder (through loneliness itself) that we are not completely alone. In solitude we may recognize a gentle face and kind gesture. But the kindness is also stern; we must be willing to go off on our own when the time comes.

There's the paradox: each of us has to find solitude alone, yet we find it through others' shapes. We learn from our guides, but at some point we part ways with them. The greatest honor any of us can show a teacher is to take off and set up shop on our own, even with gratitude, even with regret, even with a tremor, even with doubts over our tools and hands. There is no good mind that does not at some point make a break with its instructors and guides. That is its motion and life. But going forward, forward, forward is not its entire nature. It also comes back, rereads, remembers; it recalls teachers and the things that were taught. There are shivers and grins in such memory. The mind is stunned to see those old words on the page, so clear now, so appropriate for the moment, as they have been for years, and to remember the teacher's voice with all its inflections. And so it seizes those things and others and seeks to pass them on.

Mind, but never mind what others say; mind, but never mind what the times dictate. It is one thing to hear the chatter, another to capitulate to it. Solitude is not political, but it requires resistance of a sort—resistance to all those things that subdue, compromise, or dull the soul (yes, I meant soul—I won't cross it out). Flannery O'Connor wrote in a letter, "You have to push as hard as the age that pushes against you."[14] This means not rejecting the world, but instead fortifying oneself within it, so that one can be part of it and apart, the way a glowing window in a row of houses changes the view of the street but holds its private den of light.

~

Notes

Chapter 1

1. W. H. Auden, "Yeats as an Example," *Kenyon Review* 10, no. 2 (Spring 1948), 187–88.

2. Charlotte Brontë, *Jane Eyre* (London: Smith, Elder, 1847; New York: Penguin, 2006), 82. Citation is to the Penguin edition.

3. David Riesman, *The Lonely Crowd: A Study of the Changing American Character* (New Haven, CT: Yale University Press, 1950), 199–201.

4. See the University of the State of New York, State Education Department, *English Language Arts Core Curriculum (Prekindergarten–Grade 12)*, May 2005, http://www.p12.nysed.gov/ciai/ela/elacore.pdf (accessed May 22, 2011). The entire fourth standard is devoted to reading, writing, listening, and speaking for social interaction.

5. Katie Hafner, "To Deal with Obsession, Some Defriend Facebook," *New York Times*, December 20, 2009; Carl Honoré, *In Praise of Slowness: How a Worldwide Movement Is Challenging the Cult of Speed* (New York: HarperCollins, 2004).

6. Irwin Edman, *The Contemporary and His Soul* (New York: Cape & Smith, 1931), 43.

7. Mark Bauerlein, *The Dumbest Generation: How the Digital Age Stupefies Young Americans and Jeopardizes Their Future* (New York: Tarcher, 2008), 95; Nicholas Carr, "Is Google Making Us Stupid? What the Internet Is Doing to Our Brains," *The Atlantic*, July–August 2008, 57; William Deresiewicz, "The End of Solitude," *Chronicle of Higher Education*, January 30, 2009.

8. Deresiewicz, "The End of Solitude."

9. Petrarch, *The Life of Solitude*, trans. Jacob Zeitlin (Urbana: University of Illinois Press, 1924), 1.3.1, 122. Citations to this work are by book, tractate, chapter, and page number.

10. Sherry Turkle, *Alone Together: Why We Expect More from Technology and Less from Each Other* (New York: Basic Books, 2011), 242; Victoria J. Rideout, Ulla G. Foehr, and Donald F. Roberts, *Generation M²: Media in the Lives of 8- to 18-Year-Olds: A Kaiser Family Foundation Study* (Menlo Park, CA: Henry J. Kaiser Family Foundation, 2010), 2; Darren Draper, *Pay Attention* (Jordan, UT: T4–Jordan School District, n.d.), http://t4.jordan.k12.ut.us/t4/content/view/221/35/ (accessed May 22, 2011). This video was presented at a faculty meeting at one of my former schools in New York City.

11. Petrarch, *The Life of Solitude*, 2.3.12, 220.

12. Elizabeth Cady Stanton, "Solitude of Self" (address to the Congressional Judiciary Committee, January 18, 1892; Ashfield, MA: Paris Press, 2001), 9–10. Citations are to the Paris Press edition; the full text of the speech can be found on the PBS website at http://www.pbs.org/stantonanthony/resources/solitude_self.html (accessed May 22, 2011); Harold Bloom, introduction to *Stories and Poems for Extremely Intelligent Children of All Ages* (New York: Simon & Schuster, 2001), 21.

13. Diana Senechal, "Why Do We Need a Philosophy of Education? The Forgotten Insights of Michael John Demiashkevich," *American Educational History Journal* 37, no. 1 (2010): 1–18.

14. See, for instance, Roza Leikin and Orit Zaslavsky, "Facilitating Student Interactions in Mathematics in a Cooperative Learning Setting," *Journal for Research in Mathematics Education* 28, no. 3 (May 1997): 331–54.

15. Lionel Trilling, "The Situation of the American Intellectual at the Present Time," in *The Moral Obligation to Be Intelligent: Selected Essays*, ed. Leon Wieseltier (New York: Farrar, Straus and Giroux, 2000; Evanston, IL: Northwestern University Press, 2008), 287. Citations are to the Northwestern University Press edition.

16. William Wordsworth, "I wandered lonely as a Cloud," in *Poems, in Two Volumes* (London: Longman, Hurst, Rees, and Orme, 1807), 2:49, 192; Tomas Venclova, "Dar neištirpusį ledyną," in *Pašnekesys žiemą: Eilėraščiai ir vertimai* (Vilnius: Vaga, 1991), 52; my translation. A somewhat different translation of these lines appears in Tomas Venclova, *Winter Dialogue*, trans. Diana Senechal (Evanston, IL: Northwestern University Press, 1997), 7.

17. Steve Wasserman, "Steve Wasserman on the Fate of Books after the Age of Print," *Truthdig*, March 4, 2010, http://www.truthdig.com/arts_culture/item/steve_wasserman_on_the_fate_of_books_after_the_age_of_print_20100305/ (accessed May 22, 2011).

18. Ralph Waldo Emerson, "Society and Solitude," in *The Essential Writings of Ralph Waldo Emerson*, ed. Brooks Atkinson (New York: Modern Library, 2000), 668. Emerson's essay was originally published as "Solitude and Society" in the *Atlantic Monthly* 1, no. 2 (December 1857): 225–29. The quotation retains the punctuation of the 1857 version.

Chapter 2

1. Henry David Thoreau, *Walden, or, Life in the Woods* (Boston: Ticknor and Fields, 1854; Princeton, NJ: Princeton University Press, 1997, 2004), 130, 133–35, 167; citations are to the Princeton University Press edition.

2. Ralph Waldo Emerson, "Society and Solitude," in *The Essential Writings of Ralph Waldo Emerson*, ed. Brooks Atkinson (New York: Modern Library, 2000), 664–66, 669.

3. John Cowper Powys, *A Philosophy of Solitude* (New York: Simon & Schuster, 1933), 38–39; Anthony Storr, *Solitude: A Return to the Self* (New York: Free Press, 1988), 28.

4. Philip Koch, *Solitude: A Philosophical Encounter* (Chicago: Open Court, 1994), 299; Thomas Merton, *Thoughts in Solitude* (New York: Farrar, Straus and Cudahy, 1958), 81–82.

5. *The Oxford English Dictionary*, s.v. "Solitude."

6. Ibid.

7. Thoreau, *Walden*, 136.

8. Robert M. Durling, preface to *Petrarch's Lyric Poems: The Rime Sparse and Other Lyrics*, by Petrarch, trans. and ed. Robert M. Durling (Cambridge, MA: Harvard University Press, 1976), vii.

9. Petrarch, *The Life of Solitude*, trans. Jacob Zeitlin (Urbana: University of Illinois Press, 1924), foreword, 101; Petrarch, *De vita solitaria / La vie solitaire*, trans. Christophe Carraud (Grenoble, France: Millon, 1999), 34. For instances of "the retired man" or, in the Latin, *iste* or *hic noster*, see book 1, tractate 2, chapters 1–8 (pp. 109–21 of the University of Illinois edition and 44–64 of the Millon edition). Henceforth all references to either edition (except for Zeitlin's introduction and Petrarch's preface) will cite the book, tractate, and chapter, followed by a comma and page numbers (e.g., 1.2.1–8, 109–21); where Caroline Stark has provided a new translation or modified Zeitlin's translation, this will be noted.

10. Petrarch, *The Life of Solitude*, 1.2.1–8, 109–21; Petrarch, *De vita solitaria / La vie solitaire*, 44–64. The demonstrative *iste* has various connotations and is sometimes used in a disparaging sense (though here it is not).

11. Ernest Hatch Wilkins, *Life of Petrarch* (Chicago: University of Chicago Press, 1961); Morris Bishop, *Petrarch and His World* (Bloomington: Indiana University Press, 1963). Durling describes Bishop's biography as "highly readable, but unreliable"; he considers Wilkins's biography "the most reliable and complete biography, though based on a somewhat uncritical admiration." See Petrarch, *Petrarch's Lyric Poems*, 637–38.

12. Bishop, *Petrarch and His World*, 38; Durling, introduction to *Petrarch's Lyric Poems*, 4; Wilkins, *Life of Petrarch*, 76–78, 215; Caroline Stark translated the quotation from Petrarch, *Rerum familiarum libri*, 24.1l; Morris Bishop's looser translation reads, "I couldn't reconcile myself to making a merchandise of my mind."

13. Bishop, *Petrarch and His World*, 109–11; Wilkins, *Life of Petrarch*, 12–13. This translation of Augustine is translated here by Stark; the passage from Petrarch's letter is quoted in Bishop and can be found in Petrarch, *Rerum familiarum libri*, 4.1.

14. Bishop, *Petrarch and His World*, 129; Wilkins, *Life of Petrarch*, 17–18.

15. Bishop, *Petrarch and His World*, 144, 160; Wilkins, *Life of Petrarch*, 24–29, 184–86; Bishop translated the quotation from Petrarch, *Rerum familiarum libri*, 16.14.

16. Wilkins, *Life of Petrarch*, 204, 233; Zeitlin, introduction to *The Life of Solitude*, by Petrarch, 55–56.

17. Petrarch, *The Life of Solitude*, foreword, 101–2; 1.1.2, 107; the first two quotations are translated by Stark.

18. Petrarch, *The Life of Solitude*, 1.2.3, 112–14; Petrarch, *De vita solitaria / La vie solitaire*, 1.2.3, 50. I modified Zeitlin's translation of the phrase beginning with "horrible beasts"; after "unheard-of birds," his translation reads, "saturated with costly spices. Some of these, forgetful of their ancient home." Petrarch's *Secretum*, a turbulent meditation consisting of three (imaginary) dialogues with Augustine, provides ample evidence that the "busy man" is indeed an aspect of Petrarch himself.

19. Petrarch, *The Life of Solitude*, 1.1.1, 105.

20. Ibid., 1.4.7, 143–44; Stark modified Zeitlin's translation, changing "retirement" to "solitude"; "true" to "truest"; "freedom" to "justice"; "the silence of the woods" to "rustic silence"; and "faithful, trusted" to "most faithful, most trusted."

21. Ibid., 1.4.8, 148.

22. Ibid. 1.4.3, 135; 1.4.3, 136; translation modified by Stark. Zeitlin uses John Selby Watson's translation of Quintilian's *Institutes of Oratory* (London: John Bell and Sons, 1891), 10.3:27–30, 290.

23. Petrarch, *The Life of Solitude*, 1.6.6, 183; I modified Zeitlin's translation, changing "thoughts" to "cares" (*curarum*).

24. Zeitlin, introduction to *The Life of Solitude*, by Petrarch, 63; Petrarch, *The Life of Solitude*, 2.2.1, 195–96; 2.2.4, 197; Petrarch, *De vita solitaria / La vie solitaire*, 2.2.1, 190. Stark modified Zeitlin's translation, changing "period of tranquillized peace" to "tranquility of a more quiet life" and "heat of youth" to "youthful fervor."

25. Petrarch, *The Life of Solitude*, 2.2.8, 201; 2.3.5, 210; 2.6.1, 259–64; 2.7.2, 272–73; 2.8.2, 275–79; 2.8.3, 279; 2.9.4, 287. Stark modified Zeitlin's translation regarding Augustine, changing "calm privacy" to "solitude"; Stark also modified the translation of the passage regarding Demosthenes, which reads, in Zeitlin's version, "In one place he sharpened his wit, in the other he exercised his voice, but he did both in a lonely place." According to Stark, Petrarch used the word *secretum* in the sense of a private kind of solitude; his *Secretum* has many correspondences with *De vita solitaria*.

26. Ibid., 2.9.6, 291–92; Stark modified Zeitlin's translation, which reads, "The holiday which I ordain is for the body, not for the mind; I do not allow the intellect to lie fallow except that it may revive and become more fertile by a period of rest."

27. Ibid., 2.9.6, 291–92; Stark modified Zeitlin's translation, which reads, "Love knows how to make one from two, otherwise the command of Pythagoras were impossible that through friendship many should be united into one. From this it follows that any place which is capable of holding one person can hold two friends. No solitude is so profound, no house so small, no door so narrow but it may open to a friend."

28. Ibid., 1.5.4, 164.

29. Ibid., 2.3.12, 220.

30. Ibid., 2.10.9, 315; Petrarch, *De vita solitaria / La vie solitaire*, 2.10.9, 392. I have adjusted Zeitlin's translation slightly; his translation reads, "I intended to write a letter and I have written a book."

31. Petrarch, *The Life of Solitude*, 1.1.2, 106–7. Stark modified Zeitlin's translation, which reads, "For it is with a freer step, though perchance a less secure one, that I pursue my own route than I follow the traces of a stranger."

32. Robert Frost, "Take Something Like a Star," in *The Poetry of Robert Frost: The Collected Poems, Complete and Unabridged*, ed. Edward Connery Lathem (New York: Henry Holt, 1979), 403.

33. William of Saint-Thierry, *The Golden Epistle: A Letter to the Brethren at Mont Dieu*, trans. Theodore Berkeley (Kalamazoo, MI: Cistercian Publications, 1971), 19. The original title of this work (completed in 1145) is *Epistola ad fratres de Monte-Dei*.

34. Elizabeth Cady Stanton, "Solitude of Self" (address to the Congressional Judiciary Committee, January 18, 1892; Ashfield, MA: Paris Press, 2001), 15, 30. Citations are to the Paris Press edition.

35. David L. Ulin, "The Lost Art of Reading," *Los Angeles Times*, August 9, 2009.

36. William of Saint-Thierry, *The Golden Epistle*, 105. The phrase "My secret is my own" (*secretum meum mihi*) is quoted from Isaiah 24:16.

37. Merton, *Thoughts in Solitude*, 85; Petrarch, *The Life of Solitude*, 1.6.6, 184.

38. Petrarch, *The Life of Solitude*, 1.4.1, 131. Stark modified the translation; Zeitlin translates *solitudo* here as "isolation."

Chapter 3

1. Maggie Jackson, *Distracted: The Erosion of Attention and the Coming Dark Age* (New York: Prometheus, 2008), 78.

2. Laurence Sterne, *Tristram Shandy: An Authoritative Text; the Author on the Novel; Criticism*, ed. Howard Anderson (first published in nine volumes, 1760–1767; New York: Norton, 1980), 26. Citations are to the 1980 edition.

3. Susan Jacoby, *The Age of American Unreason* (New York: Pantheon, 2008), 215.

4. Neil Postman, *Amusing Ourselves to Death: Public Discourse in the Age of Show Business* (New York: Viking Penguin, 1985), 14.

5. Ibid., 166.

6. Richard Hofstadter, *Anti-Intellectualism in American Life* (New York: Vintage, 1963), 30.

7. Isaac Leon Kandel, "Alice in Cloud-Cuckoo Land," *Teachers College Record* 34, no. 8 (1933): 632.

8. Howard Gardner, introduction to the 1993 edition of *Frames of Mind: The Theory of Multiple Intelligences* (New York: Basic Books, 1983, 1993), xxi–xxiii; Gardner, *Multiple Intelligences: The Theory in Practice* (New York: Basic Books, 1993), 66, 73.

9. Daniel T. Willingham, "Ask the Cognitive Scientist: Do Visual, Auditory, and Kinesthetic Learners Need Visual, Auditory, and Kinesthetic Instruction?" *American Educator* (Summer 2005); Willingham, "Willingham: Student 'Learning Styles' Theory Is Bunk," *The Answer Sheet* (blog), *Washington Post*, September 14, 2009. See also John G. Sharp, Rob Bowker, and Jenny Byrne, "VAK or VAK-uous? Towards the Trivialisation of Learning and the Death of Scholarship," *Research Papers in Education* 23, no. 3 (September 2008): 294, 301–3, 305.

10. District of Columbia Public Schools, *IMPACT: The District of Columbia Public Schools Effectiveness Assessment System for School-Based Personnel, 2010–2011, Group 1: General Education Teachers with Individual Value-Added Student Achievement Data* (Washington, DC: DCPS, 2010), 12, 24.

11. Doug Lemov, *Teach Like a Champion: 49 Techniques That Put Students on the Path to College* (San Francisco: Jossey-Bass, 2010), 226–27.

12. Ibid., 152–53.

13. Ibid., 96.

14. Ibid., 137–38.

15. Whole Brain Teaching, LLC, http://www.wholebrainteaching.com/ (accessed May 22, 2011).

16. Chris Biffle, *Power Teaching: College; "Aristotle's Four Causes"* (video), on YouTube page "Whole Brain Teaching: Advanced Techniques," http://www.youtube .com/watch?v=x6rOIOW2Jf0 (accessed May 22, 2011).

17. Aristotle, *The Physics*, trans. Philip H. Wicksteed and Francis M. Cornford, Loeb Classical Library, rev. ed. (Cambridge, MA: Harvard University Press, 1957), 129–31; Aristotle, *Metaphysics*, trans. Hugh Tredennick, Loeb Classical Library (Cambridge, MA: Harvard University Press, 1933), 17, 211–13.

18. Whole Brain Teaching, LLC, "Whole Brain Developer: Teach-OK," http://www .wholebrainteaching.com/index.php?option=com_k2&view=item&id=164:whole -brain-developer-teach-ok&Itemid=131 (accessed May 22, 2011).

19. Tom Roberts, "TEAL Is a Step in the Wrong Direction: The Well-Intentioned Program Treats Students like Children," *The Tech*, November 5, 2010, http://tech .mit.edu/V130/N51/roberts.html (accessed May 22, 2011); Lauren E. LeBon, "Students Petition against TEAL," *The Tech*, March 21, 2003, http://tech.mit.edu/V123/ N14/14802T.14n.html (accessed May 22, 2011); Sara Rimer, "At M.I.T., Large Lectures Are Going the Way of the Blackboard," *New York Times*, January 12, 2009.

20. Arun Agarwal, "The Real Deal on 8.02 TEAL," *The Tech*, April 4, 2003, http://tech.mit.edu/V123/N16/arun16.16c.html (accessed May 22, 2011).

21. Richard Hake, "The Case for Classroom Clickers: A Response to Bugeja," December 2008, http://www.physics.indiana.edu/~hake/CaseForClickersJ.pdf (accessed May 22, 2011); Michael Bugeja, "Classroom Clickers and the Cost of Technology," *Chronicle of Higher Education*, December 5, 2008; Agarwal, "The Real Deal on 8.02 TEAL."

22. "At Universities, Is Better Learning a Click Away?" *Associated Press*, March 8, 2010, http://www.msnbc.msn.com/id/35766745/ns/us_news-life/ (accessed May 22, 2011).

23. Jacques Steinberg, "More Professors Give Out Hand-Held Devices to Monitor Students and Engage Them," *New York Times*, November 15, 2010; for more on the importance of student effort, see Paul A. Zoch, *Doomed to Fail: The Built-in Defects of American Education* (Chicago: Ivan R. Dee, 2004).

24. Martin Buber, *I and Thou*, trans. Walter Kaufmann (New York: Scribner's, 1970), 109.

25. James Merrill, *The Changing Light at Sandover* (New York: Knopf, 2003), 79–82.

26. Jackson, *Distracted*, 215, 266.

Chapter 4

1. *The Death of Gilgameš*, a version from Nibru, in J. A. Black et al., *The Electronic Text Corpus of Sumerian Literature* (University of Oxford, 1998–2006), segment E, lines 12–27, http://etcsl.orinst.ox.ac.uk/cgi-bin/etcsl.cgi?text=t.1.8.1.3# (accessed May 22, 2011).

2. *Inana and Šu-kale-tuda*, in J. A. Black et al., *The Electronic Text Corpus of Sumerian Literature*, lines 91–111, http://etcsl.orinst.ox.ac.uk/cgi-bin/etcsl .cgi?text=t.1.3.3# (accessed May 22, 2011).

3. Pennsylvania Sumerian Dictionary Project, *Pennsylvania Sumerian Dictionary*, s.v. "dili," http://psd.museum.upenn.edu/epsd/ (accessed May 22, 2011). See also the occurrences of "dili" in Herman Vanstiphout, *Epics of Sumerian Kings: The Matter of Aratta*, ed. Jerrold S. Cooper (Atlanta: Society of Biblical Literature, 2003), http://www.sbl-site.org/assets/pdfs/onlinebooks/PDF/OnlineBooks/Vanstiphout.pdf (accessed May 22, 2011).

4. Jean Stein, "William Faulkner," in *Writers at Work: The Paris Review Interviews*, ed. Malcolm Cowley (New York: Viking, 1958), 123.

5. Sophocles, *Antigone*, trans. Wm. Blake Tyrrell and Larry J. Bennett, *Diotima*, 1996, http://www.stoa.org/diotima/anthology/ant/antigstruct.htm (accessed May 22, 2011).

6. Scholars are not in agreement over the date of the first performance. See R. G. Lewis, "An Alternative Date for Sophocles' *Antigone*," *Greek, Roman and Byzantine Studies* 29, no. 1 (Spring 1988): 35–50; Robert Fagles, introduction to *Sophocles: The Three Theban Plays: Antigone, Oedipus the King, Oedipus at Colonus* (New York: Penguin, 1984), 35.

7. For a fascinating commentary on the first line, see Victor Bers, *Victor Bers Introduces the Greek Play "Antigone,"* video, http://www.youtube.com/ watch?v=RvhqXdHmb94 (accessed May 22, 2011).

8. Sophocles, *Antigone*, trans. Paul Woodruff (Indianapolis: Hackett, 2001), 54, lines 1251–52.

9. Mark Griffith, introduction to Sophocles, *Antigone*, ed. Mark Griffith (New York: Cambridge University Press, 1999), 18.

10. George Steiner, *Antigones* (New York: Oxford University Press, 1984), 177; Georg Wilhelm Friedrich Hegel, *Lectures on the Philosophy of Religion*, vol. 2:

Determinate Religion, ed. Peter C. Hodgson (Berkeley: University of California Press, 1987), 665–66.

11. Aristotle, *Poetics*, trans. Malcolm Heath (New York: Penguin, 1996), 18; Patricia M. Lines, "Antigone's Flaw," *Humanitas* 12, no. 1 (Spring 1999); Sophocles, *Antigone*, trans. Woodruff, 37 (lines 851–52); Sophocles, *Antigone*, trans. Tyrrell and Bennett (lines 859–60, 866); observation about the family curse was made by Victor Bers in an email to author.

12. Robert F. Goheen, *The Imagery of Sophocles' Antigone: A Study of Poetic Language and Structure* (Princeton, NJ: Princeton University Press, 1951), 79–80.

13. Sophocles, *Antigone*, trans. Kelly Cherry, in *Sophocles, 2: King Oedipus, Oedipus at Colonus, Antigone*, ed. David R. Slavitt and Palmer Bovie (Philadelphia: University of Pennsylvania Press, 1999), 211; Sophocles, *Antigone*, trans. Robert Fagles, in *Sophocles: The Three Theban Plays*, 84; Sophocles, *Antigone*, trans. Paul Roche, in *The Oedipus Plays of Sophocles: Oedipus the King, Oedipus at Colonus, Antigone* (New York: New American Library, 1958), 181; Sophocles, *Antigone*, trans. Dudley Fitts and Robert Fitzgerald, in *The Oedipus Cycle: An English Version* (New York: Harcourt, 1977), 210; Sophocles, *Antigone*, trans. Nicholas Rudall (Chicago: Ivan R. Dee, 1998), 28; Sophocles, *Antigone*, trans. Ruby Blondell, in *Sophocles: The Theban Plays: Antigone, King Oidipous, Oidipous at Colonus* (Newburyport, Mass.: Focus, 2002), 54; Sophocles, *Antigone*, trans. Ruth Fainlight and Robert J. Littman, in *The Theban Plays: Oedipus the King, Oedipus at Colonus, Antigone* (Baltimore: Johns Hopkins University Press, 2009), 156; Sophocles, *Antigone*, trans. Elizabeth Wyckoff, in *Sophocles: Oedipus the King, Oedipus at Colonus, Antigone*, ed. David Grene and Richmond Lattimore (Chicago: University of Chicago Press, 1954), 176; Sophocles, *Antigone*, trans. Woodruff, 21; Sophocles, *Antigone*, trans. Tyrrell and Bennett, line 510.

14. Goheen, *The Imagery of Sophocles' Antigone*, 79.

15. This translation is my own. Tyrrell and Bennett translate it, "No, be whatever seems best to you"; Woodruff, "Go on and *be* the way you choose to be."

16. For commentary on Creon's principles and piety, see Goheen, *The Imagery of Sophocles' Antigone*, 82–83; Woodruff, introduction to *Antigone*, xi; L. A. MacKay, "Antigone, Coriolanus, and Hegel," *Transactions and Proceedings of the American Philological Association* 93 (1962): 166–74.

17. Sophocles, *Antigone*, trans. Woodruff, 9; henceforth all quotations from *Antigone* will be cited by line number in the text, and will be from Woodruff's translation unless otherwise indicated. In choosing a translation, I considered several qualities: proximity in meaning to the original, readability, lyricism, and the rendition of the specific excerpts. Other translations have particular virtues; I recommend Fagles's translation for its rich language, and the translation and notes of Tyrrell and Bennett for their historical insights.

18. Hannah Arendt translates lines 1350–53 as follows: "But great words, counteracting [or paying back] the great blows of the overproud, teach understanding in old age." She comments that "the content of these lines is so puzzling to modern

understanding that one rarely finds a translator who dares to give it the bare sense." Arendt, *The Human Condition*, 2nd ed. (Chicago: University of Chicago Press, 1998), 25n8.

19. Sophocles, *Antigone*, trans. Tyrrell and Bennett, line 943.

20. See, for instance, Griffith, introduction to *Antigone*, 41–43; Goheen, *The Imagery of Sophocles' Antigone*, 75–100; Simon Goldhill, *Reading Greek Tragedy* (New York: Cambridge University Press, 1986), 168–80; Charles Knapp, "A Point in the Interpretation of the Antigone of Sophocles," *American Journal of Philology* 37, no. 3 (1916): 300–16.

21. Sophocles, *Antigone*, trans. Robert Fagles, in *Sophocles: The Three Theban Plays*, 76 (lines 332–41 of the original).

22. Goheen, *The Imagery of Sophocles' Antigone*, 53; Victor Bers, email to author.

23. R. P. Winnington-Ingram, *Sophocles: An Interpretation* (Cambridge, UK: Cambridge University Press, 1980), 171n58.

24. All remaining quotations from this ode and from the play are from Woodruff's translation.

25. *Hupsipolis* can mean both "having a great city" and "being honored in the city." Tyrrell and Bennett translate it as "lofty of city," thus combining the two meanings.

26. See Griffith's commentary on lines 370–75, in Sophocles, *Antigone*, ed. Griffith, 190.

27. Vyacheslav Ivanov, *Freedom and the Tragic Life: A Study in Dostoevsky*, trans. Norman Cameron (London: Harvill, 1952), 15–16. The original Russian manuscript of this work is lost; the English text is a translation of the German translation.

28. A fine recording of Antigone in Greek (unfortunately with some cuts) is Sophocles, *Antigone*, performed and read in Greek by members of Columbia University, with text (New York: Folkways, 1957?), FP9912, available in digital format.

29. Sandra Stotsky, with Joan Traffas and James Woodworth, "Literary Study in Grades 9, 10, and 11: A National Survey," *Forum: A Publication of the ALSCW* 4 (2010): 14.

30. Gay Ivey and Douglas Fisher, *Creating Literacy-Rich Schools for Adolescents* (Alexandria, VA: ASCD, 2006), 2–11; National Council of Teachers of English, *NCTE Principles of Adolescent Literacy Reform: A Policy Research Brief* (Urbana, IL: NCTE, 2006).

31. New York State Department of Education, "English Language Arts: Standard 2; Listening and Reading," http://www.emsc.nysed.gov/ciai/ela/elastandards/ela2a.html (accessed May 22, 2011).

32. See Diane Ravitch, *The Death and Life of the Great American School System: How Testing and Choice Are Undermining Education* (New York: Basic Books, 2010), 20; Sheila Byrd Carmichael, Gabrielle Martino, Kathleen Porter-Magee, and W. Stephen Wilson, *The State of State Standards—and the Common Core—in 2010* (Washington, DC: Thomas B. Fordham Institute, 2010).

33. Daniel T. Willingham, "The Usefulness of *Brief* Instruction in Reading Comprehension Strategies," *American Educator*, Winter 2006–2007, 39–45, 50.

34. Stephanie Harvey and Anne Goudvis, *Strategies That Work: Teaching Comprehension to Enhance Understanding*, 2nd ed. (Portland, ME: Stenhouse, 2007), 102–4.

35. P. David Pearson and Janice A. Dole, "Explicit Comprehension Instruction: A Review of Research and a New Conceptualization of Instruction," *Elementary School Journal* 88, no. 2 (November 1987): 162–63.

Chapter 5

1. David M. Herszenhorn, "Teachers Protest the Methods of a Regional Superintendent," *New York Times*, February 4, 2005; Vivian Shulman, Susan Sullivan, and Jeffrey Glanz, "The New York City School Reform: Consequences for Supervision of Instruction," *International Journal of Leadership in Education* 11, no. 4 (October 2008): 414; The Broad Prize for Urban Education, "New York City Department of Education," 2007, 3, http://www.broadprize.org/asset/2007NewYorkBrief.pdf (accessed May 22, 2011).

2. Deidre McFadyen, "Trouble in the Workshop: Mandated Model Hampers Learning in Secondary Schools," *New York Teacher*, February 17, 2005; McFadyen, "Educators in Region 4: Don't Stop Us from Teaching Our Kids," *New York Teacher*, January 20, 2005. For a description of the New York City workshop model and its effect on classroom teaching, see Andrew Wolf, "Shortcut Classics in City Schools," *New York Sun*, June 10, 2005, http://www.nysun.com/opinion/shortcut-classics-in -city-schools/15235/ (accessed May 22, 2011); Liz Ditz, "The Workshop Model," *I Speak of Dreams* (blog), September 10, 2005, http://lizditz.typepad.com/i_speak_of_ dreams/2005/09/the_workshop_mo.html (accessed May 22, 2011).

3. McFadyen, "Trouble in the Workshop."

4. Diana Senechal, "Class Discussion for Sale," *The Core Knowledge Blog*, January 4, 2009, http://blog.coreknowledge.org/2009/01/04/class-discussion-for-sale/ (accessed May 22, 2011).

5. New York City Department of Education, District 75, "Literacy Walkthrough Checklist," http://schools.nyc.gov/Offices/District75/Departments/Literacy/forms .htm (accessed May 22, 2011).

6. "Love" is capitalized in the Greek text and English translation of the *Symposium*; this suggests its divine or personified nature.

7. Plato, *Symposium*, in *Lysis, Symposium, Gorgias* (Greek and English text), trans. W. R. M. Lamb, Loeb Classical Library (Cambridge, MA: Harvard University Press, 1925), 196–97; my translation. Lamb's translation of these two lines reads, "Peace among men, and a windless waveless main; / Repose for winds, and slumber in our pain."

8. Plato, *Symposium*, trans. Lamb, 171–73, 181–83, 205–7.

9. David Coleman, "Love and Learning," unpublished essay.

10. Donald H. Graves, *Balance the Basics: Let Them Write* (New York: Ford Foundation, 1978), 5.

11. New York City Department of Education, Office of Curriculum and Professional Development, Department of English Language Arts, *Strategies for Reading*

and Writing: Grade 1 Sample Unit of Study, field test edition (2008), http://www
.ps69bronx.org/www/08X069/site/hosting/ResTeach/1st%20grade%20Strategies%
20for%20Reading%20and%20Writing.pdf (accessed May 22, 2011).

12. Ibid.

13. New York City Department of Education, Division of English Language Learners, *English as a Second Language Literacy Instructional Guide, Summer 2003: Building
Language and Literacy for English Language Learners (Grades 3–8),* field test—3rd ed.,
2003, 186.

14. Langston Hughes, "Poem," in *The Collected Works of Langston Hughes,* vol. 11,
Works for Children and Young Adults: Poetry, Fiction, and Other Writing, ed. Dianne
Johnson (Columbia: University of Missouri Press, 2003), 54; Edwin Arlington Rob-
inson, "The House on the Hill," in *The Children of the Night: A Book of Poems* (New
York: Charles Scribner's Sons, 1914), 34.

15. Lucy Calkins, Amanda Hartman, and Zoe White, *One on One: The Art of
Conferring with Young Writers* (Portsmouth, NH: Heinemann, 2005), 65, 67; Rafael
Heller, *Literacy for Amateurs* (blog), http://literacyforamateurs.blogspot.com/ (ac-
cessed May 22, 2011).

16. D. G. Myers, "The Lesson of Creative Writing's History," *AWP Chronicle* 26
(February 1994): 1, 12–14.

17. Nancie Atwell, *In the Middle: Writing, Reading, and Learning with Adolescents*
(Portsmouth, NH: Boynton/Cook, 1989), 9; Wallace Stegner, *On Teaching Writing
and Fiction* (New York: Penguin, 2002), 53–54; Joseph Barbato, "Because It Was
There," *Change* 9, no. 8 (August 1977): 51–52; Louis Menand, "Show or Tell: Should
Creative Writing Be Taught?," *New Yorker,* June 8, 2009, 109.

18. Menand, "Show or Tell," 106, 112; Michael Loyd Gray, "Speaking My Mind:
Method and Madness in the Creative Writing Workshop," *English Journal* 89, no. 1
(September 1999): 17–19; Theodore Weiss, "A Personal View: Poetry, Pedagogy,
Per-versities," in *The American Writer and the University,* ed. Ben Siegel (Newark:
University of Delaware Press, 1989), 158; Mary Oliver, *A Poetry Handbook* (New
York: Harcourt Brace, 1994), 115–17.

19. For a glowing description (and, at times, sharp criticism) of child-centered
schools, see Harold Rugg and Ann Shumaker, *The Child-Centered School: An Appraisal of the New Education* (Yonkers-on-Hudson, NY: World Book, 1928).

20. Michael J. Demiashkevich, *The Activity School: New Tendencies in Educational
Method in Western Europe* (New York: Little and Ives, 1926), 50; Diane Ravitch, *Left
Back: A Century of Battles Over School Reform* (New York: Simon & Schuster, 2001),
247–52; originally published as *Left Back: A Century of Failed School Reforms* (New
York: Simon & Schuster, 2000).

21. Raymond E. Callahan, *Education and the Cult of Efficiency: A Study of the Social
Forces That Have Shaped the Administration of the Public Schools* (Chicago: University
of Chicago Press, 1962), [iv], 25, 28–29, 68, 81.

22. Wesley Null, *Curriculum: From Theory to Practice* (Lanham, MD: Rowman &
Littlefield, 2011), 58–59, 82; Diane Ravitch, *The Death and Life of the Great American*

School System: How Testing and Choice Are Undermining Education (New York: Basic Books, 2010), 65, 71.

23. David W. Johnson, Geoffrey Maruyama, Roger Johnson, Deborah Nelson, and Linda Skon, "Effects of Cooperative, Competitive, and Individualistic Goal Structures on Achievement: A Meta-Analysis," *Psychological Bulletin* 89, no. 1 (1981): 47, 52, 54.

24. Robert E. Slavin, "Cooperative Learning," *Review of Educational Research* 50, no. 2 (Summer 1980): 325, 334–35, 337.

25. Steven T. Bossert, "Cooperative Activities in the Classroom," *Review of Research in Education* 15 (1988–1989): 226, 242–43; Stephen Balkcom, "Cooperative Learning," *Education Research Consumer Guide* 1 (Washington, DC: U.S. Department of Education, Office of Research, Office of Educational Research and Improvement, June 1992), http://www2.ed.gov/pubs/OR/ConsumerGuides/cooplear.html (accessed May 22, 2011).

26. Balkcom, "Cooperative Learning."

27. Herszenhorn, "Teachers Protest the Methods of a Regional Superintendent"; Frederick M. Hess and Andrew P. Kelly, "Learning to Lead? In Preparing Principals, Content Matters," *Education Week*, May 18, 2005.

28. Harvey Daniels and Marilyn Bizar, *Teaching the Best Practice Way: Methods That Matter, K–12* (Portland, ME: Stenhouse, 2005), 157; Slavin, *Cooperative Learning* (New York: Longman, 1983), 2.

29. Diane Ravitch, *The Troubled Crusade: American Education, 1945–1980* (New York: Basic Books, 1983), 228–66; Ravitch, *The Death and Life of the Great American School System*, 32, 47–67.

30. These are both examples of lessons I conducted with English language learners.

Chapter 6

1. Diane Ravitch, *The Death and Life of the Great American School System: How Testing and Choice Are Undermining Education* (New York: Basic Books, 2010), 3; see also Ravitch, *Left Back: A Century of Battles over School Reform* (New York: Simon & Schuster, 2001).

2. Alfred North Whitehead, "The Aims of Education," in *The Aims of Education and Other Essays* (New York: Macmillan, 1929), 2–3; essay originally published in *The Organization of Thought* (London: Williams and Norgate, 1917).

3. Whitehead, "The Aims of Education," 1, 10, 18.

4. Aristotle, *The Nicomachean Ethics* (Greek and English text), trans. H. Rackam, Loeb Classical Library, rev. ed. (Cambridge, MA: Harvard University Press, 1934), 35.

5. Benjamin S. Bloom, ed., *Taxonomy of Educational Objectives: The Classification of Educational Goals, Handbook 1: Cognitive Domain* (New York: David McKay, 1956), 10, 16, 33.

6. E. D. Hirsch Jr., *The Schools We Need and Why We Don't Have Them* (New York: Anchor Books, 1999), 254.

7. Larry Cuban, "Policy and Research Dilemmas in the Teaching of Reasoning: Unplanned Designs," *Review of Educational Research* 54, no. 4 (Winter 1984): 676n1; Council of Chief State School Officers, *Restructuring Learning for All Students: A Policy Statement by the Council of Chief State School Officers on Improved Teaching of Thinking* (Washington, DC: Council of Chief State School Officers, 1990), 1–2, 6.

8. Partnership for 21st Century Skills, *21st Century Skills, Education & Competitiveness: A Resource and Policy Guide* (Tucson, AZ: Partnership for 21st Century Skills, 2008), n.p., 1.

9. Partnership for 21st Century Skills, *21st Century Skills Map: English* (Tucson, AZ: Partnership for 21st Century Skills, 2008), 2, 4.

10. Partnership for 21st Century Skills, *21st Century Skills Map: The Arts* (Tucson, AZ: Partnership for 21st Century Skills, 2010), 4.

11. Partnership for 21st Century Skills, "P21 and the Council of Chief State School Officers Form Strategic Management Relationship," press release, August 25, 2010; Council of Chief State School Officers, Interstate Teacher Assessment and Support Consortium, *Model Core Teaching Standards: A Resource for State Dialogue; Draft for Public Comment* (Washington, DC: Council of Chief State School Officers, 2010), 15.

12. Barack Obama, "President Obama's Remarks to the Hispanic Chamber of Commerce," transcript, *New York Times*, March 10, 2009; "Tom Friedman on Education in the 'Flat World'" (conversation between Daniel Pink and Thomas Friedman), *The School Administrator*, February 2008.

13. Bruce Pourciau has pointed out two flaws in Newton's theorem; see Pourciau, "Newton's Argument for Proposition 1 of the Principia," *Archive for History of Exact Sciences* 57 (2003): 267–311. Kepler gave two nonequivalent versions of his second law in his *Astronomia nova* (1609); see E. J. Aiton, "Kepler's Second Law of Planetary Motion," *Isis* 60, no. 1 (Spring 1969): 75–90.

14. Isaac Newton, *The Principia: Mathematical Principles of Natural Philosophy*, trans. I. Bernard Cohen and Anne Whitman, preceded by *A Guide to Newton's Principia*, by I. Bernard Cohen (Berkeley: University of California Press, 1999). Readers may also wish to consult S. Chandrasekhar, *Newton's Principia for the Common Reader* (New York: Oxford University Press, 1995), as well as Pourciau, "Newton's Argument for Proposition 1 of the Principia," 267–311.

15. Newton, *The Principia*, 444.

16. Figures 6.2, 6.3, and 6.4 are simulations of Newton's own illustrations; I have created figures 6.1, 6.5, and 6.6 for additional explanation.

17. Newton, *The Principia*, 416.

18. Ibid., 417.

19. Ibid., 434.

20. Euclid, *Euclid's Elements of Geometry*, trans. and ed. Richard Fitzpatrick, rev. ed. (Raleigh, NC: Lulu, 2008), 39.

21. Newton, *The Principia*, 444.

22. Ibid., 444–45.

23. Ibid., 445.

24. Ibid.

25. Ibid.

26. Ibid.

27. Pourciau writes, "Note the beautiful symmetry, the gentle geometry, the seemingly simple passage to the limit, and the clean and easy lines of Newton's argument. But does the demonstration, ultimately, *persuade?*" Pourciau, "Newton's Argument for Proposition 1 of the Principia," 269.

28. E. B. White, "Freedom," in *One Man's Meat* (New York: Harper & Brothers, 1942), 208–9.

29. Anton Chekhov, "Doma" [At Home], in *Sobranie sochinenii*, vol. 5: *Rasskazy, 1887* (Moscow: Gosudarstvennoe izdatel'stvo khudozhestvennoi literatury, 1955), 111; I translated the quoted passage.

30. Whitehead, "The Aims of Education," 4, 23.

Chapter 7

1. Donal O'Shea, *The Poincaré Conjecture: In Search of the Shape of the Universe* (New York: Walker, 2007), 1–5.

2. O'Shea describes the three-dimensional manifold as "a set in which every point belongs to a region that can be mapped onto the points inside a clear aquarium or shoebox. In other words, the region around any point looks like space rather than a plane." O'Shea, *The Poincaré Conjecture*, 36.

3. Keith Devlin, *The Millennium Problems: The Seven Greatest Unsolved Mathematical Puzzles of Our Time* (New York: Basic Books, 2002), 182–87; O'Shea, *The Poincaré Conjecture*, 37–41. O'Shea describes the three-dimensional manifold as "a set in which every point belongs to a region that can be mapped onto the points inside a clear aquarium or shoebox."

4. O'Shea, *The Poincaré Conjecture*, 191–92.

5. Will Stewart, "World's Cleverest Man Turns Down $1 Million Prize after Solving One of Mathematics' Greatest Puzzles," *Daily Mail* (UK), March 23, 2010; PRAVDA.Ru, "Strange Russian Genius Declines Million-Dollar Prize from U.S.A.," March 19, 2010; Adam Taylor, "Grigori Perelman, Reclusive Russian Math Genius, Refuses $1 Million Prize," *Huffington Post*, March 24, 2010. The comment from "Ana" was posted on March 23, 2010, in response to the *Daily Mail* article; Masha Gessen, *Perfect Rigor: A Genius and the Mathematical Breakthrough of the Century* (Boston: Houghton Mifflin Harcourt, 2009), 175–80.

6. Jacques Steinberg, "Is Going to an Elite College Worth the Cost?" *New York Times*, December 17, 2010; William Deresiewicz, "Solitude and Leadership," *American Scholar* 79, no. 2 (Spring 2010): 22.

7. Luc Ferry, *What Is the Good Life?* trans. Lydia G. Cochrane (Chicago: University of Chicago Press, 2005), 5; for the original French version, see Ferry, *Qu'est-ce-qu'une vie réussie?* (Paris: Grasset, 2002), 14.

8. G. K. Chesterton, "The Fallacy of Success," in *All Things Considered* (New York: John Lane, 1909), 21.

9. Ibid., 21, 23, 26.

10. Scott A. Sandage, *Born Losers: A History of Failure in America* (Cambridge, MA: Harvard University Press, 2005), 99–158; quoted passages are from page 132.

11. Ibid., 117–19.

12. Walt Whitman, "I Celebrate Myself," *Leaves of Grass* (Brooklyn, NY, 1855), 14, 24–25. Originally untitled, the poem is titled "Poem of Walt Whitman, an American," in the 1856 edition and "Walt Whitman" in the 1860 and 1867 editions. In the 1881–1882 and 1891–1892 editions, it appears as "Song of Myself."

13. Yale College Undergraduate Admissions, *That's Why I Chose Yale*, video on the web page "Video: The Yale Musical," http://admissions.yale.edu/cinema-yale (accessed May 22, 2011).

14. Eric Hoover, "Application Inflation: When Is Enough Enough?" *New York Times*, November 5, 2010.

15. Heather Grossmann, "Fuzzy Math," *School Stories* (blog), May 16, 2009, http://coveringeducation.org/schoolstories09/?p=2222 (accessed May 22, 2011); Jennifer Medina, "Pressed by Charters, Public Schools Try Marketing," *New York Times*, March 9, 2010.

16. Tennessee Williams, "On a Streetcar Named Success," *New York Times*, November 30, 1947; reprinted as "The Catastrophe of Success," *Story: The Magazine of the Short Story* 32, no. 128 (Spring 1948): 71; "The Catastrophe of Success," introduction to *The Glass Menagerie* (New York: New Directions, 1949), viii. Later the word "volition" was mistakenly changed to "violation."

17. Frank Channing Haddock, *Business Power: A Practical Manual in Financial Ability and Commercial Leadership* (Meriden, CT: Pelton, 1920), 275.

18. Richard Weiss, *The American Myth of Success: From Horatio Alger to Norman Vincent Peale* (New York: Basic Books, 1969), 13, 163; Norman Vincent Peale, *The Power of Positive Thinking* (New York: Prentice Hall, 1952), 55.

19. Eric A. Hanushek, "There Is No 'War on Teachers,'" *Wall Street Journal*, October 19, 2010; Jason Felch, Jason Song, and Doug Smith, "Who's Teaching L.A.'s Kids?" *Los Angeles Times*, August 14, 2010; Jason Felch and Jason Song, "U.S. Schools Chief Endorses Release of Teacher Data," *Los Angeles Times*, August 16, 2010.

20. Amanda Ripley, "What Makes a Great Teacher?" *The Atlantic*, January/February 2010; Haberman Educational Foundation, "The Star Teacher Pre-Screener," http://www.habermanfoundation.org/StarTeacherPreScreener.aspx (accessed May 22, 2011); Dale Singer, "When Teachers Don't Make the Grade," *St. Louis Beacon*, August 23, 2010.

21. Sarah D. Sparks, "Experts Begin to Identify Nonacademic Skills Key to Success," *Education Week*, December 23, 2010.

22. Dakarai I. Aarons, "Focus on Instruction Turns Around Chicago Schools," *Education Week*, January 6, 2010; Philip N. Johnson-Laird, *How We Reason* (New York: Oxford University Press, 2006), 369–86.

23. Malcolm Gladwell, *Outliers: The Story of Success* (New York: Little, Brown, 2008), 128.

24. William James to H. G. Wells, September 11, 1906, in *The Correspondence of William James*, vol. 11: *April 1905–March 1908*, ed. Ignas K. Skrupskelis and Elizabeth M. Berkeley (Charlottesville: University of Virginia Press, 2003), 267; for James's relation to the New Thought, see Weiss, *The American Myth of Success*, 133, 139.

25. Todd Hirsch, "Is the Cult of Success Ruining Our Economy?" *Globe and Mail*, June 26, 2009; Herman Melville, *Moby Dick, or, The Whale* (New York: Harper, 1851), 416.

26. Jennifer Hochschild, *Facing Up to the American Dream: Race, Class, and the Soul of the Nation* (Princeton, NJ: Princeton University Press, 1995), 29.

27. Geoffrey Canada, "New York Politicians Who Fight Against School Choice Had Plenty of It Themselves," *New York Daily News*, March 27, 2010; Paul Tough, *Whatever It Takes: Geoffrey Canada's Quest to Change Harlem and America* (New York: Houghton Mifflin, 2008), 234–35, 240–42.

28. Hochschild, *Facing Up to the American Dream*, 30.

29. Robert Browning, "Rabbi Ben Ezra," in *Dramatis Personae* (London: Chapman and Hall, 1864), 79, 85.

30. Flannery O'Connor, *Wise Blood* (New York: Noonday, 1967), [5].

31. Mother Teresa to Father Neuner, before January 8, 1965, in *Mother Teresa: Come Be My Light—The Private Writings of the Saint of Calcutta*, ed. Brian Kolodiejchuk (New York: Doubleday, 2007), 249–50.

32. Ernest Hemingway, *The Old Man and the Sea* (New York: Scribner, 1952), 139–40.

33. Ferry, *What Is the Good Life?* 286–87.

Chapter 8

1. J. R. Piggott, *Palace of the People: The Crystal Palace at Sydenham 1854–1936* (Madison: University of Wisconsin Press, 2004), 2.

2. Fyodor Dostoevsky, "Zimnie zametki o letnikh vpechatleniiakh" [Winter Notes on Summer Impressions], in *Polnoe sobranie sochinenii F. M. Dostoevskogo v XVIII tomakh*, vol. 4: *Proizvedeniia 1861–1863 gg.* (Moscow: Voskresen'e, 2004), 332; I translated the quoted passage.

3. Theodore Martin, *The Life of His Royal Highness the Prince Consort*, vol. 2, 3rd ed. (London: Smith, Elder, 1876), 248; John Tallis, *Tallis's History and Description of the Crystal Palace and the Exhibition of the World's Industry in 1851* (London: John Tallis and Co., 1852?), 1:12, 1:22–23. Tallis does not provide the name of the journal he quotes.

4. Charlotte Brontë to Rev. Patrick Brontë, June 7, 1851, in *Selected Letters of Charlotte Brontë*, ed. Margaret Smith (New York: Oxford University Press, 2007), 190.

5. Horace Greeley, "The Crystal Palace and Its Lessons," in *Hints toward Reforms, in Lectures, Addresses, and Other Writings*, 2nd ed. (New York: Fowlers and Wells, 1855), 402, 414.

6. John Ruskin, *The Stones of Venice*, vol. 2: *The Sea-Stories* (London: Smith, Elder, 1853), 94; Tallis, *Tallis's History and Description of the Crystal Palace*, 2:45.

7. Tallis, *Tallis's History and Description of the Crystal Palace*, 2:49, 2:51.

8. Samuel Warren, *The Lily and the Bee: An Apologue of the Crystal Palace* (London: Blackwood, 1851), 8–9; W. C. Rives to the *New York Daily Times*, dated September 30, 1851, printed October 31, 1851.

9. Nikolai Gavrilovich Chernyshevsky, *Chto delat'? Iz razskazov o novykh liudiakh* [What Is to Be Done? From Stories about New People] (Vevey, France: Benda, 1867), 391; I translated the quoted passage.

10. Fyodor Dostoevsky, *Notes from Underground*, trans. Michael Katz (New York: Norton, 2001), 3.

11. Ibid., 18–19, 24.

12. Ibid., 22.

13. Ibid., 25.

14. Ibid., 25.

15. Ibid., 25–26.

16. Robert Louis Jackson, "Freedom in *Notes from Underground*," in Dostoevsky, *Notes from Underground*, trans. Michael R. Katz, 2nd ed. (New York: Norton, 2001), 187.

17. Dostoevsky, *Notes from Underground*, 27.

18. Jackson, "Freedom in *Notes from Underground*," 193.

19. David Gelernter, *1939: The Lost World of the Fair* (New York: Free Press, 1995), 369.

20. Sherry Turkle, *Alone Together: Why We Expect More from Technology and Less from Each Other* (New York: Basic Books, 2011), 65–66.

21. Emily Steel and Julia Angwin, "On the Web's Cutting Edge, Anonymity in Name Only," *Wall Street Journal*, August 4, 2010; Miguel Helft, "Google to Offer Ads Based on Interests," *New York Times*, March 11, 2009; Troy McAlpin, "Everyone Wants to Be Relevant: Why Relevance Engines Are What Matters Now," destinationCRM.com, August 21, 2010; Claire Cain Miller, "Google Unveils Tool to Speed Up Searches," *New York Times*, September 8, 2010.

22. TED Talks, *Salman Khan: Let's Use Video to Reinvent Education*, video, March 2011, http://www.ted.com/talks/salman_khan_let_s_use_video_to_reinvent_education.html (accessed May 22, 2011).

23. Louise Cowan, lecture delivered at the Dallas Institute of Humanities and Culture, November 6, 2010; quotations taken from audio recording.

24. Lauren B. Resnick and Larry Berger, *An American Examination System* (n.p.: Center for K–12 Assessment & Performance Management, Educational Testing Service, 2010), 15–16.

25. National Association of State Boards of Education, *Any Time, Any Place, Any Path, Any Pace: Taking the Lead on e-Learning Policy* (Alexandria, VA: NASBE, 2001), 4; Katie Ash, "Schools Blend Virtual and Face-to-Face Teaching," *Education Week*, September 20, 2010.

26. U.S. Department of Education, Office of Planning, Evaluation, and Policy Development, *Evaluation of Evidence-Based Practices in Online Learning: A Meta-Analysis and Review of Online Learning Studies* (Washington, DC: U.S. Department of Education, 2009), ix, xiv–xv.

27. U.S. Department of Education, "U.S. Department of Education Study Finds That Good Teaching Can Be Enhanced with New Technology," press release, June 26, 2009; Dan Lips, "How Online Learning Is Revolutionizing K–12 Education and Benefiting Students," The Heritage Foundation, January 12, 2010, http://www.heritage.org/research/reports/2010/01/how-online-learning-is-revolutionizing-k12-education-and-benefiting-students (accessed May 22, 2011); *New York Times*, "Study Finds That Online Education Beats the Classroom," August 19, 2009.

28. Neal McCluskey, "Beyond Brick and Mortar: Cyber Charters Revolutionizing Education," Center for Education Reform, 2002, http://www.edreform.com/published_pdf/Beyond_Brick_and_Mortar_Cyber_Charters_Revolutionizing_Education.pdf (accessed May 22, 2011).

29. Paul E. Peterson, *Saving Schools: From Horace Mann to Virtual Learning* (Cambridge, MA: Harvard University Press, 2010), 229–63.

30. Ibid., 251, 262–63; Laura Herrera, "In Florida, Virtual Classrooms with No Teachers," *New York Times*, January 17, 2011.

31. Anna Phillips, "Pilot of New Online Classes Earn Mixed Reviews from Principals," *GothamSchools*, February 25, 2011.

32. New York City Department of Education, "School of One @ MS131: Summer 2009" (New York: New York City Department of Education, 2009); Paul Peterson, "Adaptive Learning: Putting an Idea into Practice at the School of One," *Education Next*, May 3, 2010; Jennifer Medina, "Laptop? Check. Student Playlist? Check. Classroom of the Future? Check," *New York Times*, July 21, 2009.

33. Lisa Abend et al., "The 50 Best Inventions of 2009," *Time*, http://www.time.com/time/specials/packages/0,28757,1934027,00.html (accessed May 22, 2011); Arthur E. Levine, "The School of One: The School of Tomorrow," *Huffington Post*, September 16, 2009.

34. Fernanda Santos, "News Corp., After Hiring Klein, Buys Technology Partner in a City Schools Project," *New York Times*, November 23, 2010.

35. Beverly Woolf et al., "Affect-Aware Tutors: Recognising and Responding to Student Affect," *International Journal of Learning Technology* 4, nos. 3–4 (2009): 132–33.

36. Ibid., 133, 138; Mihaly Csikszentmihalyi, *Flow: The Psychology of Optimal Experience* (New York: Harper Perennial, 1991).

37. Beverly Woolf et al., "Affect-Aware Tutors," 137–42.

38. Beverly Woolf et al., "Recognizing and Responding to Student Affect," *Lecture Notes in Computer Science* 5612 (2009): 713–15.

39. Woolf et al., "Affect-Aware Tutors," 140, 150, 152–53; Debra Viadero, "Scholars Test Emotion-Sensitive Tutoring Software: 'Intelligent' Systems Respond to Students' Cues," *Education Week*, January 6, 2010.

40. Woolf et al., "Affect-Aware Tutors," 138.

41. Woolf et al., "Recognizing and Responding to Student Affect," 720.

42. Woolf et al., "Affect-Aware Tutors," 142.

Chapter 9

1. Evangelia Galanaki, "Solitude in the School: A Neglected Facet of Children's Development and Education," *Childhood Education* 81, no. 3 (Spring 2005): 128; Sherry Turkle, *Alone Together: Why We Expect More from Technology and Less from Each Other* (New York: Basic Books, 2011), 245.

2. Thomas Wolfe, "No Door," in *From Death to Morning* (New York: Grosset & Dunlap, 1935), 11–12.

3. Paul Tillich, "You Are Accepted," in *The Shaking of the Foundations* (New York: Scribner's, 1948), 154–55.

4. Ibid., 155.

5. Ibid., 153.

6. Thomas Wolfe, "God's Lonely Man," in *Masterworks of English Prose: A Critical Reader*, ed. John L. Bradley and Martin Stevens (New York: Rinehart and Winston, 1968), 454–62.

7. Donal O'Shea, *The Poincaré Conjecture: In Search of the Shape of the Universe* (New York: Walker, 2007), 36.

8. Gabriel García Márquez, *One Hundred Years of Solitude*, trans. Gregory Rabassa (New York: Avon Books, 1971), 25–26.

9. Ernest Klein, *A Comprehensive Etymological Dictionary of the English Language: Dealing with the Origin of Words and Their Sense Development Thus Illustrating the History of Civilization and Culture*, vol. 2: L–Z (Amsterdam: Elsevier, 1967), 889, 915.

10. Julio Cortázar, "Final del juego," in *Final del juego: Cuentos* (Buenos Aires: Editorial sudamericana, 1964); English translation, "End of the Game," in *End of the Game, and Other Stories*, trans. Paul Blackburn (New York: Pantheon, 1967), reprinted as *Blow-up, and Other Stories* (New York: Pantheon, 1985); in the English translation, the cousin's name is spelled Letitia.

11. Anthony Storr, *Solitude: A Return to the Self* (New York: Free Press, 1988), 64, 66–69.

12. Emily Dickinson, "Tell all the Truth but tell it slant," in *The Complete Poems of Emily Dickinson*, ed. Thomas H. Johnson (Boston: Little, Brown, 1960), 506–7 (orig. pub. 1945; written ca. 1868).

13. E. B. White, *Charlotte's Web* (New York: Harper, 1952; HarperCollins, 1980), 31.

14. Paul Tillich, "Waiting," in *The Shaking of the Foundations: Sermons Applicable to the Personal and Social Problems of Religious Life* (New York: Scribner's, 1948), 149–52.

15. Gerard Manley Hopkins, "Spring and Fall: To a Young Child," in *Poems of Gerard Manley Hopkins*, ed. Robert Bridges (London: Humphrey Milford, 1918), 51.

16. Jacqueline Olds and Richard S. Schwartz, *The Lonely American: Drifting Apart in the Twenty-First Century* (Boston: Beacon Press, 2009), 35, 42–43.

17. Olds and Schwartz, *The Lonely American*, 2, 6, 31; Lauren Slater, *Welcome to My Country* (New York: Random House, 1996), 188–89.

18. John T. Cacioppo, *Loneliness: Human Nature and the Need for Social Connection* (New York: Norton, 2008), 7.

19. Neil Porter Brown, "The Road to Romance: It Can Be Rocky, but Rewarding," *Harvard Magazine*, March–April 2003; Turkle, *Alone Together*, 225.

20. Alison P. Lenton and Marco Francesconi, "Too Much of a Good Thing? Variety Is Confusing in Mate Choice," *Biology Letters*, published online before print, March 2, 2011; April Masini, "Chilly Online Dating Life? Get Tips for Heating Things Up," AskApril.com, http://www.askapril.com/dating-tips-online-dating-tips-231.html (accessed May 22, 2011).

21. Tillich, "You Are Accepted," 156–57.

22. Flannery O'Connor, *Wise Blood* (New York: Noonday, 1967), 173–98.

23. Turkle, *Alone Together*, 245.

24. Evangelia Galanaki, "Are Children Able to Distinguish among the Concepts of Aloneness, Loneliness, and Solitude?," *International Journal of Behavioral Development* 28, no. 5 (September 2004): 435–43.

25. The final sentence of Nikolai Gogol's "The Tale of How Ivan Ivanovich Quarreled with Ivan Nikiforovich" (*Povest' o tom, kak possorilsia Ivan Ivanovich s Ivanom Nikiforovichem*), first published in 1835 in his *Mirgorod* cycle; the translation is my own. The story is included in Gogol, *Diary of a Madman and Other Stories*, trans. Ronald Wilks (New York: Penguin, 1973).

26. Ernest Klein, introduction to *A Comprehensive Etymological Dictionary of the English Language: Dealing with the Origin of Words and Their Sense Development Thus Illustrating the History of Civilization and Culture*, vol. 1: A–K (Amsterdam: Elsevier, 1966), viii.

27. Tillich, "You Are Accepted," 156–57.

28. Ibid., 162.

Chapter 10

1. Lionel Trilling, "Sincerity: Its Origin and Rise," in *Sincerity and Authenticity* (Cambridge, MA: Harvard University Press, 1972), 6.

2. Robert Frost, notebook, ca. 1937–1942, Dartmouth College, Rauner Special Collections Library, Robert Frost Collection, manuscript 001720; courtesy of

Dartmouth College Library; published in *The Notebooks of Robert Frost*, ed. Robert Faggen (Cambridge, MA: Harvard University Press, 2006), 456–57. The quotation preserves the punctuation of the original; "trouts" appears in the notebook without an apostrophe.

3. Rainer Maria Rilke, letter of July 16, 1903, in *Letters to a Young Poet*, trans. M. D. Herter Norton, rev. ed. (New York: Norton, 2004), 27.

4. Richard Hofstadter, *Anti-Intellectualism in American Life* (New York: Vintage, 1963), 32.

5. Vladimir Nabokov, *Nikolai Gogol* (New York: New Directions, 1961), 9–13; Henri Troyat, *Divided Soul: The Life of Gogol*, trans. Nancy Amphoux (New York: Doubleday, 1973), 58–60.

6. Troyat, *Divided Soul*, 68–69, 95, 105, 108–9. Troyat's translation of Gogol's letter abbreviates "Saint" to "St."; it has been expanded to "Saint" here for consistency with the rest of the text.

7. Simon Karlinsky, *The Sexual Labyrinth of Nikolai Gogol* (Cambridge, MA: Harvard University Press, 1976), 247–59.

8. This famous statement has been erroneously attributed to Dostoevsky. According to Simon Karlinsky, it was finally traced to the French critic Melchior de Vogüé. See Karlinsky, *The Sexual Labyrinth of Nikolai Gogol*, 135.

9. Nikolai Gogol, "Shinel'" [The Overcoat], in *Sobranie sochinenii v vos'mi tomakh*, vol. 3 (Moscow: Pravda, 1984), 121–22; I translated the quoted passage.

10. Nabokov, *Nikolai Gogol*, 145.

11. Gerard Manley Hopkins, "The Caged Skylark," in *Poems of Gerard Manley Hopkins*, ed. Robert Bridges (London: Humphrey Milford, 1918), 31.

12. St. Thomas Aquinas, *Summa Theologica* 2.2, question 179, in *The "Summa Theologica" of Thomas Aquinas*, vol. 12: *Second Part of the Second Part, Questions 171–189*, trans. Fathers of the English Dominican Province (London: Burns Oats and Washbourne, 1922), 99–100.

13. Susan Jacoby, *The Age of American Unreason* (New York: Pantheon, 2008), 247.

14. Anton Chekhov, "Palata No. 6" [Ward No. 6], in *Sobranie sochinenii v shesti tomakh* (Moscow: Lexica, 1995), 4:263; I translated the quoted passage.

15. Ibid., 4:286; I translated the quoted passage.

16. Albert E. Kahn, *Joys and Sorrows: Reflections by Pablo Casals* (New York: Simon & Schuster, 1978), 46; H. L. Kirk, *Pablo Casals: A Biography* (New York: Holt, Rinehart and Winston, 1974), 60.

17. Tobias Wolff, "In the Garden of the North American Martyrs," in *In the Garden of the North American Martyrs: A Collection of Short Stories* (New York: Ecco, 1981), 123–35.

18. Deborah Meier, "Utopia vs. 'Real Politics,'" *Bridging Differences* (blog), April 14, 2011; Eric A. Hanushek, "Valuing Teachers," *Education Next* 11, no. 3 (Summer 2011); Diana Senechal, "What Do Teachers 'Produce'?," *The Core Knowledge Blog*, April 12, 2011.

19. Jean Stein, "William Faulkner," in *Writers at Work: The Paris Review Interviews*, ed. Malcolm Cowley (New York: Viking, 1958), 134.

20. K. Anders Ericsson, Ralf Th. Krampe, and Clemens Tesch-Römer, "The Role of Deliberate Practice in the Acquisition of Expert Performance," *Psychological Review* 100, no. 3 (1993): 366–69, 375.

21. TED Talks, *Evelyn Glennie Shows How to Listen*, video, filmed February 2003, posted April 2007, http://www.ted.com/talks/evelyn_glennie_shows_how_to_listen .html (accessed May 22, 2011).

22. Tim Janof, "ICS Exclusive Interview: Conversation with Aldo Parisot," Internet Cello Society, May 4, 2001, http://www.cello.org/newsletter/articles/parisot.htm (accessed May 22, 2011).

23. Flannery O'Connor to John Selby, February 19, 1949, in *The Habit of Being: Letters*, ed. Sally Fitzgerald (New York: Farrar, Straus and Giroux, 1979), 10.

Chapter 11

1. "The Last Cruise of the Mikhail Lermontov," *New Zealand Maritime Record*, http://www.nzmaritime.co.nz/lermontov.htm (accessed May 22, 2011).

2. William Torrey Harris, "How the School Strengthens the Individuality of the Pupils," in *Journal of Proceedings and Addresses of the Forty-First Annual Meeting, Held at Minneapolis, Minnesota, July 7–11, 1902*, by the National Education Association (Chicago: National Education Association, 1902), 123; Harris, "The Relation of School Discipline to Moral Education," in *The Third Yearbook of the Herbart Society for the Scientific Study of Teaching*, ed. Charles A. McMurry (Chicago: University of Chicago Press, 1897), 61.

3. Jürgen Habermas, *The Structural Transformation of the Public Sphere: An Inquiry into a Category of Bourgeois Society*, trans. Thomas Burger with the assistance of Frederick Lawrence (Cambridge, MA: MIT Press, 1989).

4. Hannah Arendt, *The Human Condition* (Chicago: University of Chicago Press, 1958), 15, 38, 41, 64.

5. Ibid., 40, 42–43, 45–46, 52.

6. Ibid., 52.

7. Ibid., 57–58.

8. Benjamin Rush, "Of the Mode of Education Proper in a Republic" (1798), http://chronicles.dickinson.edu/resources/Rush/mode_of_education.html (accessed May 22, 2011); second quotation cited in E. D. Hirsch Jr., *The Making of Americans: Democracy and Our Schools* (New Haven, CT: Yale University Press, 2009), 22.

9. Lawrence Cremin, *American Education: The Colonial Experience, 1607-1783* (New York: Harper & Row, 1970), 550–53; E. D. Hirsch Jr., *The Making of Americans*, 22; William Deresiewicz, "Solitude and Leadership," *American Scholar* 79, no. 2 (Spring 2010): 30.

10. Cremin, *American Education: The National Experience, 1783-1876* (New York: Harper & Row, 1980), 136–40, 148–49; Cremin, introduction to *The Republic and the*

School: Horace Mann on the Education of Free Men, ed. Lawrence Cremin (New York: Teachers College, Columbia University, 1957), 8, 20–23.

11. Cremin, *American Education: The National Experience, 1783-1876* (New York: Harper & Row, 1980), 315–18, 484–85; Susan Jacoby, *The Age of American Unreason* (New York: Pantheon Books, 2008), 55–57.

12. Hirsch, *The Making of Americans*, 26, 31.

13. Hirsch, *The Making of Americans*, 23; John Dewey, *Democracy and Education* (New York: Free Press, 1916), 24, 38.

14. William Heard Kilpatrick, "The Project Method," *Teachers College Record* 19, no. 4 (September 1918): 321, 329–30.

15. Harold Rugg and Ann Shumaker, *The Child-Centered School: An Appraisal of the New Education* (Yonkers-on-Hudson, NY: World Book, 1928), 297.

16. Diane Ravitch, *Left Back: A Century of Battles Over School Reform* (New York: Simon & Schuster, 2001), 258–61; L. Thomas Hopkins et al., *Integration: Its Meaning and Application* (New York: Appleton-Century, 1937), 26, 200.

17. Hopkins, "Arguments Favoring Integration," *Teachers College Record* 36, no. 7 (1935): 605–6, 611; Hopkins et al., *Integration*, 22–26; Hopkins, "Education for Co-operative Living," *Teachers College Record* 48, no. 2 (1946): 76.

18. Hopkins et al., *Integration*, 198; Lyle W. Ashby et al., "Secondary Education for the New Day," *Journal of the National Education Association* 23 (1934): 137; W. D. Reeve, "Mathematics and the Integrated Program in Secondary Schools," *Teachers College Record* 36, no. 7 (1935): 503; E. Louise Noyes, "Watchman, What of 'Integration'?," *English Journal* 35, no. 2 (February 1946): 87–88; William C. Bagley, "How Shall We View Elementary Education as Regards: (1) Discipline; (2) The Psychology of Learning; (3) Subject-matter?," *Mathematics Teacher* 28, no. 3 (March 1935): 181.

19. Ravitch, *Left Back*, 240–41, 338–41; Alice Miel, *Changing the Curriculum: A Social Process* (New York: Appleton-Century, 1946), 40–47, 91–92; Kurt Lewin and Paul Grabbe, "Conduct, Knowledge, and Acceptance of New Values," *Journal of Social Issues* 1, no. 3 (August 1945): 62–64.

20. Common Core State Standards Initiative, *Common Core State Standards for English Language Arts & Literacy in History/Social Studies, Science, and Technical Subjects* (Washington, DC: Common Core State Standards Initiative, 2010), 24.

21. Council of Chief State School Officers, Interstate Teacher Assessment and Support Consortium, *Model Core Teaching Standards: A Resource for State Dialogue; Draft for Public Comment* (Washington, DC: CCSSO, 2010), 12, 19.

22. The University of the State of New York, The State Education Department, *Regents Comprehensive Examination in English: Test Sampler*, Spring 2010, directions for teachers, 14, http://www.nysedregents.org/ComprehensiveEnglish/english-sampler -2010.pdf (accessed May 22, 2011).

23. Ibid., scoring key and rating guide, 28–30.

24. Learned Hand, "The Spirit of Liberty," in *The Spirit of Liberty: Papers and Addresses of Learned Hand*, ed. Irving Dilliard (New York: Vintage, 1959), 144.

25. Paul Woodruff, *First Democracy: The Challenge of an Ancient Idea* (New York: Oxford University Press, 2005), 3.

26. Alexander Bain, *John Stuart Mill: A Criticism; with Personal Recollections* (London: Longmans, 1882), 104.

27. John Stuart Mill, *On Liberty* (New Haven: Yale University Press, 2003), 104, 123 (orig. pub. 1859).

28. Ibid., 137.

29. Ibid.

30. Ibid., 107; Carol Jago, "To Cherish the Interests of Literature," presidential address, 99th annual convention of the National Council of Teachers of English, Orlando, Florida, November 18–21, 2010, n.p., http://www.caroljago.com/PresAddress .pdf (accessed May 22, 2011).

31. Plato, *Republic*, trans. G. M. A. Grube, rev. C. D. C. Reeve (Indianapolis: Hackett, 1992), 155.

32. William Shakespeare, *King Lear*, ed. John Dover Wilson (New York: Cambridge University Press, 2009), 4.6.149–53. References are to act, scene, and line.

33. Ibid., 5.3.257–59.

34. John Hollander, *The Work of Poetry* (New York: Columbia University Press, 1997), 3, 5.

Chapter 12

1. W. H. Auden, "Yeats as an Example," *Kenyon Review* 10, no. 2 (Spring 1948): 187–88.

2. Ibid., 189.

3. Aristotle, *The Nicomachean Ethics* (Greek and English text), trans. H. Rackam, Loeb Classical Library, rev. ed. (Cambridge, MA: Harvard University Press, 1934), 615.

4. Diogenes Laertius, *Lives of Eminent Philosophers*, trans. R. D. Hicks, Loeb Classical Library (Cambridge, MA: Harvard University Press, 1925), 2:43.

5. Hermann Hesse, *Demian: The Story of Emil Sinclair's Youth*, trans. Michael Roloff and Michael Lebeck (New York: Harper & Row, 1989), 130.

6. Diane Ravitch, *The Language Police: How Pressure Groups Restrict What Students Learn* (New York: Knopf, 2003).

7. Elizabeth Cady Stanton, "Solitude of Self" (address to the Congressional Judiciary Committee, January 18, 1892; Ashfield, MA: Paris Press, 2001), 8. Citations are to the Paris Press edition.

8. Epictetus, *Discourses: Books 1–2* (Greek and English text), trans. W. A. Oldfather, Loeb Classical Library (Cambridge, MA: Harvard University Press, 1998), 19. The word *porphura* in the original Greek text has also been translated as "purple."

9. John Stuart Mill, *On Liberty* (New Haven, CT: Yale University Press, 2003), 138.

10. Woodrow Wilson National Fellowship Foundation, *The Responsive Ph.D.: Innovations in U.S. Doctoral Education* (Princeton, NJ: Woodrow Wilson National Fellowship Foundation, 2005), 73; Council of Graduate Schools, Ph.D. Completion Project, "Promising Practices: Program Environment," http://www.phdcompletion.org/promising/environment.asp (accessed May 22, 2011); Yale Graduate School, *Renewing the Ph.D. at Yale: The 2–4 Project,* http://www.yale.edu/graduateschool/academics/forms/2-4%20Project.pdf (accessed May 22, 2011); conversation between the author and a Yale graduate student.

11. David Glenn, "Traditional Language Programs Have Declined Steadily over Decades," *Chronicle of Higher Education,* February 14, 2011; Scott Jaschik, "Disappearing Languages at Albany," *Inside Higher Ed,* October 4, 2010; Jennifer Washburn, introduction to paperback edition of *University, Inc.: The Corporate Corruption of American Higher Education* (New York: Basic Books, 2006), ix.

12. Tamar Lewin, "Incentives Offered to Raise College Graduation Rates," *New York Times,* March 22, 2011.

13. Wen Shi's poem "Earth" and comment are reprinted here with permission of the author and her mother, Xiu Feng Huang. This and another poem by Wen Shi may be viewed at http://schools.nyc.gov/Students/PSPoem/shi.htm (accessed May 22, 2011).

14. Flannery O'Connor to "A.," July 12, 1957, in *The Habit of Being: Letters,* ed. Sally Fitzgerald (New York: Farrar, Straus and Giroux, 1988), 229.

~

Select Bibliography and Recommended Reading

Works on Solitude and Related Subjects

Deresiewicz, William. "The End of Solitude." *Chronicle of Higher Education*, January 30, 2009.

———. "Solitude and Leadership." *American Scholar* 79, no. 2 (Spring 2010): 20–31.

Emerson, Ralph Waldo. "Society and Solitude." In *The Essential Writings of Ralph Waldo Emerson*, ed. Brooks Atkinson, 663–69. New York: Modern Library, 2000. Originally published as "Solitude and Society." *The Atlantic Monthly* 1, no. 2 (December 1857): 225–29.

Galanaki, Evangelia. "Solitude in the School: A Neglected Facet of Children's Development and Education." *Childhood Education* 81, no. 3 (Spring 2005): 128–32.

Koch, Philip. *Solitude: A Philosophical Encounter*. Chicago: Open Court, 1994.

Merton, Thomas. *Thoughts in Solitude*. New York: Farrar, Straus and Cudahy, 1958.

Petrarch. *The Life of Solitude*. Translated by Jacob Zeitlin. Urbana: University of Illinois Press, 1924.

Powys, John Cowper. *A Philosophy of Solitude*. New York: Simon & Schuster, 1933.

Rufus, Anneli. *Party of One: The Loner's Manifesto*. Cambridge, MA: Da Capo Press, 2003.

Senechal, Diana. "Solitude: A Flashlight under the Covers." *Education Week*, May 27, 2009.

Stanton, Elizabeth Cady. "Solitude of Self." Address to the Congressional Judiciary Committee, January 18, 1892. Reprint, Ashfield, MA: Paris Press, 2001.

Storr, Anthony. *Solitude: A Return to the Self*. New York: Free Press, 1988.

Thoreau, Henry David. *Walden, or, Life in the Woods*. Boston: Ticknor and Fields, 1854. Reprint, Boston: Houghton Mifflin, 2004.

Turkle, Sherry. *Alone Together: Why We Expect More from Technology and Less from Each Other.* New York: Basic Books, 2011.

William of St. Thierry. *The Golden Epistle: A Letter to the Brethren at Mont Dieu.* Composed ca. 1145. Translated by Theodore Berkeley. Kalamazoo, MI: Cistercian Publications, 1971.

Williams, Tennessee. "The Catastrophe of Success." Introduction to *The Glass Menagerie.* New York: New Directions, 1949. Originally published as "On a Streetcar Named Success." *New York Times,* November 30, 1947.

Works on Education and Culture

Arendt, Hannah. *The Human Condition.* Chicago: University of Chicago Press, 1958.

Bauerlein, Mark. *The Dumbest Generation: How the Digital Age Stupefies Young Americans and Jeopardizes Their Future.* New York: Tarcher, 2008.

Chesterton, G. K. "The Fallacy of Success." In *All Things Considered,* 21–29. New York: John Lane, 1909.

Dewey, John. *Democracy and Education.* New York: Macmillan, 1916.

Edman, Irwin. *The Contemporary and His Soul.* New York: Cape & Smith, 1931.

Ferry, Luc. *What Is the Good Life?* Translated by Lydia G. Cochrane. Chicago: University of Chicago Press, 2005. Originally published as *Qu'est-ce qu'une vie réussie?* Paris: Grasset, 2002.

Hirsch, E. D., Jr. *The Making of Americans: Democracy and Our Schools.* New Haven, CT: Yale University Press, 2009.

Hochschild, Jennifer. *Facing Up to the American Dream: Race, Class, and the Soul of the Nation.* Princeton, NJ: Princeton University Press, 1995.

Hofstadter, Richard. *Anti-Intellectualism in American Life.* New York: Vintage, 1963.

Jackson, Maggie. *Distracted: The Erosion of Attention and the Coming Dark Age.* New York: Prometheus, 2008.

Jacoby, Susan. *The Age of American Unreason.* New York: Pantheon, 2008.

Jago, Carol. "To Cherish the Interests of Literature." Presidential address, 99th annual convention of the National Council of Teachers of English, Orlando, Florida, November 18–21, 2010. http://www.caroljago.com/PresAddress.pdf (accessed May 22, 2011).

Kandel, Isaac Leon. "Alice in Cloud-Cuckoo Land." *Teachers College Record* 34, no. 8 (1933): 627–34.

Olds, Jacqueline, and Richard S. Schwartz. *The Lonely American: Drifting Apart in the Twenty-First Century.* Boston: Beacon Press, 2009.

Postman, Neil. *Amusing Ourselves to Death: Public Discourse in the Age of Show Business.* New York: Viking Penguin, 1985.

———. *Technopoly: The Surrender of Culture to Technology.* New York: Knopf, 1992.

Ravitch, Diane. *The Death and Life of the Great American School System: How Testing and Choice Are Undermining Education.* New York: Basic Books, 2010.

———. *The Language Police: How Pressure Groups Restrict What Students Learn.* New York: Knopf, 2003.

———. *Left Back: A Century of Battles over School Reform.* New York: Simon & Schuster, 2001. Originally published as *Left Back: A Century of Failed School Reforms.* New York: Simon & Schuster, 2000.

Riesman, David. *The Lonely Crowd: A Study of the Changing American Character.* New Haven, CT: Yale University Press, 1950.

Sandage, Scott A. *Born Losers: A History of Failure in America.* Cambridge, MA: Harvard University Press, 2005.

Senechal, Diana. "The Most Daring Education Reform of All." *American Educator,* Spring 2010, 4–16.

———. "Why Do We Need a Philosophy of Education? The Forgotten Insights of Michael John Demiashkevich." *American Educational History Journal* 37, no. 1 (2010): 1–18.

Trilling, Lionel. "The Situation of the American Intellectual at the Present Time." In *The Moral Obligation to Be Intelligent: Selected Essays,* ed. Leon Wieseltier, 275–91. New York: Farrar, Straus and Giroux, 2000. Reprint, Evanston: Northwestern University Press, 2008.

Weiss, Richard. *The American Myth of Success: From Horatio Alger to Norman Vincent Peale.* New York: Basic Books, 1969.

White, E. B. "Freedom." In *One Man's Meat,* 205–12. New York: Harper & Brothers, 1942. Originally published under White's column "One Man's Meat" in *Harper's Magazine,* June–November 1940.

Whitehead, Alfred North. "The Aims of Education." In *The Aims of Education, and Other Essays,* 1–14. New York: Macmillan, 1929.

Willingham, Daniel T. "The Usefulness of *Brief* Instruction in Reading Comprehension Strategies." *American Educator,* Winter 2006–2007, 39–45, 50.

Woodruff, Paul. *First Democracy: The Challenge of an Ancient Idea.* New York: Oxford University Press, 2005.

Literary and Philosophical Works

Aristotle. *The Nicomachean Ethics.* Greek and English text. Translated by H. Rackam. Loeb Classical Library. Rev. ed. Cambridge, MA: Harvard University Press, 1934.

Bellow, Saul. *Seize the Day, with Three Short Stories and a One-Act Play.* New York: Viking, 1956.

Bloom, Harold, ed. *Stories and Poems for Extremely Intelligent Children of All Ages.* New York: Simon & Schuster, 2001.

Browning, Robert. "Rabbi Ben Ezra." In *Dramatis Personae,* 89–99. London: Chapman and Hall, 1864.

Buber, Martin. *I and Thou.* Translated with a prologue by Walter Kaufmann. New York: Scribner's, 1970. Originally published as *Ich und Du.* Leipzig: Insel-Verlag, 1923.

Chekhov, Anton. *Anton Chekhov's Short Stories: Texts of the Stories, Backgrounds, Criticism,* ed. Ralph E. Matlaw. Norton Critical Edition. New York: Norton, 1979.

————. *Stories.* Translated by Richard Pevear and Larissa Volokhonsky. New York: Bantam, 2000.

Cortázar, Julio. "End of the Game." In *Blow-up, and Other Stories.* Translated by Paul Blackburn, 135–49. New York: Pantheon, 1985. Collection previously published as *End of the Game, and Other Stories.* New York: Pantheon, 1967. Originally published as "Final del juego." In *Final del juego: Cuentos.* Buenos Aires: Editorial sudamericana, 1964.

Dostoevsky, Fyodor. *Notes from Underground.* Translated by Michael Katz. Norton Critical Edition. New York: Norton, 2001.

Epictetus. *Discourses: Books 1–2.* Greek and English text. Translated by W. A. Oldfather. Loeb Classical Library. Cambridge, MA: Harvard University Press, 1998.

Frost, Robert. *The Notebooks of Robert Frost.* Edited by Robert Faggen. Cambridge, MA: Harvard University Press, 2006.

Gogol, Nikolai. *Diary of a Madman, and Other Stories.* Translated by Ronald Wilks. New York: Penguin, 1973.

Hesse, Hermann. *Demian: The Story of Emil Sinclair's Youth.* Translated by Michael Roloff and Michael Lebeck. New York: Harper & Row, 1989.

Hopkins, Gerard Manley. *Poems of Gerard Manley Hopkins.* Edited by Robert Bridges. London: Humphrey Milford, 1918.

Merrill, James. *The Changing Light at Sandover.* New York: Knopf, 2003.

Mill, John Stuart. *On Liberty.* New Haven, CT: Yale University Press, 2003.

O'Connor, Flannery. *The Habit of Being: Letters,* ed. Sally Fitzgerald. New York: Farrar, Straus and Giroux, 1979.

————. *Wise Blood.* New York: Noonday, 1967.

Plato. *Symposium.* In *Lysis, Symposium, Gorgias.* Greek and English text. Translated by W. R. M. Lamb. Loeb Classical Library. Cambridge, MA: Harvard University Press, 1925.

Shakespeare, William. *King Lear.* Edited by John Dover Wilson. New York: Cambridge University Press, 2009.

Sophocles. *Antigone.* Translated by Robert Fagles. In *Sophocles: The Three Theban Plays: Antigone, Oedipus the King, Oedipus at Colonus.* New York: Penguin, 1984.

————. *Antigone.* Translated by Paul Woodruff. Indianapolis: Hackett, 2001.

Sterne, Laurence. *Tristram Shandy: An Authoritative Text; the Author on the Novel; Criticism.* Edited by Howard Anderson. New York: Norton, 1980.

Tillich, Paul. "You Are Accepted." In *The Shaking of the Foundations,* 153–63. New York: Scribner's, 1948.

Venclova, Tomas. *Winter Dialogue.* Translated by Diana Senechal; foreword by Joseph Brodsky, with a dialogue between Czesław Miłosz and Tomas Venclova. Evanston, IL: Northwestern University Press, 1997.

White, E. B. *Charlotte's Web.* New York: Harper, 1952.

Whitman, Walt. *Leaves of Grass.* Brooklyn, NY, 1855.

Wolff, Tobias. "In the Garden of the North American Martyrs." In *In the Garden of the North American Martyrs: A Collection of Short Stories*, 123–35. New York: Ecco, 1981.

Other Works

Auden, W. H. "Yeats as an Example." *Kenyon Review* 10, no. 2 (Spring 1948): 187–95.

Goheen, Robert F. *The Imagery of Sophocles' Antigone: A Study of Poetic Language and Structure*. Princeton, NJ: Princeton University Press, 1951.

Hollander, John. *The Work of Poetry*. New York: Columbia University Press, 1997.

Johnson-Laird, Philip N. *How We Reason*. New York: Oxford University Press, 2006.

Nabokov, Vladimir. *Nikolai Gogol*. New York: New Directions, 1961.

Newton, Isaac. *The Principia: Mathematical Principles of Natural Philosophy*. Translated by I. Bernard Cohen and Anne Whitman, with *A Guide to Newton's "Principia,"* by I. Bernard Cohen. Berkeley: University of California Press, 1999.

O'Shea, Donal. *The Poincaré Conjecture: In Search of the Shape of the Universe*. New York: Walker, 2007.

Tallis, John. *Tallis's History and Description of the Crystal Palace and the Exhibition of the World's Industry in 1851*. London: John Tallis and Co., 1852.

Troyat, Henri. *Divided Soul: The Life of Gogol*. Translated by Nancy Amphoux. New York: Doubleday, 1973.

~

About the Author

Diana Senechal taught English as a Second Language and theater for four years in New York City public schools. In addition to her classroom teaching, she directed her students in productions of *The Wizard of Oz, Oliver, Into the Woods,* and *A Midsummer Night's Dream.* She holds a BA in Russian and a Ph.D. in Slavic languages and literatures from Yale University; she taught Russian as a graduate student at Yale and as a Mellon Fellow at Trinity College in Hartford, Connecticut.

Senechal's translations of the Lithuanian poetry of Tomas Venclova have been published in two books: *Winter Dialogue* (Northwestern University Press, 1997) and *The Junction* (Bloodaxe Books, 2008). Her education writing has appeared in *American Educator, Education Week, Educational Leadership, American Educational History Journal,* and numerous blogs, including *The Core Knowledge Blog, The Answer Sheet, Joanne Jacobs,* and *GothamSchools.* She has contributed to several education projects, including the Common Core State Standards.

She is the 2011 winner of the Hiett Prize in the Humanities, awarded by the Dallas Institute of Humanities and Culture. In July 2011 she joined the faculty at the Dallas Institute's Sue Rose Summer Institute for Teachers. In addition to writing and teaching, she enjoys reading in various languages, playing cello, and taking long walks and road trips. She lives in Brooklyn, New York.

Index